SWEETER THAN HONEY

Ethiopian Women and Revolution: Testimonies of Tigrayan Women

"My revolution is like honey; she gets sweeter all the time"
Kiros Gebru

Jenny Hammond
Editors Nell Druce and Jenny Hammond

 **The Red Sea Press, Inc.**
Publishers & Distributors of Third World Books
P.O. Box 1892
Trenton, New Jersey 08607

WITHDRAWN

HQ
1794.5
.H35
1990

This book is dedicated to all the women who are participating with their brothers in the Tigrayan revolution and particularly to the women whose voices are heard in the following pages:

Abeba Negash fighter, medical laboratory technician
Abrahet Teklemuze working as prostitute, Endaselassie
Abrehet Teklu Mass Association, London
Ametetsion Adi Hageray Women's Association
Aregash TPLF Central Committee
Aregawit Teklemariam peasant, Edaga Hiberet
Askale ex–bank worker, Makelle
Aster Fetiwy ex–teacher, Makelle
Atsede Teklai musician, TPLF Cultural Department
Belaynesh agricultural cadre, Tsebre farm
Berhan refugee, nurse, London
Berhan Hailu REST Information Office, Khartoum
Beriha Egzigre peasant, Edaga Hiberet
Beriha Medhin peasant, Edaga Hiberet
Besserat Asfaw TPLF, Los Angeles USA
Besserat fighter, Endaselassie
Elem fighter, Endaselassie
Eysa Mohammed Afar fighter
Geday Legesse peasant, Adi Daro
Genet Negash fighter, teacher at Adi Awalla
Harnet newscaster, TPLF radio station
Kassech Asfaw TPLF, Washington DC, USA
Kebbedesh fighter, Marta School

Kidan Gebretensai peasant, *shig woyanit*, Edaga Hiberet

Kindehafte Gebremedhin agricultural cadre, Adi Hageray

Kiros Gebru peasant, repatriated after famine

Laila fighter, TPLF Information Bureau, Tigray

Lemlem Gesesse fighter, Khartoum

Lemlem Hagos survivor of Derg resettlement

Lemlem Mahmas Axum

Leteberhan Kidane peasant, Awhie

Letemariam Kunama woman, Sheraro

Letentiay Kunama woman, Sheraro

Licknesh Tekle fighter, Endaselassie

Mahta Embay TPLF Information Bureau, Gedaref, Sudan

Mebrat teacher at TPLF Political School

Medhin Gerzgiher mechanic, Gedaref, Sudan

Medhin Komo Kunama fighter, Tekezze

Neriya Wahabi fighter, Adi Hageray

Radiet Gebretensai peasant activist, Adigrat

Rahma Endaselassie

Rishan Gebremariam peasant, Awhie

Roman Secretary of WFAT

Saba fighter, Director of Marta school

Sesayt Adhanom peasant, *shig woyanit*, Sheraro

Sofia fighter, TPLF driver

Tsahytu Fekado seller of beer, mead and coffee, Sheraro

Werknesh TPLF squad commander

Yomar Endaselassie

Zafu Abraha TPLF, London

Zafu Tsehaige chairperson of Adi Hageray Baito

Zodie refugee, London

Authors' Acknowledgement

We gratefully acknowledge the support and help of the following: Solomon Inquai for help with history and background, Fessaha for comments on the text, Aziz and Mebratu for translating the poems, Berhanu and Heshe our guides and interpreters, many members of TPLF for cooperation and help, Chris Taylor for his work on the first trip, Steve Hodgson for his care with photographs, Ron Hammond for editorial help, Christian Aid for funding the first trip, and the other members of the Third World First collective for their support and forbearance.

Red Sea Press, Inc.
15 Industry Court
Trenton, NJ 08638

First Printing Red Sea Press edition 1990

Copyright © 1990 Third World First

All rights reserved. No part of this publication may be reproduced, stored in a retrieval system or transmitted in any form or by any means electronic, mechanical, photocopying, recording or otherwise without the prior written permission of the publisher.

Cover design by Ife Nii Owoo
Cover art courtesy of Tigray People's Liberation Front

Typeset and layout by Petra Pryke

Library of Congress Catalog
Card Number 90-60727

ISBN: 0-932415-55-5   Cloth
　　　 0-932415-56-3   Paper

CONTENTS

There's more to Tigray than famine.	7
Why armed struggle? The background to the Tigrayan revolution	13
Women in feudal Tigray	31
The early years of the revolution	41
On the frontline: war and the Derg	55
The support of the people	70
Knowledge is power: the women's schools	79
Changing cultural attitudes	90
TPLF and the minority nationalities	102
The land is ours!	112
Famine and migration	121
'Women can do anything men can do'	134
Liberating the towns	144
Beyond Tigray	159
New developments	169
Glossary and date outline	175
Resources	177
Links publications	178

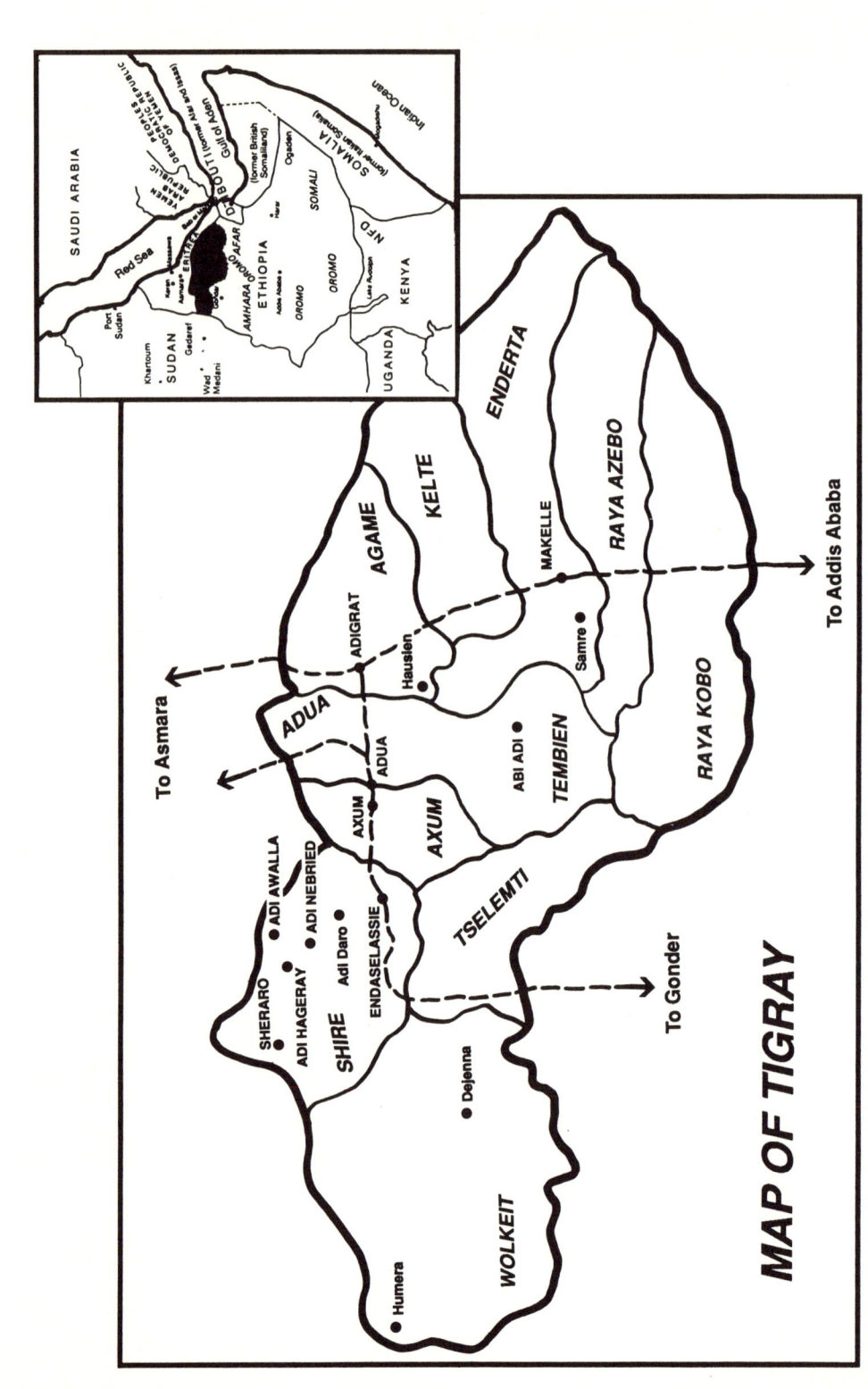

There's more to Tigray than famine...

Most of us in the West know little about Ethiopia and even less about its northern province of Tigray. The more informed have heard that there is a struggle going on between Eritrea and the Ethiopian government, without any precise sense of what it is about. Very few people know that there is a parallel struggle going on in Tigray and at least ten other regional liberation struggles elsewhere in Ethiopia which receive next to no publicity in the West. Most people will have heard about Ethiopia in the context of famine and will tend to have certain inflexible and stereotypical ideas: skeletal Ethiopians live in a baked and sterile landscape; they suffer from chronic malnutrition caused by a combination of their own shortcomings and the weather; their problems are to be solved by the benevolence and expertise of the West. How much truth is there in these widely-held perceptions? What *are* the conditions of life for the Ethiopian people? What is their hope for the future?

In 1984 the news of the famine first broke in the Western media. A common response was outrage that things could have got so bad without anyone knowing. In fact certain agencies and journalists had been trying to interest news editors in the situation for some months, but not until the suffering became 'sensational' was it considered an important story. My organisation, Third World First, based in Britain and dedicated to investigating and publicising the causes of global poverty and exploitation, worked from the assumption that it takes politics to turn a drought into famine. We produced a publication on the politics of famine in the Sahel and Horn of Africa. During the year-long campaign that followed we worked with several groups from these areas, particularly the Tigray People's Liberation Front (TPLF), the Eritrean People's Liberation Front (EPLF) and the Oromo Liberation Front (OLF).

We already had links with the Eritreans, but were relatively ignorant of the situation in Tigray. The information coming from all these groups was very different from the publicity about Ethiopia coming from the mainstream media. They had in common a concern first for the survival and then for the well-being of the poor majority in their country. In Tigray, the picture that emerged of the opposition to the Ethiopian government indicated not a bunch of 'rebels' or guerrillas, as described in the press, but a well-organised and politically mature people's revolution which was already providing an astonishing level of democratic participation, education and health-care in the liberated areas.

The TPLF invited us to investigate for ourselves the progress of the Tigrayan revolution and two of us spent December 1986 to March 1987 in Tigray. In 1989 I went back for a second visit. We did not go to Tigray the first time with the intention of writing a book. Indeed, it would have seemed presumptuous. We wanted to see for ourselves the difficulties and achievements of a revolution 'in the making'. The revolutionary rhetoric of the TPLF and the Ethiopian government can sound almost identical. They both claim a socialist revolution, sometimes in the same terms, yet they are locked in bitter conflict. Much more attention in the media and in publications had been paid to the government. There seemed no way of verifying the TPLF case without going there. We were most interested in finding out if it was in fact 'a people's struggle' and, if so, by what process it had transformed itself from the time in February 1975 when a handful of revolutionary students with a rifle and five old-fashioned pistols had gone to Dedebit in western Tigray to start the revolution.

This book has grown out of those visits. As we came to realise the extent of the ignorance and disinformation in the West about this region, it no longer seemed presumptuous, but indeed an obligation to share the information we discovered. But more than that, the extent of the achievement of this hidden revolution in Tigray was inspiring enough by any standards and deserved wider recognition for its own sake and as a model to others. Although it is only about eleven years since a measure of stability in the liberated areas allowed reconstruction to begin, already the objective achievements in the process of social transformation have a validity independent of subsequent events, successes or failures.

So, why have these developments in Tigray received so little attention in the Western press? Western people seem to be in the grip of a mindset about the nature of life in Ethiopia. Famine is in fact only one of the mythologies which govern the understanding of Third World countries and Third World issues in the public mind. More damaging even than the equation of these countries with inevitable poverty is the conviction that their people are incapable of solving their problems for themselves, made worse by ignorance of the post-colonial economic machine which has contributed to their difficulties. In Ethiopia the problem is compounded by the inaccessibility of the areas engaged in liberation struggles against the government. Journalists prefer to fly in to Addis Ababa where they can learn only the government point of view, rather than make the long and rigorous journey from Sudan to Tigray or Eritrea by night convoy over unmade roads. Perhaps this accounts for recurrent errors in reporting the aims of the Tigrayan revolution. In particular they are *not* seeking independence and secession, but self-determination within a united, democratic and socialist Ethiopia.

A common response, when I first returned from Tigray in 1987 and neighbours and acquaintances learned that I had been in Ethiopia, was to ask, with a compassionate expression, "Was it *terrible?*" When I replied that on the contrary it had been an inspiring example of what people could do for themselves, they were often reluctant to modify their image of 'Ethiopia' as a European-financed feeding camp. Sometimes they thought I was a bit simple or had been taken in. It was the question of armed struggle however which provoked the most intense resistance. We were invited to give talks and show slides to groups all over the country, in which, although mentioning the impact of the war, we emphasised democratic structures, advances in health care, literacy, the position of women. Several times and in different ways we were accused of celebrating violence. 'Violence' seemed to be narrowly defined as illegal physical force. Violence used by authority or by an established government against its own people on the other hand was somehow 'legal' and permissible. Notions that economic systems can be violent in their process and in their effects – unemployment, misery, starvation, death – seemed strangely unfamiliar. I realised that to communicate another country's culture is no simple matter. It is not just about deconstructing one's own assumptions, but also of resisting the deeply-held and media-reinforced patterns of thought in the public mind that underpin the relationship between imperialist cultures and the 'subject peoples of the earth', conveniently stereotyped through racism as victims not so much of tyranny as of 'natural' incapacity and backwardness.

The people speak for themselves

On more than one occasion I have started talks by presenting testimonies without subjective comment. The first response was silence, followed after a few moments by a tentative request for my judgement on their authenticity. I went on to give my comments, but only after I had asked certain questions. Why should I, one white woman, be believed in preference to hundreds of Tigrayans? Under what circumstances could they reasonably be supposed to have cooked up their stories together? For what purpose? International agencies, like Médecins Sans Frontières, presenting evidence of the Ethiopian government's enforced deportation scheme have been met with similar racist responses.

The fact is that for well over a hundred years Tigray has been both the focus of oppressive rule and the centre of recurrent uprisings against the central government in Addis Ababa. Since 1975, in response to this history, it has been an extraordinary example of a successful revolution – successful in the sense of transforming the lives of its impoverished and subordinated people. But it has not yet succeeded in transforming the political situation beyond its boundaries enough to safeguard its internal social and political gains. Events are moving fast however. When we first went to Tigray in 1987, almost the entire rural area of Tigray was under the control of the TPLF. Only the main towns on the two all-weather roads remained in the hands of the government. By the time I returned in May and June 1989 the TPLF had taken control of all these towns, including the capital, Makelle. The whole of Tigray had been liberated. More than this, a new Front, the Ethiopian People's Revolutionary Democratic Front (EPRDF) had been formed between the TPLF and the Ethiopian People's Democratic Movement (EPDM) to carry the struggle south of Tigray into the provinces of Wollo and Gonder.

Since the earliest days of travel, whether for exploration and trade or, more recently, anthropology and tourism, white people have mediated the peoples and cultures of the 'third world'. This has occurred across a wide range of social and educational discourses. University academics have made their careers through the objectifying of Black peoples in 'serious' and 'objective' works; tourist advertising has exoticised them in brochures which luridly distort their living conditions and culture. All this has been aided by the products of wealth and power – long-term access to education, travel, communications and technologies such as photography. So we decided to base the format largely on testimony we had gathered ourselves. In this book as far as possible the *people* speak for themselves.

We are encouraged to think of subjectivity as personal and individual. Yet this notion of the subjective is less dangerous than the shared cultural norms and perceptions which condition us as individuals and which, allied to the power of long-term imperialist success, make white mediation of Black cultures one more extension of colonial exploitation. Educational systems in the West train us in an apparent objectivity, hiding what is and must be a eurocentric perception behind third person abstractions and rationalisations. Of course, observation and comment on the political struggles and cultures of other peoples is valid (and my own have a place in this book) as long as we acknowledge the impossibility of achieving that objectively. The processes of interviewing, interpreting, selecting and editing make even testimony a relative and imperfect solution to the problem, but we hope it is a step in the right direction for those who are not Tigrinya speakers. This is why we decided to keep the supporting commentary distinct from the testimonies themselves.

Most of the testimony has been collected during the two visits to Tigray in 1987 and 1989, but additional testimony and information have been obtained through meetings with informed groups and individual Tigrayans in Europe and the Sudan over the last three years. The testimonies were made in a variety of conditions. We were given wide access and we wrote our own programme. Some interviews were arranged by our guides, but many were the result of unexpected situations such as transport delays and vehicle breakdowns which we tried to use constructively. TPLF fighters and REST guides always cooperated whenever we suggested an interview. Berhanu would encourage us to ask questions of people we met at random – sometimes meeting with resistance if we had been walking by torch or moonlight half the night or our bones ached from twelve hours in a truck eased over roads made of small boulders or pitted with craters. Interviews were sometimes in English, but in both these and the majority which were conducted through an interpreter, editing has been kept to a minimum.

Testimony is subjective, reflecting the personal experience and interpretation of the speakers, especially if they have no official role to play. We found these personal differences of memory and emphasis everywhere, but in general terms the testimonies confirmed each other. We were surprised by our own scepticism when we arrived, that so much of the ingrained and constructed Western cynicism about revolution had rubbed off on us. Now I have returned I am astonished by my own conviction. The change was brought about by the confirmation in so many ways by so many different people widely scattered over the country that it is a people's struggle; that for the people of Tigray the revolution has represented not only a new hope for physical survival which they have retained through two famine periods, but also a revelation of a society based on a different evaluation of personal worth and human dignity. For a people treated little better than slaves, for women, for Muslims, the experience of making a society in which they could be equal, of being able to have some control over their own future has been one they will not relinquish easily.

Why women?

Oppression in Tigray has not been uniform. As in all societies and particularly in a region characterised by poverty and exploitation, some groups have been even more oppressed than others – landless peasants, the minority nationalities, Muslims and all women. The extent to which women's interests are prioritised is an acid test for any society claiming democracy or undergoing revolutionary development. One way to judge the genuineness of TPLF claims to be a people's struggle is not only to investigate its popular support, but particularly to focus on the condition of women before and after the revolution.

On the other hand there are limitations to this approach. Despite the advances in the position of women, the degree of oppression was such that it would be unreasonable to expect them to have attained already a practical equality with men in positions of responsibility. It is remarkable how many have, but the fact is that much of the information we received on new systems and structures was from men in leadership roles. This information has been included in the context to the women's testimony.

The meaning of revolution

Tigrayan women are describing a revolution that is essentially a process, not an event. The strategy of the TPLF was to liberate one area at a time, eject the feudal lords, distribute the land among the peasants and lay down the structure through which the people could administer themselves. This has been an ever-accelerating process as the influence of already-liberated areas spread to those still in the hands of the government. Revolution for the Tigrayans means solving a series of problems as they present themselves and in the way that seems appropriate at the time. "Revolution is not an event for us," Meles, the Chairperson of TPLF, said to me in June 1989. "It is a never-ending process. We never had a final blueprint as to how to do things. We only had general directions and the details had to be worked out in practice through experimentation, through making mistakes and learning from them. We strongly believe in this nature of a revolution." The testimonies reflect the evolutionary processes of ideas and solutions. TPLF leaders have been open in discussions with us in acknowledging mistakes or explaining the reasons for changes of direction in the light of experience. Testimonies taken over a period of three years reflect changed approaches to, for example, women and ploughing, to women as combat fighters, to the newly liberated towns as opposed to the countryside, to medical care, education, military strategy. The base-line of principle applied unswervingly to all policies is the importance of the 'mass' as the criterion for judging tactics in all areas of struggle. The people's participation in determining solutions and their long-term well-being, particularly through the achievement of peace in Ethiopia, are the decisive factors in directing policy.

Why have the Tigrayan people been forced to take up armed struggle? The absence of any democratic structures through which to change the system and the brutal suppression of dissent forced not only the Tigrayans, but other groups in Ethiopia to take up arms. In fact it is impossible to answer this question without looking, even superficially, at the history and politics of this region over several hundred years but especially since the late nineteenth century. For this reason, but also because the history of African countries has so effectively and systematically been ignored by the West, a substantial background chapter has been included. Some of you will start there; some will want to go straight to the words of Tigrayan women themselves; others will want to dip in and out of the reference material for explanations of what the women assume to be understood.

Why should the Tigrayan revolution be important to us in the West? Why should the experiences and struggles of a remote people be of interest? Where does it get us – to identify and sympathise with their sufferings and aspirations? This book is about a process that only starts with identification. It has expanded my personal experience, although most of that has no place in it. In researching the history, in collecting the testimonies I became caught up in the efforts of Ethiopian students to compel changes in the political system of their country; I wept for the mothers forbidden to mourn over the bodies of their children slaughtered in the Red Terror; I felt the ache of long hours of grinding alongside Harnet and Román as they worked with peasant women to gain their respect and so move them to claim a better life. But identification is self-deceiving unless it leads to something more. You cannot enter human history once it has taken place, nor can a person in Britain now really recover the experience of Tigrayan people oppressed for hundreds of years. What we can do is support the struggles of people in Ethiopia, Nicaragua, Chile, Namibia and all the other places where they are transforming their lives by their own efforts, not only materially but by spreading information, by demanding more rigorous standards of news and comment, by resisting the contribution made to their subjugation by our own government and political system. More important however than what we can do for the Tigrayan people is what they can do for us. We can learn from them fundamental revolutionary principles that underlie differences of context and strategy – the meaning of 'struggle'; that, given access to knowledge and information, the people can understand and strive for the interests of a whole society and not just of a sector, and that it is possible to transform our own social and political situation by our own efforts.

Why armed struggle? – the background to the Tigrayan revolution

In 1975 the Tigray People's Liberation Front (TPLF) started an armed struggle against the central government in Addis Ababa, capital of Ethiopia. Within two or three years they had won extensive popular support, which has steadily grown until 1989 when they gained control over the entire province of Tigray. This is a revolution in every sense of the word – not merely armed protest against a regime and a system of government, but also a transformation in social and political structures, in the condition of life and habits of thought of the whole people.

The Tigrayan revolution, however, has not occurred in isolation. It is not only the Tigrayans who have felt compelled to take up arms in Ethiopia, but also the people of Eritrea, Western Somalia, Ogaden, Sidamo, Oromia, the eastern lowlands and elsewhere. There are ten or twelve liberation struggles being conducted in the Horn of Africa at the present time, representing different nationalities or class groupings. They are not all fighting for the same objectives, but have in common deep dissatisfaction with the military regime. For an explanation we need to look not only at the situation since the Addis Ababa government, usually called the *Derg* (committee), assumed power in 1974 but also at the preceding despotic reign of Haile Selassie and, briefly, at the history of the Horn of Africa over several hundred years.

'Ethiopia' in name only

The conflicts in Ethiopia today derive from its multi-national composition and from the refusal of its governments to address the complex needs and demands arising out of this. 'Ethiopia' as such is a bogus entity, actually comprised of over seventy-four distinct ethnic and language groups. The largest group is the Oromo nationality in the south, which has a present population of about eighteen million. The Tigrayans number about five million, while the Amhara people, whose rulers have retained dominance from the nineteenth century to the present day, number only some ten million out of a total population of about thirty-eight million (excluding Eritrea). The present northern boundaries have only existed since Haile Selassie's annexation of Eritrea in 1962, in defiance of a 1952 UN resolution granting Eritrèa federal status; the southern boundaries only since the 'scramble for Africa' at the end of the nineteenth century, when the

Amhara king of Shoa, Menelik II, imposed his power on the Oromo, Somali and other peoples of the south and east and on Tigray to the north.

In fact, 'Ethiopia' is used to designate a territory whose boundaries have been continuously changing over hundreds of years and whose people have been compelled by force into a paper 'unity' only in this century. The eurocentric concept of the *nation state* is an imposition which the colonial powers found expedient in sharing the African territory between them, the better to extract the spoils. The basis of Ethiopian 'unity' since the nineteenth century has not been the unified character of its peoples and their culture so much as a region *between* the European colonies which, with their help, the Amhara rulers colonised for themselves.

Successive Ethiopian governments during the twentieth century have encouraged the myth of three thousand years of continuous 'Ethiopian' history and many Western historians of the region have uncritically accepted it. The histories of the multiple nationalities which inhabit this region have been reduced to a single official version by their Amhara rulers. In particular the early history of the Tigrayan and southern Eritrean regions, seen in the highly advanced civilisation of the Axumite era, has been adopted by successive Amhara regimes to represent the history of Ethiopia and to justify an Amhara 'right' to rule the entire area from Addis Ababa. Paradoxically the independent history of the Amhara people themselves, as well as that of the Oromo, the Afar, the Somali, the Agew and other peoples, who were the southern and eastern neighbours of the Axumites, has been made invisible.

The Axumite Kingdom and its heritage

The kingdom of Axum lasted from roughly the sixth century BC to 1000 AD, reaching its greatest influence in the period from the first to the seventh century AD. Its borders extended to the southern border of Tigray and it left a rich architectural and archaeological heritage of rock-hewn churches and monuments. It was a highly literate society, soon developing an alphabet, and it is from the language, *Geez*, that modern Tigrinya, the language of Tigray and Eritrea, has evolved. Christianity was introduced in the fourth century and its monasteries, not unlike the medieval monasteries centuries later in Europe, became centres of learning, translating Greek and Hebrew works, including the Bible in the fifth century. Axum's prosperity was founded on trade relationships with Greece, Egypt, Byzantium, Persia, and the Indian sub-continent. At the height of its power it extended into the Sudan and the Yemen and controlled communications and trade in the Red Sea. By the end of the sixth century AD its influence had been eclipsed by the Persian Empire and the first wave of Islamic expansion. After its port Adulis was destroyed in 710 AD, it was cut off from trade and the outside world and began gradually to decline. Around 1000 AD the Axumite kingdom was conquered by the relatively undeveloped Agew people, who established the Zagwe dynasty.

The Axumite heritage is still important in Tigray today. The ancient Axumite obelisk symbolises the national consciousness of Tigrayans in the revolution. It not only stands in Axum still, but also in the centre of the insignia of the TPLF. The battle in February 1988, when the TPLF won control of Axum for the first time since the revolution began, has a special resonance for the people.

Until the twentieth century the name of this region (the Eritrean, Tigrayan, Amhara complex), was Abyssinia. The name may have been a corruption of *habesha*, a southern Arabian tribe who migrated to the Eritrean/Tigrayan highlands in early times, and from whose language *Geez* developed; or a corruption of *habeshat*, a 'mixed race or people'. 'Ethiopia' comes from a Greek word meaning 'burnt faces' and was used for the peoples living south of Egypt. For over a thousand years, from the decline of Axum until Amhara domination was established towards the end of the nineteenth century, Abyssinia was a shifting confederation of small kingdoms and principalities. The system was feudal and 'rule' was often more a matter of the extraction of nominal submission and the payment of tribute, difficult enough in such a mountainous terrain and in the absence of roads. The borders of Abyssinia were never the same as those of present-day Ethiopia. For example, the south, the home of the Oromo and other peoples, was never part of the Abyssinian kingdom at this time.

Ethiopia and European imperialism

Not until the mid-nineteenth century was there another attempt to impose unity under centralised control. In 1855 Teodros II became Emperor of Abyssinia establishing and maintaining his pre-eminence through constant warfare. His successor was a Tigrayan, Yohannis IV. His main concern was the defence of the Empire against external enemies and so, apart from the exaction of tribute, he allowed internal autonomy to his feudal kings and princes. It was this relative autonomy which King Menelik of Shoa exploited in order to expand his own territory, conspiring with the colonial powers, particularly Britain, France and Italy, behind Yohannis' back.

After 1869 the British were concerned to protect their interest in the Suez Canal and the sea routes to India and encouraged the Egyptians to conquer and settle parts of Eritrea. In 1875 Egyptian forces invaded Abyssinia, but were resoundingly defeated by Yohannis' forces. Under a treaty with the British, Yohannis allowed the withdrawal of the Egyptians, but the British, instead of easing the Abyssinian occupation of Massawa and Keren in Eritrea, treacherously transferred their support to the Italians who a few years earlier had established a footing in the ports of Massawa and Assab. Encouraging the Italians to expand their interest in Eritrea was part of a British effort to counteract French influence from their territory in Djibouti over the Red Sea area and was to lead eventually to the long colonial domination of Eritrea by the Italians.

Menelik, himself an astute manipulator, was not so easily manipulated by the colonial powers. He continued making use of the European powers and of foreign mercenaries, even playing them off against each other, to achieve his ends. When Yohannis' forces were fighting off the Italian invasion of Eritrea in 1885, he made a treaty of friendship between Shoa and Italy. As a result the Italians supported Menelik's bid for the throne and in return he signed the 1889

Treaty of Wichale (Ucciale) recognising Eritrea as an Italian colony. Disagreement over the terms of the treaty, however, led to conflict. The Italians claimed Abyssinia as a virtual protectorate and not until their disastrous defeat at the Battle of Adua in 1896, were they to recognise the absolute independence of Abyssinia. The myth of an uncolonised Ethiopia amid the European 'scramble for Africa' is therefore a profound irony: the Ethiopian empire-state was created in the full flush of imperialism and in complicity with the imperialist powers.

Amhara domination under Menelik

Menelik II's nationality was Shoan Amhara; his kingdom was Shoa, a province to the south of Tigray. Thus began the Amhara domination of all other nationalities in Ethiopia which is at the root of the constant conflicts in the Horn over the last hundred years. Between 1880 and 1906, he pursued his own colonial policy by conquering and annexing the kingdoms to the south of Yohannis' Abyssinian empire, so establishing the borders the new empire state was to keep until Haile Selassie's illegal annexation of Eritrea in 1962. Because of Yohannis, he saw Tigray as the main threat to domination and was determined to destroy it. He tried to impose his own governors on Tigray, but met massive resistance. The British diplomatic mission of the time reported that Menelik's governor, Ras Mekonnen, was having difficulty obtaining rations:

> *He has already asked Italy to send him rations for his troops. He has by proclamation already ordered the farmers to plough and the traders to trade. They have refused to obey, saying that they are not going to plough to feed the Shoan army for nothing. His proclamation of establishing a peaceful government for them has only had the effect of rousing the population to worse conduct and increasing the number of rebels.*
>
> *(Foreign Office, 403/284 No.419. Mr Harrington to Viscount Cromer, Addis Ababa, May 31st 1899)*

The despotic regime of Haile Selassie

Haile Selassie continued the process Menelik had started. First as regent from 1916 and then as Emperor after 1930, he followed European models by reducing the power of the feudal lords, separating the legislature from the judiciary and setting up a national army and a centralised administration and bureaucracy. The education system was expanded to provide educated officials to staff the new ministries.

These new or expanded institutions, however, did not improve the quality of life for the impoverished and illiterate majority. On the contrary, they were staffed largely by Amharas and were used unremittingly to enforce Amhara supremacy over the other nationalities. Amharic, a minority language, was declared the official language; all other languages and cultures were ruthlessly suppressed and the people were denied all basic human rights.

Under his despotic and feudal rule, the various regions of Ethiopia were seen merely as opportunities for exploitation and plunder, especially Tigray because it was still regarded as the major threat to Amhara supremacy. During centuries of feudalism there had been no agricultural development, but under Haile Selassie oppression of the peasant farmers intensified. Peasants had to pay up to three quarters of their production as taxation in kind to the landlords and further tax in cash to the Emperor. The Christian Orthodox Church itself held huge tracts of land and cooperated with the Amhara rulers and the feudal barons in the oppression of the people. Muslims were particularly severely oppressed in the Christian areas. They were not allowed to own land and had no legal rights.

Land rights under feudalism

No account of Ethiopia can ignore the persistence of feudalism and its effects. Haile Selassie was perpetuating and intensifying a system which has oppressed the peoples of the region throughout its history. The domination of the other nationalities by the Amhara has been accompanied by the added oppressions of feudalism, so that alongside the nationalities question the issues of land rights and land reform have been of central importance in the Tigrayan revolution.

Under feudalism there were two kinds of land rights. With the *gult* system, which was widespread in the south, *gulti* land was granted as fiefs to the aristocracy and servants of the state.

When Menelik conquered the Oromo land in the south in the last quarter of the nineteenth century, he gave huge grants of land to his Amhara military leaders. These *neftegna*, as they were called, extracted large surpluses as taxation from the peasantry, often as much as three-quarters of their production.

In the north, including Tigray, the majority had land rights through the *risti* system. This granted, not ownership, but cultivation rights through birth to a kinship ownership system, traced genealogically to a first ancestor. However, multiple descent groups and the absence of written genealogies meant that competing claims were common and, as access to courts was determined by power and wealth, these were also the determinants in the development of a class of rich peasants who held the cultivation rights.

Poorer *ristegna* would often have to promise a proportion of their harvest for the hire of plough oxen, to pay taxes or meet family needs. In times of drought or locust plague, there would be no harvest and the land would have to be sold to settle the debt. Also many holdings became fragmented through division between family members. Landless peasants and those whose plots were too small to feed their family had to work the land of *ristegna* who held the cultivation rights. They too often had to give up to three-quarters of their harvest to the *ristegna* who themselves paid tribute to the *gultegna*, the nobility or clergy who held the fief from the Emperor.

The First *Woyane* of 1943

The oppressions of the peasantry under Haile Selassie's regime led to the First *Woyane*, or revolution, which was to erupt across the province in 1943. Before that, however, in 1935 the Italian fascist army had invaded Ethiopia and a few months later Haile Selassie fled into exile in Britain, where he won a place in the popular imagination as, incongruously, an enemy and victim of fascism. In 1941 the defeat of Mussolini's colonial ambitions in north-east Africa allowed his return.

After the excesses of the fascist occupation, the people had welcomed him back, but this acceptance was short-lived. In 1943 the people of Tigray rose in spontaneous and wide-spread revolt in an armed struggle which united them across class divisions. After significant victories it was put down with the help of British personnel and aerial bombardments by RAF planes from Aden in South Yemen. Reprisals were swift and harsh. After the ceasefire the Ethiopian army was sent through Tigray on a punitive campaign of looting, burning and rape against subsistence farmers who had dared to protest against their enforced poverty and degradation. Far from social reforms being initiated, the only response to the uprising was further repression.

The 1943 resistance to Haile Selassie's oppressive rule is given immense importance in revolutionary Tigray. They see this first Woyane as an essential precursor to the revolution inspired by the TPLF in 1975. It is valued as irrefutable evidence of the strength of resistance to oppression by the Tigrayan people, as well as proof that intensified oppression eventually intensifies the people's determination to resist again.

But the First Woyane also taught important lessons for the future. Despite its fervour, in the judgement of the TPLF it lacked the two essential ingredients for successful revolution — *organisation* and *political consciousness*. These lessons had an important influence on the development of a revolutionary method both leading up to and after the 1975 revolution or Second Woyane.

After the 1943 revolution the minimal development input which Tigray had received was reduced. There was no agricultural development and the population of over 95% subsistence farmers was still trying to grow enough to pay huge feudal dues and feed their families with the same few primitive tools they had been using for hundreds of years. The population of the rural area was entirely illiterate, yet thirty-six of the forty-nine town schools were closed in 1949 on the grounds that Tigray did not bring in enough revenue. The peasants had no access to health care. For a population of nearly five million people, there were seven doctors in four poorly equipped hospitals, two of them the remains of Italian field hospitals in shacks. There was no industrial development, only exploitation of gum arabic, incense and sesame from the west for processing outside Tigray.

The 'Amharisation' of Tigray

The oppression which Tigrayans recall most vividly, however, was the enforced 'Amharisation' of their culture and the suppression of all regional languages and cultural traditions. Autocratic rulers have always founded their exploitation on the suppression of language and culture and Menelik and Haile Selassie were no exceptions. All non-Amhara nationalities became second-class citizens. Education and public communication had to be conducted in Amharic. The tiny minority of Tigrayans who achieved school or university education found it increasingly difficult to find jobs as the government was virtually the only employer. Tigrayans were not allowed to write or publish in Tigrinya: "We had to use the Amharic language," a TPLF member who was a student at this time told me. "I would write to my mother in Amharic and she would have to ask a student to come and write a letter to me. She would say it in Tigrinya and he wrote it in Amharic."

After the illegal annexation of Eritrea by Haile Selassie in 1962, resistance there broke into open revolution and this provided an important model for the Tigrayans. As repression increased through the 1960s and 70s, the Tigrayans, as well as other oppressed nationalities in Ethiopia, began to organise clandestinely.

Organised resistance

The *edir*, the traditional Ethiopian mutual support groups based on nationality and kinship networks, provided a natural meeting point for Tigrayans and an outlet for national feeling. The most powerful and organised resistance, however, came from the Tigrayan National Organisation (TNO), an association of progressive Tigrayan intellectuals and students. It was essentially a Tigrayan rather than a student movement and drew on the long history of Tigrayan national resistance. The organisational impetus of TNO probably had its roots as far back as the 1943 Woyane. Certainly the importance ascribed now to the First Woyane by TPLF would support this.

When TNO emerged as an organisation in 1972, it began to play a crucial role in mobilising and politicising Tigrayans in the main towns. Its agitation for political and economic change made a decisive contribution to the popular uprising which was to topple Haile Selassie from power in February 1974. This was the organisation which was to form the basis of the TPLF.

The Ethiopian student movement before 1974

The student population in the towns was also becoming increasingly vocal in its opposition. Haile Selassie's modernisation programme had contributed to the growing discontent. He had expanded the educational system to meet the needs of the new government bureaucracies, only to create a source of opposition in the students themselves. In a country where there was 95% illiteracy and so few had access to education, 'students' included the higher grades at school, not just the minute proportion able to attend college or university.

The grievances of students extended beyond differences of nationality and the Ethiopian student movement before 1974 unified Amhara and non-Amhara students behind a number of demands, particularly the slogan 'land to the tiller'.

Active protest extended even to the schools, so that in the early 1970s education was on the point of breakdown. Berhanu Abadi, our guide and interpreter, was a student in a Makelle high school at that time:

> We had many uprisings in the schools. The students were mostly demanding better education, equipment and materials, and only sometimes political demands – in fact in some places the student movement was not politically conscious enough. In 1973 we shut the schools for two months and in 1974 for the whole year. Even the teachers decided not to teach. It was then the mass movements started. Then the military started to oppose the Haile Selassie regime in different parts of Ethiopia.

Political argument flourished in underground cells and anti-government songs circulated clandestinely. Tartarow, a fighter who now organises TPLF cultural troupes, told us:

> In 1974 I came to realise my national identity through the songs. They stirred emotions in me. I saw the discrimination against students in Tigray – no books, no good teachers, no materials, not a single thing. But Tigrayans in Addis brought back political thoughts to us. They made us realise we were oppressed in school, where the police, the 'White Guard', beat us up, although we just wanted to study peacefully and help our families where we could.

The end of Haile Selassie

The revolution which toppled Haile Selassie was a popular revolution. The frustrations caused by the suppression of all political activity, let alone opposition politics, were compounded by the government's failure to deal with or even acknowledge the existence of a terrible famine in Wollo and Tigray in 1971-73. There was dissatisfaction too among the bureaucrats in Haile Selassie's modernisation programme, now emerging as a professional class whose interests were opposed to those of the feudal aristocracy who had held power for so long. A wave of strikes and demonstrations involving all sections of society broke out throughout Tigray. The mainsprings of the uprising were the Ethiopian student movement, the TNO and the workers' movement. Workers in several factories played a major role and price increases in petrol, for example, made it impossible for the taxi drivers in the towns to make a living. Workers, taxi drivers, students and teachers came out on the streets.

The army at first supported the Emperor. However, as the uprising grew more serious, there were signs of dissatisfaction among the junior officers. Twice within a few weeks the government gave in to the soldiers' demands for salary increases, but disaffection spread as the army found itself unable to contain or crush the people. Two units came out against the government and were joined by elements in the airforce. The army decided to side with the people and in February 1974 Haile Selassie was swept from power.

A time of hope

Accounts of the few months until the following September give us an idea, at least in the major towns, of a different Ethiopia from the one that has evolved since. People who were there speak of the general feeling of unity and hope. For the first time in their history, concerted action of different groups, across religious, national and class barriers, had succeeded in bringing down a repressive government. There was euphoria on the streets.

Solomon Inquai, now chairperson of the British branch of the Relief Society of Tigray (REST), described the atmosphere in Addis:

> In that moment the press was free. You could discuss anything. Freedom dawned on the people. They felt the chains were broken and that the people were united, that a democratic atmosphere was unfolding. It was beautiful.
>
> During this time I joined a big march by Muslims from the Grand Mosque to the office of the Prime Minister. I went to the Grand Mosque early in the morning. The march was Muslim, but the streets were lined with Christians, cheering and ululating. I was crying with joy. If anybody had told me that as a Tigrayan I could not be happy, I would not have believed them. I could see a new Ethiopia where it didn't matter whether you were Christian or Muslim, Tigrayan or Amhara.

These few months were of profound importance to future developments in the struggle for freedom. The opposition movement had had a taste of success and a glimpse of a different kind of society. When their hopes evaporated and were finally shattered by the repressions of the military regime which seized power later in 1974, they realised there was no going back to the old ways of underground resistance. Better organisation would be required if they were not only to mobilise the people but also successfully assume power. Different factions were to develop different strategies in response to the new situation.

In February and in the following months none of the opposition groups, however, was strong enough to provide an alternative government. Political repression had enabled protest, but disabled the growth of any practical political experience. At that time the army was neither organised for power nor politically conscious. Its last minute support was more a facing up to the inevitable than a statement of an ideological position. However, after Haile Selassie's fall, each unit had elected representatives to a military committee in support of the revolution. Among these was Mengistu Haile Mariam, known for his drunkenness and brawling. Most were non-commissioned officers with no knowledge of politics. This was the base of the group of army officers who were able to step into the political vacuum.

On 12th of September 1974, they seized power in Addis Ababa. They dissolved the civilian government, appointed as prime minister a member of the nobility on the political right, and established themselves as the Provisional Military Administrative Council (PMAC), usually referred to as the *Derg* (the Amharic word for 'committee').

But the Derg lacked a popular base. Although a popular uprising had swept Haile Selassie from power, this clique of mostly Amhara soldiers and officials had not been the leaders of any popular movement and did not represent the interests of any group but the military. In this new Ethiopia in which people's power could sweep away unpopular rulers, how were they to secure a base in the people?

Expediency had influenced their support for the revolution; expediency seems to have been a factor in the choice of an ideology. Since the political atmosphere was dominated by the socialist thinking of the student movement, the military government responded to the mood of the times by taking up socialism as its professed ideology. Yet they were still ambivalent about the way forward; they had laid down no structures as yet and were still appointing civilians to important posts. Most importantly, they were led by Mengistu Haile Mariam, who would turn out to be as dangerous an autocrat as his predecessor.

The Derg in power and the growth of opposition

The basis of the seething discontent throughout Ethiopia and Eritrea which produced the 1974 uprising had been on the one hand the punitive conditions of feudal deprivation and taxation of the poor peasants and on the other the larger context in which feudal oppression took place – political suppression of the diverse nationalities. Yet, despite its Marxist rhetoric, the new regime proved as little inclined as the preceding one to encourage either the development of the poorest classes as a political force or to offer any political participation to the various national groups. It was always improbable that any degree of political autonomy which would threaten the authority of the central government and its Amhara domination would be granted to the regions. Not only was the urban middle-class of administrators, army officers and students still predominantly Amhara; the Derg itself was dominated by the Amhara. Despite a proclamation in April 1976 that 'No nationality will dominate another one, since the history, culture, language and religion of each nationality will have equal recognition in accordance with the spirit of socialism', the new government not only continued but intensified the same policies of Amhara ascendancy and extinction of the cultural and political expression of other nationalities.

Once again the mainstay of opposition was to be the students. Workers and teachers made a limited contribution, but the vast peasant majority and the urban mass had no voice whatsoever. Even the students, although representatives of an expanding and relatively privileged class, were still very restricted as far as practical political participation was concerned. Because non-Amhara nationalities were also required as administrators in the regions, students were also drawn from the Tigrayans, the Oromos and other nationalities. These had good reason for discontent, but opposition was not only dictated by self-interest. The Amhara ruling-class had unwittingly produced more than servants of the state; they were assisting the creation of a new intelligentsia in the sense of a growing body of educated, politically committed and socially responsible people who were prepared to sacrifice personal interest to work with their oppressed people for a more equal and socially just society.

Disunity among the student opposition

After the Derg's military coup had dashed all hopes of a successful transformation of Ethiopian society, different strands in the student movement began to break into various factions, influenced by students in exile in Europe and the USA who had begun returning to the country after Haile Selassie's downfall. The largest group, centred on students in Addis Ababa, became the Ethiopian

People's Revolutionary Party (EPRP); a smaller faction was MEISON, an Amharic acronym meaning the All-Ethiopian Socialist Movement.

Divisions were about tactics rather than ideology, but no more resolvable for that. The MEISON group argued that in the absence of a popular base, it would be unwise to condemn or antagonise the army; they should work with it and use it as a springboard to a popular base. The EPRP view was that it was impossible to collaborate with a reactionary movement like the army; a coalition government made up of students, teachers, workers, the army and other classes should draft a constitution which would provide for an elected government.

EPRP was the largest and most influential group but was to make two mistakes. Their class analysis excluded the nationalities question and their adoption of a policy of urban terrorism after 1976 encouraged reprisals from the Derg. Although working for a revolutionary mass struggle for political and democratic rights, EPRP was politically unable to solve the fundamental problem of the suppression of the nationalities. MEISON was never more than a minority faction but, although at first closer to the ideology of EPRP, after 1974 it formed a close alliance with the Derg and became its ideological wing, when the military government proclaimed itself socialist.

Persecution under the Derg

The suppression of all opposition groups turned into open persecution soon after the Derg take-over. In the later months of 1974 arrests and disappearances increased as the Derg began systematically to eliminate all who questioned the legitimacy of its power. All opposition political organisation went underground. Even the *edir* mutual-support groups were banned by the new government. Solomon Inquai describes this time:

> Both the right and left were lumped together as reactionaries and counter-revolutionaries, and decimated. Many were slaughtered in cold blood, others were taken into custody only to vanish without trace – many more still languish in prison. Ethiopia today has the highest number of political prisoners in Africa, perhaps in the world.

However, the military regime moved particularly forcefully against the proletariat. Although the workforce was relatively small, it was the only sector of Ethiopian society with a modicum of organisation, in the form of the Confederation of Ethiopian Labour Unions (CELU), which could mount an effective opposition to the regime. When they called for a general strike in support of the demand for a popular government, their leaders were arrested and imprisoned. Throughout the following year, the trade union movement was under constant attack; all activities were banned and all collective agreements suspended.

In the new labour code of December 1975, the word 'class' did not appear and workers' rights and working conditions were defined by conventional bourgeois standards. It included neither a minimum wage nor any social security measures and strikes were only lawful if the High Court failed to give a ruling about the dispute within fifty days. CELU was replaced by the authoritarian and hierarchical All-Ethiopia Trade Union (AETU), facilitating government control of labour. Spontaneous worker protests were met with shootings and imprisonment.

The founding of the TPLF

Not only did increasing intimidation, arrests and executions shatter any expectations of social or political reforms; they also provided the final impetus for open revolt. As the Derg repression increased, it became apparent to Tigrayans, as to the Oromo and all the oppressed nationalities in Ethiopia, that the 1974 take-over by the Derg did not represent any fundamental change in the distribution of political power. TNO once more took up its leading role as an underground organisation, constructing an analysis of oppression, politicising and mobilising its growing numbers in study groups and cells.

There was of course nothing sudden about TNO's decision to move from agitation underground to open revolutionary struggle in the TPLF. Accumulated resentment against Amhara domination, whether under the Derg or the Emperor, was widely felt. The Tigrayan petty bourgeoisie could not expect the same privileges as the Amhara. Tigrayan businessmen, workers and students still experienced constant discrimination against them. Able young Tigrayans were allowed to be students, but needed higher grades than Amhara students to qualify in examinations. Applicants with non-Amharic names failed to get jobs.

This made them sensitive to the even greater oppression and misery of the peasants. Awareness of the enforced and needless impoverishment of the Tigrayan peasants seems to have been a factor in the consciousness of the Tigrayan intelligentsia from the time of the First Woyane, maybe earlier. In any case there is not in Ethiopia the distinction between town and country that we are used to in the industrialised countries. Only Addis and Asmara are towns in the Western sense, with the beginnings of an urban industrial society. Tigrayan towns are essentially market places and part of the economy of the countryside. Land is the basis of the economy and the economic status of those in the towns was based not only on employment, if they could get jobs, but also on land-holdings in the countryside. Country relatives would provide them with cereals, milk, vegetables and eggs; the town family would expect to help out if crops failed, cattle died or the taxman called. Tigrayan students came from a range of backgrounds, but all had close connections with the land and the peasantry. It was TPLF's insistence from the beginning on the importance of the peasant 'mass' and on their eventual participation in determining their own future which served to broaden the base of its appeal and to make them so different from the other opposition movements in Ethiopia.

So it was that, one year after Haile Selassie's fall from power and six months after the Derg take-over, when all other means of pursuing their democratic aims were closed, TNO took up arms and started the struggle for national self-determination. On February 18th 1975, a small group of ten Tigrayans left for the Dedebit area and took the struggle for Tigrayan self-determination out of the towns and into the rural area. TNO had become the Tigray People's Liberation Front.

Fighting the feudals

Competing with TPLF, however, were other organisations that united Tigrayans against the central government across class barriers. Several resistance groups emerged, not all of them on the side of the poor and exploited. In early 1975 the Derg used the Land Reform Bill to dismantle the power of feudal landowners. These 'feudals' began to arm themselves as an organisation of landlords and peasants in the Ethiopian Democratic Union (EDU). Although led by a Tigrayan prince, Ras Mengesha, EDU was not a Tigrayan organisation and encompassed both reactionary Amhara and Oromo.

In Tigray EDU exploited Tigrayan nationalism and at first had great appeal for a peasantry conditioned in feudal relations and encouraged to blame external oppressors for the miseries of their lives. In the short-run it did manage to rally mass support, but it was led by a nobility more interested in preserving the privileges of the Tigrayan feudal aristocracy against Amhara encroachments than changing the conditions of the peasants. *Terranafit*, another feudal-nationalist group also had a large following in the north-west of Tigray.

TPLF had to challenge and defeat both EDU and Terranafit, in order to rid Tigray of its feudal landowners and start the process of freeing the minds of Tigrayan people from feudal sentiments. This was the period of 'the early years' when TPLF went off into the rural areas or 'the Field' and gathered support. News of the activities of TPLF gradually spread among Tigrayan students and organised underground support increased in Addis and the Tigrayan towns, particularly in the capital, Makelle.

The Zemacha campaign

The Derg took the threat of this organised and politicised student movement in the towns seriously. Soon after coming to power, it started to enrol many students in a campaign called *Zemacha*. The Zemacha purported to send students into the countryside to explain the political developments in Addis Ababa, and to help carry out the radical land reforms announced in March 1975. In reality it was a pretext for emptying the towns of these inconveniently vocal opponents of the military regime and dispersing them widely over the rural area. The more politically conscious students in the towns saw through the campaign and opposed it from the beginning; others were politicised by other students or through the experience of the campaign itself. Berhanu described his experiences to us:

> The politically conscious students in the university opposed the campaign, but most of us weren't so aware and we joined it. But I had a good friend – we were friends even at school and we were both sent to the same place in Korem. He knew much more about politics than I did. He was very inspiring. He shared his experience and information with me and I became involved in politics consciously. We started to oppose the Zemacha campaign openly. So after one month and a half, they imprisoned thirty-six students from Korem. They took us by truck to Addis Ababa and threw us with many others into an underground prison –

> *more than a hundred and seventy students. Really we suffered a lot. They flogged us and tortured us. When we were in prison there was a big student demonstration in Addis – it was May Day 1975. One of the slogans of the demonstration was 'Release the imprisoned students'. So not more than a week after this demonstration we were released and I was transferred to southern Ethiopia.*

The ironic paradox was that for many students, the Zemacha experience did not so much diffuse their political energy as clearly show them the Derg's lack of any serious intention to increase political freedoms. The issue which most intensified their opposition to the Derg however was that of land reform.

The Derg's land reform

The Derg's 1975 land reform bill announced the nationalisation of all rural land and its redistribution to landless tenant farmers, sweeping away the economic base of Ethiopia's feudalism and earning the new government a reputation for radical reform.

Its tenets would have had very radical effects *if* they had been fully implemented. In practice it was only paper radicalism.

The *gult* system which prevailed in the south was abolished and every farmer was promised up to ten hectares of arable land, but the principle of equal distribution was never followed through. Redistribution of 'land to the tiller' was widespread, but rich peasants remained in positions of power. In the north, peasants were given possessory rights over their existing plots, but existing inequalities were compounded, leaving petty landlords and rich peasants with economic and political power.

Land reform was intended to be implemented through peasant associations set up by the Derg. The progressive element among the Zemacha students took the edicts of the land reform seriously and, though they were met with great suspicion, began to work with these newly-formed associations, to arm the peasants in the face of recalcitrant landlords and to redistribute the land.

The cosmetic nature of the Derg's socialist pretensions again became apparent. As soon as the students began to work closely with peasant activists to implement land reform, the military tried to curtail their activities and to accuse them of sabotage and ultra-leftism. They were especially castigated for upholding the national rights of the oppressed peoples of the south. The Derg's strategy had only aimed to destroy the power-base of the old regime, not to transfer power to poor and landless peasants. In cases of open confrontation the Derg sided with rich peasants and in fact alliances with the local notables and rich peasants became the basis of its control in the rural area. In these conflicts many of the Zemacha youth were killed.

Peasant associations were far from becoming the basis of the political and economic power of the peasantry within a framework of socialism. The declared aim of making them the spearhead of a socialist agriculture came to nothing. They became instead organs for the *depoliticisation* of the peasantry, where, for example, the participation and organisation of women were systematically marginalised. Like the urban associations, or *kebelles*, they were gradually transformed into instruments of state control, with law and order, conscription, revenue collection and suppression of dissent as their main functions.

In this savage crackdown on progressive Zemacha elements, both students and peasants, there were reports of Tigrayan and Oromo students being reviled and attacked by fellow Amhara students. Many students began leaving the campaign and, like Berhanu in 1976, made contact with TPLF, so that, in effect, the campaign became a training ground for future members of TPLF, the Oromo Liberation Front (OLF) and other liberation movements. Berhanu again:

> *The TPLF was well-organised. There were communication links with the field, with the public relations workers in the TPLF. They smuggled leaflets into the towns, even cassettes with revolutionary songs. We tried to send back information about military secrets.*

The departure to the Dedebit forest to start the armed struggle was the precursor for the flight from the Derg's persecution of first hundreds, then thousands, of Tigrayan women and men over the next few years. For these revolutionaries, the guerrilla struggle in the mountains, patiently winning the support of the peasants and enduring every kind of hardship, was the most important politicising aspect of the early years and severed them completely from their petty-bourgeois past.

The real nature of the Derg

Despite their claims to the contrary, the Zemacha campaign revealed the true nature of the Derg again. Judging their claims to socialism by their treatment of the three key sectors, the workers, the nationalities and the peasantry, there has been a persistent contradiction between rhetoric and practice; in their response to workers' demands and workers' rights, in their continued suppression of the nationalities, and finally in their cynical depoliticisation of the peasantry.

The story of Suhool

The story of Suhool, one of the first members of TPLF, told to me recently by his daughter, Lemlem, describes vividly the growth of opposition in the last years of Haile Selassie, the emergence of the TNO/TPLF as the major focus of opposition to the Derg and the process of the Tigrayan revolution:

My father's name was Gesesse Ayele. His name in the TPLF was Suhool. He worked for the government of Haile Selassie in charge of a gum arabic company in Tigray. In 1968 he had a confrontation with the government. My father was insisting that the government open up local processing factories but they absolutely refused. He rebelled against them and began mobilising the people, so when they came to arrest him, he had to escape to the forest. I was eight years old when that happened. Immediately the government started all kinds of harassment and arrests against the whole family and my aunt took me away to Adigrat so that nothing would happen to me. It was the first time I'd been separated from my family, from my mother. It was the hardest time of my whole life. I hated it.

Everything we had was auctioned by the government. My mother, my grandmother and my uncles were put in prison. My relatives in the countryside were arrested and either put in jail or forcibly moved to town and put under house arrest. They were separated from their wives and their cattle were slaughtered.

There were so many atrocities against my family that my father agreed to a deal with the government. The provincial governor came and took him to Makelle where he was made executive director of the only gum arabic company in Tigray. Later he was transferred to Dire Dawa in Harar province as chief executive of both companies.

We stayed there three years and I started school. Then he returned to Tigray where he was elected to parliament and went to Addis. Even there as a member of the Senate, he was under continuous surveillance by the government. We were always afraid of what might happen to him and to us. We always expected him not to come home in the evening. There were always camouflaged government cars around our house. Even though we were living comfortably and had enough to eat, we always had this fear in our minds that they were going to do something bad to our father. Once they killed his bodyguard, Mahdi, mistaking him for my father. Another time they kept him in prison for a month. There was never any explanation, no one was ever accountable – and he was a member of parliament!

During this time our house was open to all to come and talk. He was always ready to talk to everyone and always writing. I used to wonder what he could be writing about. While in Addis my father was a member of an *edir* committee. Most of them were university students and this connection started a political process. He started, along with other students, the Tigrayan National Organisation (TNO), an association of progressive Tigrayans, which later became the TPLF. That's how my father came to be a member.

When parliament was dismissed in 1974 and the Derg took over, my father was selected to represent the Tigrayans on the new Derg committee in Addis. After about seven months the Derg started arresting people, killing and torturing. He heard he was to be arrested so, when there was trouble in Axum between Christians and Muslims, he offered to go and quell the situation. That's how we came back to Tigray.

As soon as we got home to Endaselassie, he got in touch with many people. I knew something was happening, that he was acting outside the government and without their approval. The Derg demanded my father's return and announced on the radio and in newspapers that he was refusing to go back to Addis to represent the people. All he would tell us was that he wouldn't go. After three or four months my father was sure the Derg were going to arrest him. They had given up on my father. Not only that, they knew all about his activities. Then my father with other members of TPLF went to the field. They left from our house. I was about fifteen then.

Then came what happened to every family whose family members joined TPLF. They asked what had happened to our father – as if they didn't know! We said we didn't know. "Your father has become a bandit. We know you know where he is. You must take us to him." "How can we know where he is? You say he has gone to the forest – you find him." They called us together, all the relatives in one group and Christian and Muslim leaders in another. We were told to beg the TPLF to return. We children refused, but the group of elders did go. The TPLF told them they hadn't taken up arms just to go back when begged by parents and religious leaders. Their stand concerned political principles and they were going to fight for them.

He was only in the field for one year. He was martyred fighting against the EDU.

GRINDING SONG

*Hear me, my grains, my grains of wheat –
While I tell my tale.
When we brought you from the harvest fields
You filled the basket to the brim;
But after all that labour on the land,
When you come to the grindstone,
Instead of ten donkey-loads,
You are only a few handfuls.
The feudals have taken it all.*

*My hands, hear me as you grind,
Hear me and take care
Not to let fall the smallest grain
And waste it on the floor.
The Lady in the feudal's house
Sits idle, with her hands
Adorned with gold and henna.
But my hands are ground down
With work, and fighting
With this stone –
To ward off hunger.*

*Why am I born a woman?
For a priest, I make do with a hen;
My grindstone is my only friend.
I can open my heart to no one near.
Whether they are home or the house is empty,
No-one speaks to me.
My priest is a hen and my friend a grindstone.*

*How do you feel, my husband,
As you labour for nothing on the land?
The fire burns bright in the feudal's home,
Where there is soup and meat and milk;
Coming home from the fields
To a house cold and dark
With no fire and no food –
How do you feel, my husband?*

Prerevolutionary women's song

Women in feudal Tigray

"Take a stick to your oxen, but a stave to your wife" Tigrayan proverb

"To understand the position of women in Tigrayan society, you have to understand feudalism," says Besserat in her opening testimony. Before we can understand the massive support of women for the revolution, we need to know what life was like for them up until 1975. Then, as now, 95% of the population were subsistence peasant farmers with no other source of food or income than the land. The difference then was that in a rigidly hierarchical society in which most of their production was taken from the producers, poor peasant farmers could never take survival for granted even until the next harvest. They were illiterate, without health care and with an average life expectancy before 1974 of forty-seven. Women were at the bottom of the hierarchy of oppression. They had no rights of any kind, but the worst deprivation was the absence of rights to land. This condemned peasant women to the kind of dependency normally associated only with domestic animals.

We know that from time to time in Tigray before 1975 resentment flared into sporadic rebellion among both the peasants and the intelligentsia. But what do we know about women's response to the harshness of their lives? Evidence for active resistance from women is scanty. A prominent member of the Ethiopian student movement and of the Tigrayan resistance was a woman called Marta. In 1972 with other university students she tried to hijack a plane, but the attempt failed and they were arrested and executed. One of the places we visited was Marta school for women, which is named after both that Marta and another who was the first woman fighter to join TPLF.

"Women's plans are fit only for the latrine" Tigrayan proverb

The most important evidence of articulate resentment, if not of active resistance, comes from songs, many of which show clearly that the people were well aware of their oppression. Various kinds of professional musicians made their living from singing and playing at weddings, funerals and feastdays. The *mase* in the Adua, Agame and Adigrat areas, were men only and their songs fall into two groups, highly complimentary songs for the houses of the feudals and subversive versions for the peasant listeners. Sometimes in one song double-meanings and codes would allow two opposing interpretations of the same words, intended to be relished by the peasants while going over the heads of the lords paying the bill. The professional poet-singers and social critics at funerals were called *melkesti*. Many were women. They were engaged at every social level to sing the *melkes* or funeral ritual. But once the formalities of celebrating the life and deeds of the dead person were over, they were free to criticise openly any aspect of society, even the feudal lord. They were protected by the culture from all reprisals; the only comeback for the lord was to have his own singer on hand to give a counter view. Famous women *melkesti* at the courts of the most powerful feudal lords were Maskale at the court of Ras Seyoum, and Weyzoro Tekle and Weyzoro Te'ebey in the service of Dej Gebreselassie.

The most open expressions of resistance to the daily conditions of life under feudalism are found in work songs. The different stages of the agricultural year and even of times of day had songs ascribed to them, the rhythms of which corresponded to the kind of work being done. The harvest songs were the most bitter. Every member of the community would be engaged in the fields, even the children – everyone except the family of the feudals, who would then take almost the entire crop. The grinding song at the beginning of this section reflects not only the hard labour and isolation of women, but the problems of the whole community in its relations with the landowner. Women had to labour in the fields, as they still have to, as well as for the house. Their special responsibility was weeding and at this time of year there were many songs sung by men and women together in a sort of 'conversation'. Some of the most striking in a society so repressive of sexual expression are the ones in which the woman's social inequality and her sexual inequality come together in a joint lamentation. *Hemsi* is her vagina:

> *O this hemsi of mine,*
> *How unlucky I am to have it!*
> *If I say, 'No,*
> *I don't want to do it!'*
> *I get beaten anyway*
> *With a big stick.*
> *How I wish I didn't have it.*
> *God is unjust*
> *To give us this hemsi*
> *Which we can't call our own.*

Her *hemsi* complains of the bitter treatment it gets from her husband, but he is not sympathetic and replies:

> *All of you hemsis,*
> *Not only of my woman,*
> *But of all the women,*

Gather together
In the village square
And cry.

Other songs equate a woman's sexual obligations with her female tasks and the penis with the big stick that beats her if she is lazy. Even the wives of priests were allowed to sing these songs. Iyassu, head of TPLF cultural department, quoted a priest as saying: "As long as you sing songs like this in the fields and nowhere else, God allows it."

Despite the many changes already achieved by the revolution, the feudal past interpenetrates the present. The conditions of life before 1975 were very present in the consciousness of everyone we met. Women still in their twenties had been brought up and reached marriageable age under feudalism. These included women we interviewed who had joined the revolution after the Red Terror in 1978 and were now playing leading roles in TPLF. Kebbedesh, who was only thirty-one when she was interviewed, had endured many years of bare survival before becoming a fighter. Older women found it hard to break years of prohibition on speaking in public to do more than smile and cover their faces with a shawl. Women over forty carried the scars in their faces of years of labour and inadequate nourishment – they looked nearer seventy to us. Yet at the same time the profound changes that had taken place sometimes made it hard to remember that the Haile Selassie era was so recent. In part this was a problem of perception. Words like 'feudalism' for British observers belong to remote periods of history; other words like 'biblical' offer themselves as a means of describing an agricultural economy while in fact obscuring the unpardonable anachronism it represents in the late twentieth century.

"A pot made by a woman will shatter at a hyena's bark" Tigrayan proverb

In many respects women's material position and the hardness of their lives remain little altered. Their lives are still spent in time-consuming and back-breaking tasks like grinding, cooking the traditional meals, gathering fuel and collecting water. One typical image, still, of the Tigrayan peasant woman is indeed 'broken-backed', typically bent at the hips at an angle of forty-five degrees beneath the burden of a child, a clay water pot, a cloth-wrapped bundle or an enormous pile of wood fuel. But images are unreliable and the camera can lie. The political and social context has completely changed; the structures of feudal oppression have been lifted. Now the people own the land; their labour contributes directly to their own survival and that of their communities and does not fill the granaries of a landowner; women are talking in the people's council (*baito*) about practical ways of improving their lives in a country still shackled by material poverty and primitive technology.

I don't intend to comment on all the testimonies. The women speak for themselves. But Tigrayan peasant women have no habit of self-expression, of attributing importance to their experiences or their emotions. Those who have become fighters have in addition dedicated themselves to a cause which prioritises the revolutionary struggle over the private emotional life. These life-stories are spare and concise, without any embroidery or self-indulgence. Those who expect harshness of experience to be reflected in expressions of emotion will be disappointed. Readers from a different tradition may read too fast to catch the resonance or they may unconsciously impose their own cultural norms and miss the meaning altogether.

I'll illustrate what I mean by reflecting on Kebbedesh's story, one of the first in this chapter. It is for me the most important and fundamental of these testimonies. In the Tigrayan context it is not extraordinary, but typical. I heard many similar stories. Her experience shows in its details what life under feudalism was like. Bandits of the kind who murdered her father were widespread. Lawlessness in an unequal and unjust society is another means to survival. People subjected to feudal exploitation had to face bitter dilemmas to survive which became preserved in cultural practice. Sons were productive and through marriage could bring wealth into the household in the shape of goats or oxen; girls were not only another mouth to feed, but upon marriage would take wealth out of the family. The alternatives for women were marriage or prostitution. In both institutions they were commodities for sale or barter. Banditry and prostitution were the more visible economic consequences of an exploitative social and political system. With the redistribution of land to the peasants, including women, they have died out in the longer-liberated rural areas. Thousands of prostitutes have, like Kebbedesh, responded to the TPLF principles of equality and participation for women by returning to Tigray from surrounding countries to support the struggle.

> "A busy woman will even wash her husband's bible" Tigrayan proverb

Kebbedesh approached us in Marta School for women. She came to where we were sitting with Saba and Román and after a while said she would like to hear about the struggle of women in Britain and tell us about her experiences. The others, who knew her story already, were obviously moved by it. They saw it as a triumph of women's strength and spoke of Kebbedesh as a model for fighters. When I used the story in subsequent talks in Britain I found that some British people responded very differently from Tigrayan fighters, whether men or women. Western readers or listeners tended to interpret it in the light of their own cultural experience. Kebbedesh, instead of appearing as a strong woman whose life shows from the beginning a clear pattern of refusal to submit and of a series of choices leading to seeking out TPLF and becoming a fighter, is seen primarily as a victim, an abandoned child of a 'bad' mother and a 'bad' society. Prostitution was sometimes seen as a less than acceptable way out of her miseries.

For Tigrayan listeners on the other hand, this seems to be a story about women, not one woman. It is as much about Kebbedesh's mother, possibly only a child herself in her early teens, for whom her daughter was a 'heavy burden'. It is about the aunts, turned into instruments of social pressure by an extra mouth to feed, by a society which had no place for a woman without a husband and which measured husbands in terms of the oxen they could provide, and by public opinion which regarded a child brought up without a father as 'rubbish'. It is about the prostitutes, perhaps the nearest we get to independent women with their jewellery, 'good clothes' and their freedom to travel, who take her to the Sudan. It is also about the women fighters at Marta School who have rejected the oppressions both of imposed marriage and of prostitution and who are working for ways of constructing more equal lives for women.

Melkes chant sung at funerals

O God, don't come down,
Don't come down from your holy place.
We are beaten and tortured
By the priests and the feudals.
If you come down here
Their boots will trample you too.
Don't come and make more trouble.
Just keep watch from heaven
And when their time is over,
When the lord has exchanged his gold
For a rope and a shroud,
Then will be your chance for vengeance.
He will slip through the thin line
And fall to the fires of hell.
Now we are waiting for the guns,
The guns of the oppressed
In the hands of the peasants.
Your time is near!

"To understand the position of women in Tigrayan society, you have to understand feudalism"

Besserat: To understand the position of women in Tigrayan society, you have to understand feudalism, where women are treated as second citizens. In Tigray women were never allowed to own land, which means they were excluded from the most important source of economic livelihood. They were not allowed to participate in political activities. Culturally, there were a lot of traditions that put women on a very low level. It was dictated that women were lower than men and must be treated only a little better than animals.

"No one knew more about women's oppression than I did..."

Kebbedesh: My family were peasants. I never knew my father – he was murdered by outlaws when my mother was pregnant with me. My mother faced many problems after his death. She was shocked and her health was not good. Because of her troubles she called me Kebbedesh, 'a heavy burden'.

After a while my mother remarried. She left for another village but I went to live with my aunts. When I was seven, my aunts arranged for me to be married to a wealthy neighbour. He was rich, chauvinistic and rather foolish. He was huge, with a beard, and he seemed like a giant to me. My uncles told him not to have sex with me. They made him promise in front of a priest that he would wait until I was mature, but this did not work.

I went to his house, which was strange to me. I saw him for the first time inside the house. He was like a giant, like something that makes you afraid. At that time I didn't know what marriage, or being husband and wife, meant. After three terrible nights I escaped back to my aunt's house. My family insulted me, shouted at me, "Why did you come back, you stupid girl?" They forced me to return.

After some weeks I escaped again, this time to the forest. I passed several very difficult days there. I was hungry and thirsty and I just wanted to die. I fainted and a peasant found me and took me back to his house. He knew me and knew my family were angry so he kept me in his house. He gave me milk because I couldn't eat *injera*. After a few days he took me back to my home. My family took me in but then they tried to persuade me to return to my husband. They said he was rich and owned many cattle. They wanted me to go and live with him again.

They took me to him for the third time. I lived there for some months, maybe a year, but then I escaped again. I felt it was too difficult to live in the world. I took a rope and went to the forest to hang myself. A neighbouring peasant who was tending his cattle in the forest found me standing under a tree. He was surprised and asked me what I was doing there with a rope. I told him I was collecting wood. He didn't believe me and tried to take me back to my husband. I refused to go – I said I was looking for wood.

After two days in the forest, I became so hungry that I returned to a neighbour's house. They tried to reconcile me to my family. When I was eight, one year after I was married, they made me return to my so-called husband. My husband forced me to have sex when I was eight years old. I was sick for many days after that. I just didn't know what to do or how to help myself. All paths seemed closed to me. All the people in the area were against me. They said I should stay with my husband because he was rich. They couldn't see it from my point of view – they thought it was natural.

I continued like this until I was eleven, escaping and being returned by my family. At last my mother learned what was happening to me. She came back to the village, divorced me from that man and took me away with her to her village.

But once I was there I faced another problem. The people there insulted me. Because I didn't know my father, they said I was undisciplined. They said I was rubbish because I had been brought up by a woman, without a father. They said a woman could not bring up a child properly, that I was undisciplined to divorce my husband and so they teased and insulted me. Things weren't easy for my mother either. She also felt insulted because I had left my husband. So I decided to go to Asmara. A friend had come to visit us from Asmara, so I went to her and begged her to take me away with her. I was fifteen at that time.

But when I reached Asmara I didn't like it. There was nothing for me there. After a miserable time there I went to T'senay near the Sudan border and got a job in a bar. In the bar I was badly treated – men came and kicked me, spat in my face. They could do whatever they wanted. The owner of the bar also was cruel. If I broke a glass she would not pay me. I worked there for two years but was not even able to buy any clothes. The male customers cheated me. They said they would give me money to pass the night with me, but after they slept they would leave without paying.

At last some women came to the bar from Sudan. They had jewellery and good clothes so I asked them about their life in the Sudan. They encouraged me to go there with them, saying I could have a good life. So I went to Sudan after two years in T'senay. I lived in the Sudan for ten years. I rented a room and worked as a prostitute for ten miserable years. The life of prostitution is clear to you, so I don't need to explain it.

In 1977, TPLF members were trying to agitate the people in Sudan and to establish underground movements wherever there were Tigrayans. I became interested in this news. TPLF didn't need to politicise me – I had led a terrible life. No-one knew more about women's oppression than I did. I became an active participant in TPLF activities and worked for two years with them. I learned sewing and then, in 1980, I decided to come to the Field as a fighter. After I finished training, I was assigned to the workshop as a tailor. Then, three years ago, I was assigned here to Marta School. I am a student and I teach sewing. I am also a fighter.

I feel proud and happy to be here. We are many women with different miserable experiences. We discuss our past lives all the time. This gives me a very special feeling. Before I came here I was fighting without a full consciousness. I understood more than anyone that women are oppressed by men and by class oppression, but still I was not fighting consciously. I had not examined the 'woman question' scientifically. Since coming here I have studied the 'woman question' and have come to realise that the solution is to struggle and to bring about a new society.

It makes me happy that I came both to learn and to teach. I feel so happy to be teaching my sisters, to be producing skilled sisters. I feel joy and happiness when I see the results of my teaching.

"To have a girl born in the family was like a curse"

Besserat: One of the signs of oppression of women in Tigray was the number who were prostitutes in neighbouring areas, in Sudan, in Ethiopia. There were so many prostitutes because women were not allowed to own land. On top of that, woman had to pay money to get married. Now if you were a poor peasant and you had daughters, you couldn't marry them off because you didn't have dowries to give them. A lot of women were left without any provision for life. In most other countries the dowry is paid by the man, but in Tigray it's the girl who had to pay her oppressor, the man. He had to be paid to get married to her! So what happened was all these girls would be hanging around the villages with nothing. They would migrate to the next town, from there to the bigger towns, and from there to Eritrea and the Sudan. In the Sudan alone, there are one hundred and fifty thousand Tigrayan prostitutes.

To have a girl born in the family was like a curse. If she had a dowry, the family would be poorer, whereas if she'd been a boy, they would have received a dowry from another family. Tigrayan girls were brought up in a family that openly showed them they didn't want them. Tied up with this we had some of the most appalling traditions you can imagine. A girl used to be circumcised at eight days old. We had two types of circumcision, one is where you remove the clitoris, the other is where they remove the whole thing, pharaonic circumcision or infibulation. This was one of the reasons why infant mortality was higher in girls than in boys, because they were exposed to all sorts of infection – huge wounds at the age of eight days. OK, so boys were circumcised, but not the removal of the whole thing.

Then there was child marriage, one of the terrible feudal traditions we had. My own grandmother married when she was five years old. Eight, nine, ten was the age of marriage for girls, and then they married men as old as fifty! Divorce was the right of the man alone. Among the Muslim Tigrayans, a man could be divorced three times. The woman would receive about four pounds. That's all!

Then there was wife-beating. Any man who was supposed to be macho, who had to stand among his friends as a man, was expected to beat his wife at least once a month, or if he was a very good strong man at least once a week. Rape was not even a crime, it was just something men chuckled about.

"I am less of a human being than a man"

Mahta: You cannot understand the changes brought about by our revolution unless you know something about what life was like for women before. Culture in Tigray has played a big role in women's oppression especially as, before the revolution, so many women accepted it. Women had very low status, reflecting traditions brought about by the feudal system of government as well as religion. Women saw *themselves* as inferior: "I am less of a human being than a man" or "I have to do domestic work, because my husband has to work outside, or do an election – he is important!" Even in eating she had to wait for her husband to finish. Without being invited by her husband she could not even eat after he was finished. Among the Afar people, she couldn't eat with her husband at all, but only his leftovers. In Christian families, she could eat with her husband, but only when invited.

She had to marry at twelve years old at the latest and often at nine or even eight, but if she was unmarried at twelve it was a disaster for the family. "She is twelve already, she is not married – oh what can we do?" Always her parents would be talking about her: "Why should we still be feeding her? Why is she still dependent on us?", and in one way they would be right because they were so poor and, according to custom, she should be able to feed herself. Sometimes, a girl would leave her parents and her village and go to the Sudan – that would be resistance!

It was essential for a woman to be a virgin when she married. If no blood was visible on the wedding night, the husband could send her back to her parents dressed in black as a sign of shame, riding on a donkey. For her, for all the family, it was a terrible disgrace – "Oh what can we do? How can we go on?" All her sisters became unmarriageable too. Physical abuse was also traditional. If she complained to her parents, she was told it was normal and to go back to her husband.

After marriage, women were not happy to give birth to girls, who were considered weak, only half a man. "Boys can protect us and work. Girls are just for the kitchen." When a child was born, the women gathered to ululate, seven times for a boy, but for a girl only three times. Her parents would say, "She is a girl. What are we going to do?"

Education was not allowed for women at all in the rural areas where 95% of Tigrayans live. But even in towns boys and girls were treated differently. Education was not seen as necessary for girls because they were destined for domestic life. This meant that in primary schools, 40% of the pupils might be girls, but in secondary schools maybe only 12% because by that time the women might be married or working.

In the countryside, a woman did 40% of the work outside the home, but it was not recognised by society. She had to do the hoeing, the tilling, the harvesting, and to prepare food, but especially the weeding is women's work in Tigray. She would be engaged in subsistence farming and supplying food for the family. She could be blamed if things went wrong – if there was a drought; "God is sad, because women are touching the plough, or harvesting." During ploughing and harvest, she was not allowed to go near the fields. She had to stop two kilometres from the workplace in order not to interfere with the harvest. She would have to call out to her husband, "I am coming. Can you please come and get your food?"

In the towns only low status service jobs were available to women, sometimes shop assistants or bar work, but more often domestic service or prostitution. If women were raped or ran away to the towns from the rural area, there was little open to them but prostitution. Prostitution was very high in the towns.

Women could not be called as eye-witnesses to give evidence in legal cases. Although her husband or her brother could use the courts, she was not allowed to complain to a court. In fact, she was not allowed to speak in public at all and so had no voice in affairs.

Religion and the priests had an important influence on women's oppression. They wanted women to accept it. With no knowledge of science and technology, the church and religion were very powerful and women were constant church goers, so those laws and traditions were also very powerful. During menstruation women were not allowed to go to church. In Axum there was a separate church for women and a separate burial ground. Men could go to the women's church, but not the other way round. All the oppression was strengthened by religion, especially the conviction that a woman was not equal, only half a man. Among the Muslim population this was intensified. Clitoral circumcision was practiced throughout Christian Tigray, pharaonic circumcision among the Muslim Afar people. Women were thought to be uncontrollably sexy, if they were not controlled by circumcision. This was generally carried out between one and ten days after birth, but always before eighteen days. Boys in the Orthodox Church were circumcised, a much more superficial operation, some time before their baptism at forty days after birth.

Superstition was very high and especially connected with women's oppression. Women had no power to express themselves and their needs were never fulfilled so they would often turn to superstitious beliefs. In our culture blacksmiths ('budda') were seen as sacred. If you argued against them you would be killed, or possessed by some magical force. Women were seen as the victims of the 'budda'. They were unable to have any real power at all, even rights over their children. So if they wanted something, they would resort to curses and hysteria, because people's fear of their frenzied state would obtain for them more material reward. Women resorted to familiars and fortune-tellers more than men because they had no capacity for solving their problems. Now women are stopping these practices, as they get more control over their lives.

The early years of the revolution

To the sun's scorch or the lash of hail
We are indifferent;
Whether we dry with thirst or drown in marsh –
We do not care.
Our pillow is a stone; a cave is our home.
Our strength is in our people and our politics
And we will not submit.
TPLF song

The revolutionary struggle started on the February 18th 1975 when the first fighters went to an area known as Dedebit in western Tigray near the Eritrean border. The aims of the revolution had already emerged in the theoretical debates of the Ethiopian student movement and TNO. It was against exploitation from within Ethiopia – the Amhara rulers and the landlords – and from without – the imperialist powers who had supported Haile Selassie's regime. They were fighting for national self-determination within a changed Ethiopian political system, but not, unless they were forced, for independence. Within these broad aims, the priority was to free the peasants from the exploitation of the landowners. But first they had to secure the support of the farmers for the struggle and establish a mass base. For this, practical strategies were necessary and the practical difficulties were immense.

Their numbers went up from day to day, but by the end of the first year there were still only about a hundred and ten fighters altogether. They were impoverished; living conditions were harsh and they often went hungry. Accounts of this time all reflect the same contrast between the rigorous physical life and the joy of the early stages of a revolutionary struggle. Iyassu tells us:

That was the time when we felt very happy and very free in our free nation. But the forests! It was very hard – not the same as sleeping in comfort. You had to walk

> *at least ten hours a day; even if you were going in the hottest area you only had one drink; there was no soap and you didn't have a chance to wash for a month or to cut your hair. We had lice; we were almost naked. But everybody was happy, everybody was singing, everybody was discussing. We did not have quintals of wheat to eat, but we had knapsacks full of books, Marxist books, a typewriter, and a griddle to bake our bread if we could get hold of any flour.*

But what part were women playing in the revolution at this stage? They receive no mention at all in the historical books and papers I have drawn on for this brief survey. Presumably they are subsumed within the usual terms used to describe the range of human beings without responsibility ('people', 'peasants', 'students'), but not in decision-making categories ('military', 'government' or 'Derg'). We know from the first chapter that women as a class were so oppressed that our expectations of their participation have to be low.

However, the oral history I have gathered in Tigray itself suggests that women did take part in the struggle for change from very early on. The first woman fighter was a peasant called Marta, who migrated to Eritrea and found work in a factory. While she was there, she was influenced by the women fighters in the Eritrean struggle and then went to the Field to join TPLF only eight months after the struggle began. Marta is now a legend in Tigray. She was killed in battle but she lives in the imaginations of women fighters as a model and her name has been given to a school for women fighters, Marta School. Lemlem was one of the first two or three women to join the struggle and her story gives us many insights into the difficulties of being a woman in a guerrilla force at this early stage. So who were these women? What motivated them?

Except for Marta, at first they were drawn from better-off, better-educated families in the towns and came under the influence of radical groups in universities and schools. Families who believed in education for sons saw it as unnecessary for their daughters. Zafu makes quite clear how unusual was her mother's insistence on education for her daughters. They were a Muslim family and her mother had to defend herself against the criticism not only that education was an unnecessary extravagance for daughters destined for a domestic life, but that it was likely to be morally corrupting. When we read these testimonies, we have to see the importance of women like Zafu's mother, whom we can almost miss at the margins of the revolution, but who in fact play a central part in influencing the process. By far the largest number of women were working in the underground political movements in the towns. Women like Lemlem, influenced from a young age by her father, exposed to the frequent visits of political activists to the house, began to work first in the underground support groups, carrying messages and food to the Field. Increasing harassment from the Derg pushed her towards joining the struggle as a fighter, only to find women were not very welcome at that stage.

It is remarkable how these women overcame the disadvantages of their background; in some senses it seems as though they were showing men the way. We met in Tigray continued astonishment from men at the achievement of women. A basic principle of the revolution is that the people have to *claim* the revolution for themselves. "Socialism must be built by the people," Meles said to us, "not for the people by somebody else. Any system that is given in charity can be taken away by force." Women fighters demanded a place in the struggle. Lemlem stresses the importance of refusing to admit inequality, that physical equality was easier to demonstrate than mental equality. Mebrat and Zafu have to trick their way out of the towns to the liberated area. Kebbedesh refused to submit to a miserable life. In later testimonies, Belaynesh, Atsede and Lichy decide to be fighters and refuse to be put off.

The Red Terror

The first three years of the struggle were taken up with fighting the feudal landowners in the Ethiopian Democratic Union and ousting the Ethiopian People's Revolutionary Party (EPRP) from Tigray. The Derg was essentially weak and without effective strategies for dealing with the multiple opposition movements in Ethiopia, until in 1977, it turned from courting the USA, Ethiopia's historical supporter, to the USSR. Timely and massive assistance from several socialist states orchestrated by the Soviet Union utterly changed the balance of power and gave the Derg, under the dictatorship of Mengistu Haile Mariam, both the resources and the confidence to launch a campaign of state terror.

On February 3rd 1977, seven Derg members were executed; the following day the Red Terror began in Addis Ababa. I have heard accounts of how Mengistu addressed the crowds in Red Square, with a bottle of blood held high in his fist. "We will spill the blood of the reactionaries like this," he shouted. Many thousands died in his attempt to exterminate once and for all everyone who opposed him and terrorise everyone else into passivity. Young people were especially targeted as they were the most vocal element in the social agitation for a people's government. Families lost four or five children at once. Most of the EPRP leadership and many TPLF activists were killed.

On May 1st at least fifteen hundred students were massacred while taking part in a peaceful demonstration. I heard many eye-witness accounts of the bodies left in the streets as a lesson to the townspeople. Mourning was forbidden; mothers were threatened with arrest as sympathisers if they wept; families could only bury the bodies of their children if they bought them back for the price of the bullet that killed them. This was set at about two hundred and fifty birr, a month's salary for a teacher and totally out of reach for most of the population. Between May 19th and 21st, in the midst of the Terror, the EEC confirmed massive aid to Ethiopia and, ever since, the Western powers in one form or another have continued to keep a foothold in this strategic area by financial support. That September a second wave of terror was launched. From Addis it spread in 1978 to Makelle and other Tigrayan towns like Axum. On my recent visit to the newly liberated towns I discovered that for many families the scars of the Red Terror are still fresh.

Ironically, the Red Terror drove thousands of new recruits from the towns to fight with TPLF in the countryside. This was the time when waves of women went to the Field. Their role as underground activists in the towns could no longer be sustained – too many had been slaughtered. From the beginning, the importance of the mass base was an essential part of the ideology of struggle and from this emerged a fighters' code of practice. Bitter experience had taught the peasants to be suspicious of outsiders and that people who carried guns were of two kinds – either they were in the service of the feudal landowners or they were bandits. Both inspired hatred and fear. At first, TPLF with their guns seemed no different from bandits, so the first necessity for the fighters was to gain the trust and confidence of the people. If they were against exploitation, they had to start with themselves. "Don't take so much as a needle from the people when you go among them," was their code. "When you need goods or food from the peasants, you must pay and pay well."

From now on there were the numbers to intensify the process of consciousness-raising in the rural area. 'Consciousness' is now an important word in Tigray. Women, for example, refer to the time before they were 'conscious', and what happened to make them 'conscious', their desire to bring consciousness to other women. But in the beginning it was an uphill task, as Iyassu describes:

> *They don't know anything about what struggle means by itself. In our culture if someone has a gun and stands against the government, he is called a bandit. People having power had never been seen before in Tigrayan society. So that when we tell them that we are going to overthrow the Derg's government and have power in our own hands, power of the people, they can't imagine it. If we talked theoretically, they would never accept it. So, for example, when we taught them about the tactics of guerrilla fighting, we told them about the dog and the flea. The flea jumps on the dog's back. The dog starts scratching. The flea jumps to another place. Soon everywhere there are fleas. They suck his blood and the dog becomes skinny and in the end it will die.*

From the first, song and poetry were an important way of raising consciousness. Before they were able to accumulate or carry musical instruments, songs would be accompanied by a peasant on a bamboo flute and by the fighters on a *mogogo* or baking griddle. Marta was the first woman fighter and her first song was:

> *Women! Get up off your knees;*
> *We knelt beneath the feudals' rule;*
> *We were only speaking tools.*
> *Now we as well as men have guns*
> *And one day we'll be free.*

Lemlem's story

Lemlem: My parents lived in Shire, one of the eight districts of Tigray. I was born in the town of Endaselassie. We were seven children. I was the third of four daughters and I had three younger brothers.

After my father left for the Field, I contacted TPLF in Axum and began working for the underground there. I was still living in Endaselassie, but the government was keeping a constant watch on me and others in my family. Because of this I couldn't work there, so I went back and forth to Axum. I worked like this for a year and nobody knew I was working for TPLF, not even my mother. Then in 1976 I went to the Field myself. When I joined TPLF, women were not welcome as fighters, but only as underground workers in the towns. The TPLF felt they didn't have the facilities to accommodate female fighters. They told me to go back where I came from. But I refused. I said the Derg knew I had left and if I went back I would be in trouble. They wouldn't accept me, so for a while I was roaming about on the fringe of the urban area. After a while they came to understand.

I was one of the first woman fighters to join TPLF. Marta was already in the Field and there might have been one or two others, but we were very far apart, working in different areas. At that time TPLF organisation was weak, to say the least – practically none! Can you imagine? – coming from the town to those sandals fighters wear. You know those ones made from old rubber tyres! My feet were swollen all the time, with pus coming out. I was famous for my foot-problems! My sandals would come round to the top of my feet while I was walking. You see, when I did my training it was the winter, the rainy season. We had no shelter of any kind and only one piece of clothing made of something, not cotton, which was neither warm in winter, nor cool in summer. The training was dreadful – there are no words to describe it. We were always on the move and had no household items, so when we got flour we could only make one kind of poor quality bread, always the same. The guns were very heavy – there were no Kalashnikovs then as the Soviets had not started to support the Derg. We carried these old rifles and, since the guns were more important than life itself, we used our clothes not for us, but to protect the guns. I used to carry one of the heavy guns – at every step it banged my calf muscles. But with all the hunger, without enough clothes, with so many difficulties, you could not believe the comradeship there was between us. We were always kind to each other; there was no grumbling, no complaints. It was what kept you going. And we didn't know each other before – we were all from different parts of the country.

During training I was assigned to guard duty with a young boy. I don't know why we were put on guard duty – he had never shot a gun, we didn't know how to shoot. He was very excited and kept taking aim at things. I told him not to do that, to take the bullets out. Then I practised taking aim myself. I pulled the trigger, thinking it was empty, but it fired! I fell backwards one way and the gun fell the other way. That was my first experience of shooting. Towards the end, I had proper firearms training of course, but my first shot was an accident! As soon as my three months training was completed, I was assigned to a TPLF battalion and sent to the war against EDU and *Terranafit*.

There were hardly any women in TPLF. Their acceptance of women was a long process. At first all I knew was that the organisation was reluctant to accept women fighters because the natural things that make us different from men were seen as an obstacle. The discussions went like this: "We are poor. We often have to do without food. We have to travel fast. How can we provide such things as panties or pads for menstruation? Even if pads cannot be provided, there have to be clean clothes and this is not possible. If people are starving, how can an organisation provide pads, when we have not even enough clothes to cover ourselves from the rain?" I don't believe they were saying women have no role to play, but at that early stage of organisation it seemed a great problem. In fact it has never been solved completely.

In principle there were rules and regulations. Every unit had a physician or a person responsible for health and medical equipment. We were supposed to tell him if we had our periods and if the towns were not far away then someone was supposed to buy what we needed. So at times we did get supplies of pads or tampons; at other times we didn't. We were in a war situation and constantly on the move. It wasn't possible to keep a stock and it wasn't a priority. But the TPLF had a clear policy that if a woman told the medical officer that she was menstruating then she didn't have to fight. This meant we *never* told him until later because we didn't want to be excluded.

After they accepted and trained the first group of us, including Aregash, there was a long period when they didn't accept any more women into TPLF. We had to prove ourselves so as not to be excluded, especially physically. There was a policy that a woman did not have to carry so many rounds of ammunition as a male fighter. We fought that vigorously. It was easier to prove our equality to the men physically than mentally, so we refused to carry less than the men. There were very few of us, widely scattered, but if we met, the first things we gave each other were words of encouragement: "Never show you're tired. Don't let them make you carry less." We not only helped each other physically, but gave each other moral support as well. There was no way we'd stay behind in war. Even if men had to stay behind for some reason, we were in every battle. In addition to our own guns, female fighters always helped with the heavy guns. During our periods of rest we were always doing something, teaching our fellow fighters to read and write, never just sitting still. If we were staying in a house, we would always share the woman's work. We wanted to teach her everything we knew and learn from her. In fact we did more than the men did.

I was injured in battle with the EDU and went to hospital for a while. When I was better I was given first aid training and I worked there for a short time before rejoining my unit. I stayed a combat fighter until the war against the EDU was over in 1977—8. In 1978 I was assigned to work in the Mass Bureau. By this time the Derg had started the Red Terror. The TPLF underground organisation was being hounded in the towns and many people fled. Then women going to the Field became the norm. Before that it was the exception. Most of us who had joined the TPLF by that time were those who had worked very vigorously in the urban underground, had contributed a lot to the Front and then became military and political leaders. That was the time that women fighters made a difference.

My happiest time was working with the mass associations. I worked in Agame in Central Tigray, in Afar areas, in the west, almost all over Tigray, when I was working with the Mass Bureau. I did it until 1983. You are really in touch with what is happening when you work with the people. You are involved more, you think more, you learn everything from their daily activities. You cannot really know the people from just being in Tigray – you have to work with them. It gives the real meaning of why you have to struggle. We used to make decisions, not because we thought we were good judges, but because we had the trust of the people. Of all the things that surprised me most, it was that the people of Agame never hesitated to accept the decision of a woman fighter, more so than of male fighters. I really don't know why. The people of Agame respected the women fighters. I only have experience of Agame, but later I compared my experience with that of other woman fighters and they said the same of other areas.

The Mass Bureau was just being formed. The people brought a lot of problems to us, problems from Haile Selassie's time as well as the Derg. The culture was different then and attitudes were still rooted in the ways that existed before we started the struggle. All the land was not yet distributed; relationships were still feudal. Nearly all the claims and counter claims were to do with land. "Give us land!" was the cry of the people. "Prove to us you are for the poor peasants! We are hungry – give us land!"

In 1983 the first Women Fighters' Conference of the TPLF was held. I was elected a member of the Committee of WFAT and so I left my work in the mass associations. It was after that conference that Marta and March 8 schools were established and all the issues concerning women were taken seriously by the organisation. I did this work until 1986. Women are not symbolic in TPLF. Women are half of the struggle. Women have contributed so much from top to bottom of the struggle. If the struggle were to continue without women, if that were possible, then it would only be half a struggle. When I talk about women, I am not only talking about women fighters, but about the women of Tigray. They are raising their kids, producing their grain, protecting their revolution. I don't think they would have done that without the participation of women in general.

Now you see everywhere women who are fighters, in all positions from guards to high commanders and department heads. Without the participation of women this struggle would have been paralysed. But the *mothers* in Tigray have changed more than anyone else. Today a mother doesn't cry when a son or daughter wants to join the TPLF. In fact she prepares them for the TPLF. When she has done her work she takes part in the literacy campaign or trains to become a cadre. That is a more visible change than even those in the women fighters.

In 1986 I caught malaria. I was travelling all the time, but they carried me on a stretcher. I took the full dose of chloroquine tablets and I should have got better after four days. They gave me another medicine, the last resort when malaria won't improve. I felt better for a time. When I was convalescing, I started working again, but I was not really getting better. I attended a conference for a month and when it was over I fell sick again with a very high temperature. The only difference I noticed from before was that I couldn't urinate. I was taken to the nearest hospital – it was five hours away on a stretcher. I was able to urinate again after a day and a half, but they were not able to diagnose my sickness so I was sent as an emergency to Sudan. I was in a lot of pain. I was not conscious when I was admitted as an emergency patient in Khartoum. They discovered I was paralysed from the waist down. I stayed there six weeks, then the hospital referred me overseas. It took two years to make the arrangements to come to Britain and I came in January 1989.

Before I got sick I was a very healthy person. I don't remember ever being sick for a prolonged period. I used to get malaria but I always got over it very quickly. In '86 when I got so ill I was very shocked. At first I thought it was a temporary problem and that I would get better and I'd walk again. I admit to you I was very angry. I was not ready to accept it, especially when I discovered that I was not medically curable. It hurt me that I couldn't do simple things for myself. I accepted my illness but I was not ready to be dependent on someone else. For two years I lay on a bed and had to have help even to go to the toilet. My next concern was that I was not able to contribute to the struggle as much as I had done before. I had been very active all my life. I was very bitter on two counts – I felt excluded from the struggle and I couldn't take care of myself.

Our Front has clear policies and procedures for people in my position. As you know, we are in a war and there are many people like myself. The organisation takes care of us as far as it can and of course that care is relative to our society's development. Some of us do work according to our abilities, so I knew that gradually, if I could get some independence I could work with them and I could contribute something. That's how I came to realise that I need not be separate from the struggle. I have learned these things since I came over here to Britain. I am now a bit far from the struggle physically, but I know my role and I am clear what I am going to do on my return.

One of the things you learn from this long experience of struggle is that you're ready for anything. I never thought I would survive this long – I have seen so many battles, so many comrades have died. You learn many things on a personal level. I am no better than the people who have died. You learn courage and that your life has meaning, even as a handicapped person. I never expected to be disabled through sickness, but I know now that disability comes in many forms. I can tell you now that if my feet fail me, I still have two hands to work for the struggle. We say in the Field, "Do your share for the people. That is what the people expect of you." This applies whether you are disabled or not.

The Derg takes power

Besserat: In 1974 there began a popular uprising of the whole of the Ethiopian people against the rule of Haile Selassie, which had been supported by the Americans. The oppressed nationalities felt that they were under the Amharas and they suffered and wanted to be free from it. Haile Selassie was toppled and the soldiers came and took over, but basically nothing had changed because we were still under the Amharas. The Amharic language and culture is imposed on every nationality in Ethiopia. Their history is supposed to be our history. Our kids were never allowed to go to school and learn in their own language; our culture was supposed to be lower than theirs; we were treated as second citizens during Haile Selassie's time, and we are treated as second citizens during the reign of the military fascist regime today. So, when the Selassie regime fell, there was a power vacuum, and as with all underdeveloped nations, the soldiers were organised and took power. So basically there was no change for the oppressed – it was only a change of who was on top, Selassie to the military.

It was a hundred years since all these oppressions were started by the Amharas. People knew and understood – our parents and grandparents had seen better days and they told us what had happened, the source of the poverty, the destruction, the oppression. A child going to school doesn't have a chance like an Amhara child because he has to learn another language; the Tigrayan is systematically demoralised – 'the Tigrayan is low by nature', that kind of thing. Our parents taught us to be proud of our history – we could see that a better world could be created. We were furious about the oppression, we wanted change, we wanted justice. We wanted education, medical facilities, science and technology, and we understood from our lives that unless we struggled, unless we stood up and said 'no!', then we were going to perish as a people, and you know as well as I do that no human society perishes quietly. It is in our nature, and I think it is one of the most positive things about human beings, that we do struggle to survive, and this is *our* struggle to survive.

Fifteen years ago in 1975, ten revolutionary intellectuals with four outdated guns went into western Tigray, and started the revolution. They took on ideas of human liberation from whatever is unjust and they took up arms and started to organise the people. It was important to see their problems. It's not enough to say, "Well, OK, we will have self-determination; we will not be under the control of the Amharas any more" – you also have to have a programme that answers the questions and needs of the oppressed people themselves. This meant distributing land in a just way, with an economic programme, a social programme, and a cultural vision of a world where there will be justice and equality between men and women, and between all human beings.

So they went into the forest to organise the peasants – not only peasant men, although it was easier than organising the women, because we were a society which was extremely oppressive to women. New ideas had to be spread, new education had to be given. The first woman joined the TPLF when it was only eight months old. We organised peasant associations, women's associations, youth associations. Even though we didn't have any industries, we had a small number of workers in cottage industries, so we had workers' associations too.

Then the oppressors – the feudal chiefs, the government bureaucrats – came, organised as a force against us in the Ethiopian Democratic Union (EDU). We fought them for three years. It was a very bitter war. The EDU were destroyed because the people didn't back them, for naturally they couldn't stand with their oppressors – it's very natural for human beings to hate their oppressors. So we went on growing and growing and we're here, nearly fifteen years later in 1989.

Zafu's story

Zafu: I was born in Adua in northern Tigray. We were seven in the family – five children, and I had a twin brother and sister younger than me. My name is Zafu, but my mother used to call me Samhale, which is a fragrant herb we have in our homes for feast days. My father and mother were Muslims, but they were very liberal and sent us all to college, both boys and girls. I had two brothers who were teachers and one teacher sister. My eldest sister married when she was nine years old, so she didn't go to school. My family regretted that afterwards – she was so sharp, yet she didn't have any education.

My father died when I was five years old and after that my mother had all the responsibility of bringing us up. She decided to continue the education for the four of us. She had a lot of trouble with Muslim relatives who thought we should be married as soon as possible. "You are only a woman," they said. "You can't control them. They will be like Christian women, like prostitutes." But my mother didn't like the culture of the Muslims for women. "I just want my daughters to be independent," she said. After that my older sister finished at high school and became a teacher. In our country, high school takes you up to twelfth grade. After that some people go on to university in Addis. When we finished school, at eighteen years old after twelfth grade, my mother wanted us to get married, but she didn't put pressure on us and my sister chose her own husband when she married. I kept telling her lies, saying: "OK, I'll get married," and so on. I was recruited by the TPLF at that time, but because she was my mother I didn't want to upset her.

By 1973-4 the students had become the strongest opposition movement to Haile Selassie in Ethiopia. In 1975, when the Derg came to power, they broadcast the decision over all the media that students had to go out into the villages and teach the peasants about land reform and literacy. It sounded good, but it was a very hot revolutionary time and the real intention was to get Ethiopian students out of the towns and dilute the resistance. The Derg called it the *Zemacha* campaign. The people were not armed at that time, but the government saw the danger if the students continued their opposition. Although they called themselves the *people's democratic government*, they were not – they had introduced military government and wanted to counteract the severe opposition. There were so many democratic questions being raised at that time, such as women's rights and land rights.

I had to serve in the Zemacha campaign, but I didn't go when it started in 1975, because the area where they had assigned me was under the control of the TPLF. So one year after the start of the campaign I was sent to Makelle. I was sixteen years old. I had heard about TPLF because they were agitating the students in Zemacha so that some of them were leaving the campaign because it was not in the interests of the people. When we tried to carry out the literacy campaign, there were no pens, no paper or materials. Only the rich peasants or those who had been administrators under Haile Selassie were holding positions of responsibility. The representatives of the people who should have been distributing the land were the rich peasants, so they took all the fertile land themselves.

I heard all this and several of us started working underground. Many students were arrested for leaving the Zemacha campaign. In 1977 I too went back to Adua and started eleventh grade. Working underground, we collected information and held many meetings. The sort of questions we discussed were, "Why are we oppressed? What is TPLF? What are its aims? How can we help our organisation?" TPLF's only help at that time came from the underground supporters, so we raised money for TPLF through knitting. Most of us girls used to knit – making jumpers, bedcovers, pillows to sell. We also had to be in the Derg women's associations. All the women were told they had to spin cotton and make garments to be collected and sold to make money for the Derg. But, underground, we were getting the materials from the Derg and selling half for TPLF and only half for the Derg. We also made tea and coffee and different kinds of bread and sold them. Our mothers too gave us money to make things to sell and gave food for TPLF, like flour or lentil stew. If it had been discovered we would all have been arrested, and our mothers too. They had endured so much oppression from the Amharas for so many years. They were not very politically conscious and so they hated all Amharas, but we used to teach them who was our friend and who was our enemy – and all Amharas were not our enemies. The Derg was not strong then. We put the story of our oppression and the background of our struggle into plays. Even some of the Derg cadres were TPLF members, so it was easy to teach the people.

In 1977 the Derg got help from the Soviet Union and that changed everything. At the end of 1977 they started the Red Terror in Makelle and by the middle of 1978 it had reached full force. The Derg was like something that is bitter and poisonous inside, but covered in honey to be swallowed more easily. They were saying good things, but at the same time killing the people. Most of the people could not support the Derg and most of the students, if their activities had been exposed, would have been killed. Some of them were not TPLF but were killed all the same. That was the time I joined the TPLF. Many educated women did, but we did not fully understand the issues, although we had many political discussions.

I left for the Field with my younger brother, one of the twins. After we left, my older brother who was a teacher was arrested and killed by the Derg. He was twice in prison but wasn't killed for four months. He was thirty-two. His body was thrown onto the street and my mother was forbidden to cry because the guards said if the mothers cried it proved they were sympathising with the traitors. Nine others were killed with him. She could not take his body for burial.

It was thrown down like a dog. My youngest sister saw his body and the guards hit her for crying. My oldest brother who was also a teacher was sad and sick because he was unable to show his feelings. He shouted, "Where is my brother?" and they arrested him, saying, "You are against the government!" They accused him of being in the TPLF and of coming from a TPLF family. But my oldest brother was not active in TPLF because he had children and responsibilities. He was released after a few months, but he was ill, always upset and depressed, till his death in 1986. He was only thirty-five.

Just as the Red Terror was starting, we were warned that it was beginning the next day and we should save our lives, so we escaped to the Field before the worst. All of us escaped in different ways and the next day they started the killing. I had to deceive the soldiers. We said we were going to a village where someone had died. I dressed in the long clothes of a housewife instead of the shorter ones usually worn by students. A worker disguised himself as a peasant carrying hay, but in the hay was money collected for the TPLF. We took money too, hidden in tea. We took whatever we could which might be useful to TPLF – laboratory equipment, even a typewriter – because it was better that these things should work for the people. We women weren't suspected so much, so we could take things in different ways.

The TPLF organised people so they could save themselves during the Red Terror. We were all linked up, but for security reasons each person only knew one other person. We got out of the town and they took us to safety. I was eighteen when I joined the struggle. I joined at the same time as Harnet. First I had to take training and after a few months I served with the mobile forces. I also took a course to work with the mass associations in different places.

I became ill with headaches and an ear infection, so I was sent to Cairo in Egypt for two years for medical treatment. I went to Rome for further treatment and I also worked there with the mass association. Habtom came to work there too. From there I went to the Sudan and then to the Field for the discussions about marriage for fighters. Marriage was not allowed in TPLF at that time. Habtom and I got to know each other and when marriage was allowed and when we were in Sudan again, I chose Habtom for my husband.

(Zafu's story continues in *Beyond Tigray*)

What was it like for the first fighters working in the villages?

Aregash: We want women to be free from oppression of all kinds, politically, socially, economically, culturally free. We want them to participate in activities which are useful to society. We aim to make them equal to the male and participate in all that the male participates in. We had these aims from the beginning, so, when the struggle started, we started to organise the women in the villages.

Before, for women to see a woman with a gun was very bad because of their experience of police, the military, even bandits in the village. So fighters with guns also made a very bad impression. [laughs] There were only twenty-five or thirty of us then. First we approached them individually in church or in places women could go. We tried to show them that we weren't bandits or police. We said we are women who have taken up guns. At first the women did not believe we were women at all. We had to prove it.

Laila: When we first went into the villages, the women there would say, "How can you come to fight? Is it possible to travel around with male comrades? Our place is only in the kitchen."

Harnet: At first, when we were a few, when we were starting as fighters, wearing trousers, shorts, carrying guns, with short hair, without any decoration, they didn't imagine that we were women. When they first saw us they thought we were men – "How can a woman hold a gun? How can a woman go fighting? You are not women." To prove we were women we had to show them our breasts! [laughter] After this they believed us, but they didn't believe that all women could fight, all women could struggle, all women could go to the Field. "After some time you will be like us," we said to them. "We go to the Field, to the frontline, and we fight with our guns. We kill the troops of the Derg," and so on. They didn't believe us. "Maybe when your comrades go to the front line, they leave you at home," they said. [laughter] We showed that we had a gun or a wound or we said that we were married at home, or that we had children. Comrades who had a child before they became fighters told them that they had children but they left them at home, "Because leaving them at home is necessary at this time because we are oppressed. It's as if we were blind, because women have no rights, no right to learn, no right to teach or to go anywhere because they are women."

Román: In 1975 we were going from house to house, teaching people. In our religion, they have got angels and saints, St Michael, St Mary and so on. So the women make special celebrations. They prepare beer and bread for the feast days. We'd go there and take part in these St Mary groups and discuss with them their problems. They'd talk about how they are going to dance in their group. We would do the same – even if we didn't know how. Then at the end we'd throw in something about the struggle, about our aims. They really wondered how we became fighters. They were very polite to us, but they were in doubt. We had our guns on our backs. They always asked, "Are you really a fighter? How are you going to go with men, equally?" But after some time they came to know that a woman can be a fighter and have a gun in her hand and try to liberate herself.

Aregash: We said we were against anyone who exploits peasants, so then the women became very interested in us. We went into their houses and showed concern for their problems. We discussed their difficulties of health and housework; we gave them guidance about their children, about sickness and so on. We travelled around, two days here, two days there. We returned again and again, discussing daily problems and why we had been forced to take up guns. Gradually they gained confidence in us. They became very interested to hear about organising women. It was very hard to persuade them to go to meetings because they thought they were forbidden to leave the house for such things.

Zafu: For a time there were problems between women and their husbands. The men didn't want them to take political education. They thought that if the women were politically conscious there would be disagreements in the family. Women were beaten, they were forbidden to go out. We had problems in making the men understand. But I was really interested when I was working with the mass because when we taught the people, they understood and began to participate.

Laila: The first time they were called to take part in a meeting, the women said, "How can we come out to the stage to speak? How can we be organised?" The men were saying, "How can women go out?" We started little by little like this and now there are so many of us, women in the peoples' councils, in the hospitals, as teachers, even administrators. So many women now, so many women fighters.

Aregash: After that, we began women's associations in their locality. Of course they didn't start at the same time everywhere. Fighters would clear the villages of the enemy and we would start to politicise the peasants and establish associations. This is still going on.

The liberation of women goes hand in hand with the general liberation process. We set up clinics and gave 'land to the tiller'. This was a very big demand – to get land from the landlords. We made an effort to involve women at every stage in setting up the administrative structure of *baitos* (people's councils). The number of women taking part goes up every year.

On the frontline: war and the Derg

Our beautiful bull has been slaughtered;
Our plough has been turned to ash;
Our faces burned with soot and smoke;
With bombs instead of seeds our yard is sown
Our hay washed away to dam the flooded river.
They are out to destroy us.

But we, the mothers of heroes, have given birth
To lions who don't shrink from death.
Our children we have given to the revolution
And we have become as poison to the enemy;
Our husbands, the militia, give them hell.
Their bombs pour like winter rain,
Yet can an elephant be killed if it is guarded by lions?
TPLF song

The harsh realities of war are obvious from the first moment of crossing the Sudanese border. All convoys have to go by night because of the danger from MiGs. On our first visit fighters with AK 47s slung across their backs walked ahead of the trucks in some places in case the road had been mined. Bombardments had recently forced the Information Bureau, complete with book production and printing equipment and research library, from the valley floor into caves up the mountain. TPLF hospitals and schools were semi-nomadic within a network of wooded river valleys. On one occasion we had to run for cover from a helicopter gunship and on another we were caught in a heavy bombardment by three MiGs in an area where there were many training schools and workshops. When I returned in summer 1989 the whole of Tigray was free from the Derg and security was more relaxed, but the danger from the air remained, so travel still took place only at night.

The fighters can move their base area, but of course the peasants cannot disappear so easily. In the small towns in the liberated countryside, we frequently saw bombed houses and market places, and air-raid shelters were dug outside every house. Market places on market days have been a favourite target of the Derg and several now have monuments commemorating the dead and wounded. Bombings are deliberately increased at certain times of year, such as sowing and harvest times, contributing to food shortages, and MiGs are particularly active around the annual celebrations of the revolution during February. If the intention is to demoralise and weaken the resolve of the people, then this military policy is counter-productive, because every raid intensifies the peasants' hatred of 'the fascist Derg' and hardens their resolve to work for its defeat. Sometimes the peasants use evacuation to outwit the military. In 1983 the Derg soldiers occupied Sheraro for over a year, but the entire working population of the town moved into the hills, leaving their houses to the soldiers and a few old people. Zafu, the chairperson of Adi Hageray *Baito*, told me that all her community have been evacuating the town daily because of the danger of bombings. One of the worst atrocities was the total destruction in June 1988 of the town of Hausien, killing over eighteen hundred people and wounding seven hundred. I lost count of those I met who had been imprisoned and tortured as suspected supporters of the TPLF. Ironically, many only began supporting the revolution whole-heartedly after spending time in prison.

The aim of the revolution from the beginning has been to transform the economic and social lives of the people. TPLF believe this cannot be done without a change of government, which, in the absence of any democratic structures, means armed struggle. Yet the war constantly disrupts efforts to effect social change or even to grow enough to eat. Overcoming all obstacles, whether physical, military, psychological or emotional, is what the Tigrayans mean by *struggle*. Nothing can be achieved without a fight, even if it is with yourself and your own weakness. Every Tigrayan I spoke to seemed to feel *in struggle* as well as involved in *the* struggle.

The fighters play a crucial role. The Tigrinya word for 'fighter' does not mean 'soldier' and the concept of fighter is much wider than combat fighter. Most are drawn from the peasants; so they are not an elite, but a vanguard who can guide the people in the revolution. The fight is not just against the physical enemy, but also against food deprivation, ill-health, ignorance and superstition, powerlessness, and every kind of exploitation. The early fighters were all in combat units, but later the departments were established: Education, Agriculture, Health, Mass Bureau, Information, Propaganda and so on. The TPLF began training programmes and to use skills appropriately, so although all fighters are given basic combat training and continuing political education, they are found all over Tigray working with the people as teachers, medical and health workers, vets, researchers and writers, musicians and cultural workers.

This policy is being intensified and, as Aregash explains later in this chapter, will involve more women fighters. "We are trying to keep the ties between fighters and society very close." Peasants, even if they are TPLF activists, remain in the community, tied to agricultural production. All fighters, on the other hand, dedicate their whole lives to the struggle and to the TPLF, taking on whatever role the organisation assigns to them. There has never been any need for conscription; in fact one of the difficulties is that too many people want to be fighters. Only a proportion of the sons and daughters of each family can be accepted; the majority have to stay behind to safeguard agricultural production, the basis of the economy and therefore of the war effort, or as peasant activists responsible for mobilising the people.

Although Tigrayan nationalism is an important element in the revolution, the TPLF have never been narrowly nationalistic. Through political education, they have extended the non-exploitative approach to the people in their 'Fighters' Code', even to the soldiers of the enemy. They encourage the people to see the Amhara ruling class as the enemy, not the Amhara peasant, nor even the Amhara soldier, whom they see as victims as much as themselves. I heard before I ever went to Tigray that their code of conduct forbade any unnecessary killing of enemy soldiers and prescribed the giving of water, food and medical care first to prisoners of war, before their own fighters. I must admit I was sceptical of these claims. Yet the prisoners of war I interviewed in the central hospital confirmed this treatment. All prisoners are given compulsory political education about the struggle, and then a free choice to return to their homeland in Ethiopia, to stay with TPLF or to go as a refugee to the Sudan. The ones I spoke to were very young, had all been forcibly recruited from market-places or schools and, despite the probability of persecution, wanted to go back to see their families. A proportion of these return to join TPLF – I met several Amhara fighters.

The testimonies that follow show how policy towards women combat fighters is developing. Earlier contributions show the importance to women of sharing in the armed struggle as combat fighters. Both Werknesh and Lichy played an important role in the decisive battle of Endaselassie in February 1989. No wonder there has been heated debate and such resistance to the decision to withdraw women fighters gradually from combat roles.

The testimonies also show the different factors that have led women to become fighters. The dislocation of Mebrat's family is typical. It is the dislocation of civil war, with brothers fighting on both sides, family members scattered through different countries, husbands divided from wives and children, a chronicle of arrests, flight and psychological trauma. Another example is Genet's story of her experiences of torture and imprisonment while still a young girl. Such heroic individualism appeals to the Western reader, but the women fighters who were present were shaking their heads in rueful disapproval as they listened. They admired her bravery but for them it was an example of spontaneous rebellion without 'consciousness or organisation'. Her one-girl rebellion, like the First Woyane, brought pain to her and suffering to her family, but achieved nothing for the revolution. "We have had to make too many necessary sacrifices for the struggle," said Román. "Not a single unnecessary sacrifice can be justified." Their response was an important lesson for me in revolutionary consciousness. But Genet's experiences were the beginning of a process of politicisation for her. She had returned from Italy to become a fighter and the following day she went to the training camp. Two years later we bumped into each other by chance in newly-liberated Makelle and she is now a fighter and a teacher.

A fighter's family

Mebrat: My mother ran away from my father into the forest for years and years. I think it was because she was very young and there was a big difference in age. I have never seen him in a bad mood or harsh in any way to her or to us. Her family chased her back all the time. She ran away continuously right up until she had three children. Then she decided that divorce was out of the question and she went on to have seven children. I was the fourth.

My oldest sister is forty-five. She has five children and is in bad health. Her husband was about to be imprisoned by the Derg, but he fled to Saudi before they could arrest him. He has been very unhappy at the separation. I write to him constantly to support him and also to win him to a greater political consciousness. Now he is a member of the Eritrean Democratic Movement in Saudi. My older brother, next up from me, is closest to me and is most responsible for the family. He is in Sweden. Another brother is in Somalia; another brother is in Addis and has no class consciousness.

The one in Somalia was an agricultural cadre for TPLF, but was physically too weak and got permission to leave TPLF. Then three years ago he joined the Derg, but fled to Somalia with a guilty conscience. My father and the brother in Sweden couldn't stand him working for the Derg and helped him to escape. My sister's son – I call him my younger brother – has an interesting story. He was not a TPLF supporter, but was working with two others, one of whom was a Derg spy. Somehow the spy was killed and the others were accused of his death and of being TPLF members. They were beaten so badly that the other one died and my brother was almost paralysed. They took him to Addis. He thought there was no way out. He kneeled down and became a cadre. He was afraid he would be killed if he resigned, but he did anyway and they transferred him to office work in Adua. Although he had no contact with TPLF at all, they started suspecting him and a month ago he escaped on foot. He said, "I know I will never be free from the fact I have worked with the Derg, that I have been a Derg cadre. I was responsible, but, knowing this, I have come to TPLF." He is in Makelle now, since it has been liberated.

My family background helped me. My father had run away from home when he was only seven years old. His father was a peasant and my father a shepherd boy. One day he lost a sheep, or through him it got killed. He was so fearful of his father's anger that he ran away. He then wandered for years and his connection with the land was severed, which made him unconventional and different from other men. My family never supported Haile Selassie or the feudals. My mother had much more connection with the land and hankered after it more than my father did. My father had always been in cities and so I suppose the feudal spirit had no hold on him. He was never educated and never learned to read and write, but he was a very innocent and kind and I was very close to him.

My family were sympathetic to the TPLF from the earliest days but they didn't know very much. Like most students, I was opposed to Haile Selassie and the Derg. I joined the Zemacha Campaign, but we didn't have a clear idea of what was going on. The Derg's intention was to disperse the students and I was sent to southern Ethiopia. I learned a lot in Harar from the Oromo people about the national oppression. After that in 1976 I decided to go off and join the TPLF in the Field. A contact told me to catch the bus from Makelle, where I lived, but to get off at a certain town on the way and to go east. I was twenty then, but I was frightened of being caught by the Derg soldiers. The liberated area was very small in 1976. TPLF was very small then. Anyway, I left Makelle, alone. On the bus I carefully prepared a story – I lied to the peasants, so that they should not suspect me and betray me to the Derg. I knew I was different from them because I was from the city. I wouldn't be able to fade into the background, so I engaged their sympathy by telling them I was going back to a village to see my relatives, about leaving my parents, my hopes and fears. "I heard there are bandits around here," I said, "so maybe I won't ever reach my family." But they said there would be no problem. They were so interested in me and very concerned.

After I got off the bus, I turned east as I had been told. I knew the name of the village, but I didn't know how to meet up with TPLF and I couldn't ask anyone in case they betrayed me to the Derg. I made up this story that I was going to the village to be a teacher. I had to ask a peasant the way and he was suspicious of my story. "Are you sure you're a teacher?" he asked, "There aren't any teachers in that village."

He showed me the way, but all the time I thought he was a supporter of the Derg. In fact he was sure I was looking for the TPLF, so he took me straight to them. When we came to the TPLF, I didn't know who they were and went on sticking to my story. I didn't expect TPLF to have guards. "Come on now, aren't you looking for TPLF?" one said. "Haven't you come to join them?" But I denied it. Later they told me they were the TPLF and had seen through my story from the beginning.

For six months I was a combat fighter. There were very few women fighters at that time, only three of us in that force. I was with Román and Aregash. In the beginning I was so weak and I had such difficulty in walking. But the other fighters understood what it's like for a new fighter and always distracted attention if I was slow or getting left behind. My first problem was walking, but my second was putting on my shoes in the dark! In a military situation, fighters have to move very quickly at night. But I never minded the rough food and sleeping conditions.

My baby son is in Makelle with my family. The organisation thinks it is better for a child to grow up in society and not in TPLF camps. My mother was impressed with that because it matched her own ideas. My youngest sister, Genet, is like a mother to him. Now I am back in the Field working in the political school. We teach the new fighters after they have finished their basic training. I really enjoy it.

The Women Fighters' Association of Tigray (WFAT)

Román: The Women Fighters' Association of Tigray is for women fighters only. As you know, most people in this society are peasants and so most fighters are peasants too. Just as we were backward compared to the men in the society, so we were behind when we came to fight. We won't always be held back by these cultural restraints. So the aim of this organisation is to raise the consciousness of women, especially concerning our question, to avoid cultural backwardness and to participate in everything equally with our comrades.

Because we have always been inferior in our society, a woman cannot explain how she feels at a meeting or in public. If she can have separate discussions about our question or participation – anything at all – she will have the enthusiasm to challenge everything, to participate in everything.

We can discuss problems in our organisation and in our association and then we can write about them in our magazine *Mekalih* (Echo) or in our other newspaper *Arena* (Unite). There is a programme for discussing women's issues among all the fighters, so during that time we can make everyone understand much more about the issues.

Aregash: Our association elects its leadership. It has its own coordinating body and internal laws common to all women's associations, although there can be local differences.

Genet's story

Genet: My name is Genet Negash. I am twenty years old. I was born and brought up in Makelle. From about 1980 my local *Kebelle*, the Derg's urban association, forced me to go to youth meetings. From the beginning I didn't like it. I was thirteen and I told them I was too young to be a member. I've always been a good football player because I used to play at a Catholic mission, so they elected me onto the team. So I started to play for the women's football team. Then they asked me to make a payment to the youth organisation. I refused, but they forced me. In our culture, if someone dies you give a gift in kind, sugar or salt, called *debes*. So I gave them twenty-five cents as an insult.

The next day they came to my home and arrested me. I hadn't done anything but they really had it in for me! They took me and flogged me with a stick on my back, my knees and arms. My parents tried to apply for my release, but the officials refused to see them. They were in tears. They tried to visit me but the guards refused to let them because I had scars. After two weeks my elder sister begged them to release me and they did.

From that day I declared war on the committee. I insulted them whenever I saw them. I would shout 'you bastards' at them in the street. I refused to go to any meetings or to pay the subscription. That year my eldest brother was taken forcibly from school to a training centre for troops in Addis. This made me even madder. I could not control my anger.

Two months after that they arrested my uncle. I went with my family to ask about him and the guards said he had been taken somewhere else. This was how we learnt he had been executed.

It got worse. One time I deliberately quarrelled with the chairman of the Youth Association. He kicked a stone at my forehead, so I went to his house and threw stones through his window and kicked him. Then they arrested me. They flogged and beat me again. My sister, who is ten years older than me, went and bribed the guards to get me released. She was my eldest sister – her name is Letensia.

I started my own protest movement. Some of my family came from Samre, a TPLF area – so I had some idea about the TPLF. They tried to politicise me. They told me about the women fighters, their courage and their relation to the mass. I began to sympathise and begged them to take me to Samre. They said I was too young and told me to stay at home.

I started to write slogans against the Derg and distribute them. The secretary of the Kebelle was a neighbour of mine – he looked after the Kebelle seal. I went to his house and stole the seal. Then I wrote two anti-Derg slogan-papers and stamped them and returned the seal to his house. I decided to distribute these slogans and then escape to the Field. I went to the meeting with the slogans in my pocket. My plan was to ask to leave the meeting, then drop the papers and run away.

When I was outside I put the two slogans by the gate and left. I went home. But before I could leave, the meeting finished. The cadres had been told it was me who'd left the slogans and they went after me. When I knew they were following me I went home and bolted the door. They demanded that I open the door but I refused. Then the military police arrived – they arrest people and are notorious killers and executioners. They came in their red helmets, broke down the door and took me to the Central Investigation Department. This was in May 1981 when I was fourteen.

They asked me whose paper it was. I told them I didn't know, that I wasn't even a Kebelle member so I had no access to the seal. They told me to tell the truth and confess, but I refused. So they tied my legs and hands together behind my back with a rope tied through my mouth and around my head. I think they electrocuted me and I became unconscious.

After three days they tortured me again. When they beat me, they kicked me in the head and made me unconscious. After that they threw me outside the room. I lay there from ten in the morning till three. My clothes were covered in blood, and stuck to my neck. I didn't know what was wrong. In the afternoon the investigators found me and realised I had internal bleeding. This made them scared and they took me to the health centre outside the prison. I saw a physician who checked me over, washed my ear and gave me ear-drops. I was escorted back to CID with four guards. When I returned, my mother was queuing outside, waiting to bring me food. When she saw me, she was shocked and ran out to hug me. But the guards hit her with a stick and pushed her back into the queue. We both cried.

When I was back in prison they asked me again to confess. I refused and they threatened to torture me again. I was afraid because of my ear and my foot which were in agony. So I confessed that I was a member of TPLF, although I wasn't, and that I'd written the slogans. I confessed I was working for TPLF and I wanted to kill the Party Chairman. They said "How could you do this? – you are not militarily trained." I said, "Oh yes I am. I have a gun and have been training in a village five kilometres away. If you want, we can go there." This pleased them a lot.

My plan was for them to take me outside Makelle where there were TPLF soldiers, in the hope that I could escape and the officials would be arrested by TPLF. Unfortunately there were no TPLF soldiers there. They said to me, "Where is the gun you have hidden?" I told them where to dig, but of course there was no gun. They accused me of trying to get them captured by TPLF, but I said that in the two weeks since my arrest, TPLF must have come and taken the gun. They beat me for this.

Then they wrote everything on a statement: that I was in TPLF, I had a gun, I tried to kill the Party Chairman and that I was signing of my own free will. Then they made me sign it. It was a very great crime which I hadn't done. After I had signed the statement, the Head of Tigrayan Police, Colonel Tilahun came. "You donkey, how do you dare to kill these people?" "You are the donkey not me!" I replied. [laughs] He was Amhara and this is a traditional insult by Tigrayans against Amharas, but I meant it only against him; I said this in Tigrinya and he couldn't understand, but a Tigrayan official told him what I'd said. He was furious. He wrote that I was a very dangerous member of TPLF and should be executed. Then he signed the paper and left.

I was sent to the main prison. When I reached it I could not walk properly or sit because of the torture. I had to squat because of my back. I suffered for six months. I went to the clinic, but they didn't treat me, although my ear was still bleeding and discharging. So my sister, Letensia, brought drugs from a pharmacy and smuggled them into the prison. I really thought the Derg would kill me so I didn't use the medicine, I thought it was useless. I just passed the time in pain. Psychologically I had real problems. The investigators used to come at night so I had bad nightmares. I would scream in my sleep, which worried the other prisoners.

My sister tried her best to get me released. She went to the CID chief and other officials and tried to convince them I was innocent, that I was too young to be involved in politics. They agreed to go to the prison and check. But I wouldn't say that I hadn't done it. My sister was very shocked. She had begged for my release and she'd expected me to say I'd been tortured. In prison I used to insult the guards and say whatever I wanted. After that my sister went to Addis Ababa, even though she was married. She spent three months there, trying to get me released. She gave them bribes and did whatever they asked. After three months they said I would be released and that she should go back to Tigray.

They released me and took me to the Tigray Administrator. This was after two years. I stood in front of the Administrator with my family. He said they were releasing me because I was so young. They wrote a statement saying if I did the same thing again I would be killed. They made my father sign this instead of me. I said, "OK – but you have tortured me so severely I still have a head injury. You must write a statement on that, and say I will never go to your kebelle again."

After I was released I had many problems. Spies were following me everywhere and I had severe headaches. Eventually physicians referred me to the psychiatric hospital in Asmara. I went there and then returned to Tigray. My sister went to Rome to find a job. She sent me a document to enable me to get a passport, but it was confiscated when I tried to get a pass paper to leave. So I went to Addis and bought a passport. Then I went to Rome – my sister paid for the flight.

In Rome, I had two months treatment for my head and body injuries and then I started working for TPLF. Now I have come back to Tigray and have decided to train to be a fighter.

[Two years later...]

I joined the TPLF military training centre and was trained in theory and practice. After finishing my training I was assigned to the educational department of TPLF and was sent on a three month teacher training course. First I was assigned to May Day School, an MLLT political education school. I was teaching academic subjects only, but the students helped me to develop my political understanding and it became much deeper. After that I was chosen to teach in the people's public school in Adi Awalla in Adi Abo zone in Region One.

Their political background was very strong, so that when a call came from TPLF to join the fighters it was easy to agitate them to volunteer for military training to be fighters. Almost all of them went except for women with education below grade five, since the policy doesn't allow them to become fighters. But they are allied with TPLF and are encouraged to give support by providing things that are needed or by working in the frontline in the health clinics or by becoming agricultural cadres.

Soon I'll be going to Adi Awalla to take part in a yearly evaluation by our teachers of our work, in our own districts, and in the whole region. It will take about fifteen days. The schools are all closed now because it is the beginning of the agricultural season.

I still play football. I play with my students and train them in football and volleyball. We have matches with other teams in the area.

I have come to Makelle to see my parents. I last saw them in 1984, five years ago. My sister Letensia has gone to Canada, and now she is a strong supporter of the TPLF too.

The Derg invasion of Sheraro 1983

Tsahytu Fekadu: In 1983, the Derg invaded Sheraro. There had been a heavy war around Sheraro which lasted for five or six days. TPLF pushed the Derg back, so the Derg bombed the market place, killing thirty-one people. Then they brought in reinforcements from Eritrea. This included about forty tanks. At this point TPLF retreated and the Derg took the town.

Everyone left the town except for about fifty old people who were too weak to travel. They were treated badly and their standard of living deteriorated. They were denied the right to go to their land because they were suspected of spying or running messages to the TPLF. They had to pay eight birr for just one kilo of sugar!

The Derg stayed for thirteen months. The people simply left the town and made a temporary settlement in the hills. We still refer to it as 'Sheraro in the Hills'. We had shops, we taught school lessons and went on as normal. But the Derg had many problems. They had no way in and out of the town, and no food because the surrounding area was liberated and in the control of the TPLF. The Derg was totally encircled, imprisoned.

The destruction of Hausien 1988

The mother of Almaz [remembering the day her daughter was killed in the bombardment of the town]: Those who died here – Teklu Buru, that's two. Desta Woldu's son, three, a merchant called Gebremedhin Buru and his sister, five. I spent most of the day digging for them. Then one man came and told me she was buried under the rubble in our house. Yes, my daughter who left five children behind, she is dead.

We were digging here and I didn't know what was happening at that house. There were many people there and about thirty injeras and three gallons of beer. One of my youngest granddaughters came and told me our house was destroyed and her mother, my daughter Almaz, was buried. I ran quickly to the house. All I could see were pieces of human bodies, legs and hands everywhere. I called out for my daughter. I went crazy.

One of the men trapped in the ruins tried to calm me, saying my daughter was OK. I heard one of her young sons who had been buried by rubble screaming, "We are here! We are here!" My daughter was also buried in the rubble. She was screaming for water, "Water! Water!"

We dug the whole day and still the planes were bombing us. Towards evening some more people came and helped us get the bodies out. We took four bodies out before we came to my daughter. By then she was dead.

"This was a special thing and I felt it very deeply"

Werknesh: I am twenty-one, and I come from western Tigray, from Adi Awalla. I have been a fighter since 1984, and I have a position of responsiblity, as a commander of a squad.

In particular what made me a fighter was the oppression of our feudal society. I was a part of that, and a woman too, so the oppression was not the same as for men, but a double oppression of class and also of sex. After TPLF emerged I learned how to free myself and my society.

I trained for two months in military tactics and arts, with specific reference to our terrain. We covered types of terrain, how to attack in a guerrilla fashion, enemy tactics, how to read maps, how to manipulate the ongoing battle and give decisions. This enables us to fight the Derg in an efficient and flexible way. Broad military teachings are not enough. Since we have a political aim and since all our activities come from our political beliefs, we also learn political education.

I went into battle at once after my training in Megalle in East Tigray in 1984–85 in the Eighth Offensive during the drought time. During that severe famine time, the Derg thought it had us in its power because we were scattering in different directions out of control. The whole infrastructure and even the mass associations stopped working. Most of our fighters were focusing on famine and even our militia gave up their arms, which was to the Derg's advantage.

At Endaselassie, my last battle, I felt very strong and glad to be a fighter. The number of Derg soldiers was many more than before. It used to be unique for a woman in Tigray to be engaged in battle, so this was a precious thing for me and I felt it deeply.

Since the attack was continuous and fast I had no rest, but had to run with the speed of the battle. We mixed with the men and attacked with them, since our organisational position is not separate. We viewed it equally and we shared it equally.

The Derg was using artillery and sophisticated automatic machines and had overhead support from MiG planes. They began attacking heavily and intensified their shooting at the place they expected us to be. They always use the same moves; they focus on mechanised tactics which are no match for our scientific and carefully planned guerrilla strategies. Our force is democratic; all our decisions are discussed at every level. Derg soldiers are conscripted, and have no voice in the battle.

Since we fighters come from society, and are the people's army, we follow a very disciplined approach towards the people, towards the decisive and powerful masses. Our organisation does not teach us a segregated approach; we're all people alike. For example, when we go among the people we follow the regulations of the baito, and try to give an example in agricultural activities. In the same manner we do not separate the Amhara and Tigrayan people. When we take prisoners of war, once they are freed from the generals they no longer wish to fight. We approach them in a positive and democratic way. Even on the battle site, even if my comrade has been killed, we never take revenge. From the very beginning of the battle we try not to kill people, and only do so if we are forced into it. We are trying to capture, not to kill. Our slogan is, "Don't kill but let the bullet whip past his ear!"

"Of course what pushed me towards the TPLF was marriage"

Lichy: My fieldname is Lichy, which means light. My real name is Licknesh Tekle. I became a fighter seven years ago when I was thirteen. Our village was near an area under Derg control, and my mother and father did not even allow me out of the door.

Of course one of the reasons that pushed me towards the TPLF was marriage. When I was a child my parents forced me to marry in 1980. I stayed with my husband for nearly three years, and then I told my father and mother that I couldn't go on with the marriage because I couldn't cope with him and the household responsibilities; I was always upset. At that point the Derg troops came into our village, and eleven houses including my father's were burnt to the ground. The Derg is still doing things like this. In December in a village called Adi Zeresenay, the Derg burned all the villagers' piles of harvested grains awaiting threshing. Those who tried to defend them from destruction were taken to a nearby valley and shot. After this the whole village was burned. Everyone who could, escaped, but many women, children and old people were killed.

Then I decided to run away to the fighters I had heard so much about. There were always a lot of rumours, and one day I heard that some fighters were passing nearby. There were many of them, and they were responsive towards the people. Their weapons were very unusual, not like any seen in Tigray before. Also we had heard that in central Tigray they had shared land equally, so everyone was impressed by that. I started to build up emotional support for them. Sometimes when I went to the market with my husband, I used to see them there, and my feeling for them increased.

I have been a combat fighter until recently, and now I'm waiting to be reassigned to a non-combat role. I'm sorry to be out of combat. I was injured in battle and the wound still bothers me. I can only eat very digestible and bland foods like plain pasta or rice. I was a fighter in both battles for Endaselassie, in 1988 and in February 1989. I guess there were about thirty-two to thirty-three thousand troops at Endaselassie, since it was chosen as a military garrison. There were also many other troops from Eritrea, and other parts of Ethiopia.

The mass helped us in the second battle. The fighters' responsibilities were to fight face to face with the enemy, and the people were to supply ammunition, water, food and to take the wounded and PoWs to safety. Many women were involved also, some of them participating in these things. They had been told about it before the operation started, and the baito and the associations had discussed it; they were organised in regiments, and called into the battle to play their roles. The second time, they were given an explanation about who to attack and who to help, and what to do inside and outside the battle zone. They were not on the frontline and had to respect all orders given. I was very glad of the people's participation, as they really wanted to do their share. They prepared for it. They're real friends to us fighters. We have estimated that about thirteen thousand of the mass took part, excluding those involved further back in the villages and fields who captured fleeing soldiers.

I'm not sure how many women were involved in the battle. The proportion of women combat fighters has dropped since the new policy. There's only about five or six in my unit now. Before the adoption of the new policy I was very strongly opposed to women not being combat fighters, but after a time I realised the drawbacks of the original policy for the TPLF and for women, so now I accept it and support it.

I married in 1987, again. My husband was a combat fighter in the same division, but now he's in another division. Many women fighters are now married. I don't have children, but know many women fighters who do. Before we used our full capacity but giving birth has reduced us to a very limited capacity. When a fighter is about four months pregnant, she is sent to the base area, and looked after by the medical workers until the birth of the child. She breastfeeds her child for two years. Women with children cannot be combat fighters any longer. Personally I don't want to have children because I believe that it hinders my activity.

The role of women fighters in the TPLF

Harnet: My name is Harnet. I became a fighter in 1979 when I was seventeen years old. Before that, I was a student in Makelle, the capital city of Tigray.

Laila: I have been a fighter since 1978. I was eighteen and a student in Makelle too. We've been together since then, but in Makelle we were not together – only after we joined the TPLF.

Harnet: Our role as fighters is not simple – it covers so many things. Some of us work in information and book production; some of us teach in schools; some of us fight against the Derg in the army. Our role is to cover the work of the organisation. As fighters, we teach women in our society who are not fighters to participate in the revolution, to know about their rights, to fight against their oppression – and not only women – because we believe in class struggle, we teach men also, our class friends. If we want our revolution to be victorious, the participation of women is necessary, because women are half of society. In our organisation, TPLF, we share in every part of the work of the revolution, military, economic, and political.

My own work is in the TPLF radio station as a newscaster. Also I have a baby now. She is four and a half months old. Her name is Niat. Laila is expecting a baby in three months. Being a mother will not make any difference to our role in the organisation, because taking care of this child is not only my responsibility, but the responsibility of all my comrades, the responsibility of the organisation. Then everyone helps, you know. The organisation brings me everything necessary for the child. If I have work to do, I cannot be with her. My comrades who are around me, help me.

Laila: Fighting for our rights is not about having babies or not being pregnant. We can fight, we can work as guerrillas, as mothers, as a part of the society. I work in the Information Department, in the personnel section, and I am having a child in three months time. Fighting to liberate ourselves from oppression is one kind of struggle; reproduction of society is another way and we accept this, as everybody does. Sometimes it can be difficult for a mother. Because of the equality we have gained, when I have to work, the baby's father will help me. For a short time in the beginning we will look after the baby together. But after that, when it is old enough for other people to take care of it, everybody will help us, the organisation, the people, our comrades. They are our society's children, not our private ones, so we won't have any problem.

We have different kinds of maternity leave. For a combat fighter, it is hard to stay after three or four months of pregnancy, especially if the army is on the move, but if we are working in an office, we can go on working until seven and a half or eight months. Legally, we have three months before and after the birth, but unless we need to stay in hospital, there is little division between our home and our department. We need the hospital to take care of us, but after that it is simple for us, if we are in the base area.

It is now more than a year since we started this scheme of child care and marriage for the fighters. Later on, there will be mothers' care schools for the children and for the mothers.

Harnet: The women combat fighters come to the base area after three months pregnancy. After delivery they will stay for two years, taking care of the child, because the baby must have the mother's breast-feeding for almost two years if possible. After that, the mother will go back to her work, either in the army or elsewhere. Then the child will go to the organisation's nursery. This is for the women fighters who are mobile either in the army, the frontline, or any kind of work requiring mobility.

This kind of law is only for women fighters. Marriage has only been allowed for fighters since 1985. Of course there has been marriage for the rest of society.

Women and combat – the new law

Aregash: Women's involvement in military activities has been an issue. As fighters, we have revised our stand. Before, we were trying to involve women in the combat forces, which was seen to some extent as making them equal. It was one means of showing that women are equally as capable as men. But having women as combat fighters doesn't necessarily prove that they are equal. Actually, if too many are involved, their equality could be adversely affected, as far as their general involvement in society and political and economic advancement goes. Now we think that our first policy was narrow; that we were emphasising the combat side too much.

Many women couldn't cope with the physical conditions of the combat forces, although the ones that are fit for that activity should still be involved. In fact the effectiveness of the revolution is made through the people, both men and women, using their capabilities as well as possible. Men are not all as physically capable as each other and not all should be involved in combat.

At first there was resistance from women comrades, especially those who were combat fighters, as they thought it was one way of balancing their inequalities. So they were furious. We discussed it a lot in local associations of WFAT and finally we called a conference. In general the new policy directed that women should be involved in the liberated areas, which means a reduction in the total number of women fighters, because combat activity was the major role of women in the Field.

We are now accepting fewer women as fighters in non-combat activities. These tasks demand both skills and academic background, so therefore the qualification has to be fifth grade education, which means reading and writing perfectly. Then they can be involved in training for office work and health work and so on. The problem is that we already have too many peasant women in the organisation, because being a fighter is such a liberation for them. We are obviously involved in teaching them. The men on the other hand could be illiterate and handle the combat activities perfectly well. Combat doesn't demand education, although political education is necessary.

So the proportion of women is now lower that the old 30%, but there is an expanding area involving women outside the combat force. Opportunities for women to be involved in health activities, for example, are very extensive since the towns were liberated. So the level of recruitment for women fighters is a little reduced. But this has created resentment among the women in the villages. We have by ourselves created those feelings through the way we have conducted the course of the revolution. It has demanded an effort to make them understand that change of policy and that the change is eventually in the interests of their equality and of the struggle in general.

Fighters and society

We are trying to keep the ties between fighters and society very close. There is a danger in any country involved in combat; the fighters can become uprooted from the active life of society, forming their own groups and sections. We are trying to handle the problem very consciously, with the fighters always discussing and contributing to solving the problems of society. We are trying to keep the mentality of the fighters and society at the same level. The fighters and the peasants are each doing their share, not separately, but as organically linked bodies. The fighters are prepared to involve themselves in building a new Ethiopia, and will be farmers or factory workers if necessary. However Ethiopia will always need an armed force, even after the revolution.

The support of the people

We see their footprints in the dust.
Did they pass by –
Our children?
The sound of distant firing
Guides our footsteps
As we bear them food.

We hear the distant firing of their guns
And we must follow.
Be strong, our children!
We are bringing food and drink to you.
Can a needle sew without thread?
Can children fight without their mothers' support?
TPLF song

We know there has been widespread disaffection in Tigray and elsewhere in Ethiopia for decades, maybe for hundreds of years. But so is there in many other countries, where the impetus for revolutions has evaporated in the mishandled efforts of intellectual 'leaders' to compel support from oppressed people. It's not difficult to conclude that injustice and exploitation provide the justification for revolution, but at the same time deprive the people of the energy and self-confidence necessary to carry it out. What turns disaffection into revolution? How did they manage it in Tigray?

'Organisation' and 'political consciousness' for the TPLF are the two elements that distinguish spontaneous rebellion from successful revolution. In Tigray there were sporadic uprisings, but, in general, resentment was unfocused and unorganised until TPLF began to provide an analysis and leadership. Yet everywhere we travelled the peasants referred to the revolution as 'our struggle' and to TPLF as 'my organisation', so how was an illiterate, conservative and suspicious peasantry persuaded to support so whole-heartedly what must in the beginning have seemed an unequal struggle?

We have seen how important consciousness-raising was in the early stages, how the early fighters were prepared to work alongside the peasants, learn from them as well as hope to teach them, and to see persuasion at whatever pace was appropriate as the only possible means of gaining support. I tried to discover more about this process in many conversations in Tigray. Meles, TPLF Chairperson, told me:

> There is no point in trying to speed things up. We can't enforce anything. If we try to force anything on the peasants and at the same time fight the Derg then we are stuck. So we let the peasants go their own way. We try to convince them through practice in a protracted process. Once they hold it through this protracted process they are sure not to forget it, so when they hold it they hold it fast, and we want it to be held that way, so that any problems that may be created, any defeats that we may have to face would not dismantle what we have done.

Every political decision in Tigray is based on lengthy discussion. The *mass associations* are the most important element in the 'protracted process' which Meles refers to. In a newly liberated area these associations are formed at the instigation of the TPLF as soon as possible. Membership is voluntary, but everyone we spoke to indicated that most people are very keen on attending. They are based on natural interest groups, farmers, women, youth (divided according to gender), merchants, workers and so on, according to the constituents of a particular area. Within their associations the people are encouraged to gain an analysis of their past oppression and discuss their specific interests and solutions to local problems. These are political organisations; they are about raising consciousness, including understanding of new policy directions, but they do not implement policy. Administration is the responsibility of the locally-elected people's councils, the *baitos*, which are independent of TPLF, but as all the members of the baito will also be members one of the mass associations, the discussions and understanding gained in the associations will influence decisions of the baito.

The definition of 'political' is very wide. In a region where survival is equated with winning the war against the central government, everything has been geared to the 'war economy'. The basis of this is a self-reliant agriculture, so that techniques of terracing and water-conservation are political issues to be discussed in the farmers' mass association. The importance of literacy, preventive health and solutions to the burdens of women's work are political issues in the women's associations. Peasants, whether men or women, who are particularly active in their communities, are given the opportunity to have special training as community leaders or cadres. There are special cadre schools where they can be taught intensively to read and write, to understand the aims of the revolution and how to lead the mass associations. There are agricultural cadres, health cadres, education cadres, political cadres and so on, but they all work within the mass associations to further people's understanding of and participation in the social transformation of their society. The most important kind of cadre are the *shig woyenti* ('torches of the revolution'). Unlike fighters, they stay within their communities as farmers or housewives, but they have special political training and their responsibility is to 'agitate' the people, an expression which sounds strange to Western ears.

Every baito selects local men they can trust with arms to defend the security of the community as *woyenti*, or militia. The shig woyenti, the militia, cadres and the fighters are all members of TPLF and so they dedicate their lives in different ways to the revolution. As members of TPLF they have the right under the constitution to be elected to the TPLF Congress which decides policy every four years. The fighters and TPLF members from mass associations elect representatives in equal numbers, so the mass associations influence the TPLF and the TPLF influences the mass associations. The Mass Bureau is responsible for overseeing all the affairs of the mass. It is organised into eight departments, including one for the mass associations. There is a department for the administration of the baitos and others for the women's associations, for the nationalities and for the towns. We spoke to Bitew of the Mass Bureau and asked him about the relationship between TPLF and the mass associations:

They don't have a direct link with TPLF. We won't order them to do anything. We have discussions with the different associations. They have the right to oppose or make suggestions. The organisation (TPLF) can suggest things, but after discussion they have the right to reject proposals or to accept them. They are free discussions.

A fundamental tenet of the revolution is the right of women to organise separately within their associations, but, more than this, the women's associations are the whole basis of the strategy for gaining women's equality. Through the regular meetings women have largely managed to overcome the lack of confidence instilled in them by centuries of suppression. When we heard them speaking out strongly in congresses and at huge events, it was difficult to believe that before 1975 they had been forbidden to speak in public or to take any part in political affairs.

We attended several hot debates in both baitos and mass associations. In Sheraro we attended a woman's association meeting. There were about a hundred women there. They were sitting on the ground in the shade of a three-sided barn. Many had children with them at the breast or in slings on their backs. I noticed at once how many older-looking women there were, including several with infants. Peasant women have a double role working in the fields as well as being mothers and housewives. In Tigray they go on having children over a long period of time, but their appearance also reflects the hardness of their lives. The leader of the session was a woman called Medhin. She was also a member of the baito and we had met her earlier in the day. She was giving a question and answer session on an aspect of political education.

Medhin presented a text which was then discussed by the women present. The theme was 'prison': "When there is oppression there is also struggle. When there is struggle there is also prison." The session gave them an opportunity to pool their personal and family experience of prison and torture and so convert it from individual experience to a shared political analysis of long-term oppression by the government. The discussion brought together points from the whole history of struggle from Haile Selassie's time to the present, from the First Woyane to the Agazi operation (when, in February 1986, a few TPLF fighters released over fifteen hundred prisoners from Makelle prison). Leteberhan recalled her experience of the First Woyane, when she was eight years old, when "so many innocent Tigrayans died and the blood of people in the market place was deeper than a horse's hoof." Here there were peasant women from the whole community and they were contributing to the discussion. "Under the Derg," said Hiwot, "even a baby is assumed to be a supporter of TPLF." Berhanu took notes for us and after the main session I joined in the discussion with the help of an interpreter and the women extended the theme of prison to their own domestic experience and spoke about the captivity of the house and the 'chains in the head' which prevent women from developing a revolutionary consciousness.

"It is necessary to separate women to learn about their own oppression"

Román: The women's associations were at first – by the end of 1977 – just meetings of the women in some places. In 1978 the Women's Mass Associations were started and developed. Ever since then, if we liberate the land, we go there and lead associations. Some of the women will have heard our aims and what we are doing, so it is not too difficult.

Laila: When we taught our people at first, we didn't identify men from women. We taught the same to everyone about their revolution. Then we realised it is necessary to separate women to learn about their own oppression. They learn first with their oppressed brothers about class struggle, then, separately, how their oppression has arisen out of that class struggle. Now they organise their committees and everywhere, in every district, in every village, there are women's associations. The adult women are separated from the younger women. The younger ones are also in the youth association.

Aregash: One of the most important achievements of the revolution has been the raising of political consciousness. Among the peasants there are women cadres who raise consciousness. The first requirement for a cadre is physical fitness. Then they should know the life of the people and be able to organise and discuss the issues. They receive political training at a training school for one and a half or two months and then return to their villages where they try to raise the consciousness of women and of the general public. They try to involve people. They call people to meetings. The women of the villages feel confidence in these local women. They can relate to them and respond to their own organisation.

Román: So the plan is – first getting a few local women interested, and then giving them education and training. Then they set up women's associations with our help. Political consciousness is mainly taught in the schools, the cadre school, the political school, so the women go there together. Besides that, they go to the women's schools, like the March 8 School, to learn about women's questions. The women who have particular political education at March 8 women's school and at the political school (which is mixed) become shig woyenti and then go back to their villages and help teach the mass.

The membership of the mass association is voluntary. If a woman has a problem in taking care of a child or a lot of work in the house, sometimes she will not come to the mass association meeting, but everyone else in the village will come. Women often have no confidence that together they can discuss political things about their country, about their society. They assume that this is not *their* work. It's always somebody else's work, especially the men's, so it sometimes really is a problem to make them believe that they can join in meetings. At first none of them came to the women's association. We used to go to every house, and discuss something which didn't seem political, but underneath it was, for example: "Are you OK? How are your children, your family? How is your harvest?" – something like that. She'd discuss these issues because they are her immediate problems – and then at the end we'd say, "This is all part of the struggle too," or something like that. It's different in most areas now, because they know about us and they come to join the mass association by themselves.

Now we are trying to suggest that in one mass association in the *tabia* (village), especially in the nearby houses, that two or three can stay with the children, so that the others can follow the meeting, but we have not yet implemented it – we are still discussing the problems. A woman must be convinced that it is right to give her child to somebody else, if she is to go freely and follow the meeting attentively.

Aregash: The women's associations meet at least once a month, but usually twice. They discuss political things which concern everybody and also their problems – mainly women's political issues, but it's not limited to that. They even discuss the village and its administrative, social and economic problems and how they can be solved. They discuss these with fighters who if they are asked can help them work towards a solution. If there are women who are active in women's associations and among fighters we take their history and their experiences, and use them as teaching material and as propaganda.

There is a baito, a people's council, in each area. There are women members in each one who are also in women's associations. These are elected by the women's association. The leaders take note of important things and take them to the women baito members, so the baito can discuss them and if necessary adopt a policy and set a programme.

Some people fear that separate women's associations will disrupt the revolution, but so far we haven't found this problem. If the leadership and political organisation is well-founded in its understanding of women's struggles, I think it can lead the struggle properly so that we can have separate women's associations. We hear there are parties who don't believe in separate women's associations. We don't accept this. Women have special problems arising from their history and experience, therefore separate organisation is essential so they can become a part of the general struggle of the people.

It's necessary to have women's associations to discuss programmes, to discuss women's problems, to organise and solve these problems in a coordinated way. The women's association has the aim of destroying oppressive structures of society, but we don't believe women's associations alone can solve the problems of women and of class society. They should be a coordinated part of the larger struggle, led by political organisations.

"Without class struggle we can't liberate ourselves"

Laila: As we told you before, our aim is class struggle. The reason that class struggle is important is that it unites everybody, not just women, not just men – they are not separated. Teaching is organised so that people know consciously about their struggle, know their enemy. Women are also included in this.

Without class struggle, we can't liberate ourselves. If you fight quite simply, without any radical consciousness it will not achieve anything. Although the Derg has passed so many amendments and new laws, without true class struggle there is no solution for women or for any oppressed people.

Harnet: As we have double oppression, abolishing class oppression and sex oppression must go side by side. The first aim or principle of our women's association is leading class struggle in order to abolish all kinds of oppression which deny democratic rights, including the woman question, the religion question, and the inequalities between nationalities within Tigray. We solve the problems in getting national equality and sex equality and all democratic questions with our struggle. In our women's associations, the aim is to achieve women's equality in the organisation and in the society through struggling for the women's rights, whether we are fighters or in the society. Then the role in society of the women fighters who are in WFAT is to teach women in society and also Tigrayans and Ethiopians who are in the foreign places.

Adi Hageray Women's Association: "We have three hundred and seventy members"

Ametetsion: I'm a member of the Adi Hageray Women's Association, and I want to tell you a bit about us. Our association was founded ten years ago, and we now have three hundred and seventy members – it's only a village here really. The only women who are not involved are about thirty of the oldest and most traditional.

We are proud to have you come to see our struggle. Before the revolution started we were oppressed, but now we are struggling for the total emancipation of women. Because of the feudal-bourgeois situation we weren't keen to start the association and get organised. When we were approached we would close our doors. But the fighters persisted and eventually they taught us to understand our oppression. After this we started the association. In the past, we were never able to sit with men and discuss things. It was forbidden. So there was male-supremacy and we weren't eager to get involved in the women's meetings.

I am very happy because at last we are participating alongside men. Because of TPLF we have come to realise how women can struggle and participate in the revolution. We discuss our political progress. We discuss women's problems, the source of women's oppression and how to struggle against it.

The situation for women has changed over the last ten years. Now we have the right to discuss issues and to be elected to any position. And we are being elected. We know that male-supremacy will never be able to return; we have overcome 75% of it. There are other sisters who don't have the rights that we have and we will fight for them.

Fewer women than men are free even now to attend the school and this is because of marriage. Before, they used to marry girls at less than fifteen but now, because of the women's association, the age is fifteen or over. We are trying to raise it to eighteen or twenty to relieve the burden on women in the home.

A 'torch of the revolution' – a shig woyanit

Kidan: My name is Kidan Gebre Tensay, and I'm twenty-seven. My family and others were helped a lot by the TPLF after the famine. We now live near Edaga Hiberet town in Marmaz Wahta village.

Before liberation we were highly oppressed and dominated; we could not even look at men. We would have to hide if we saw them coming. Women could not go to meetings or make any decisions or suggestions. Muslim women were even more oppressed than us. The revolution has put an end to all this and we have become free and equal like our class brothers. The organisation has shown us the way and now we participate in all areas. From my personal point of view, before, I was an insignificant woman and now I have been given political education and I am a shig woyanit.

Before the famine, I was living with my two sons. I owned some land. My life was not that good because of my personal situation, but I had no special problems. It's awful to think back to the famine. At that time we suffered so much – we even ate roots or leaves just to save our lives. Since the famine we have got on well. TPLF helped us and gave us money for seed. I grow enough food, but I still don't have any cattle.

Being a shig woyanit, I teach political education to the mass. This is my contribution. As we all know, political consciousness is the key to the revolution. Our main purpose is to challenge the people who don't believe in equality or who believe in superstition.

I teach with the baby on my back and my mother looks after the other boy. Before I had a child I was very active. After the birth I had six months leave, but now I have started teaching again.

"Shig woyanits are chosen by the people: they choose those who are most voluntarily active"

Sesayt: My name is Sesayt Adhanom, and I'm twenty-five. I come from Sheraro. I am married and I have one daughter of three months old. My parents are peasants and their land is here. My husband is a fighter, at Adi Hageray where he works for the agricultural department. I was eleven when I got married, the year the struggle began. At that time we didn't think it was good or bad, but I know now that it was not the right time to marry. I don't want my own children to marry until they are mature enough. I began to participate in the revolution because for me it started from the problems in my own house. As a woman I had a lot of sexual oppression – my husband quarrelled with me, shouted at me and wouldn't let me out of the house. Bit by bit I began to understand what was happening and now I am one of the strong supporters of the revolution.

My husband became a fighter in 1979. He has improved and even encourages me! But now I don't have him to help me, as well as all the problems of being a woman. He says, "Don't feel loneliness. We are fighting for a better society. Be strong and work with your organisation." I like him very much because he is always at my side in spirit.

I became a member of the women's association in 1980. First I was an agricultural cadre, and learned in Asregar how to plough, how to conserve soil and water and make simple terracing. When we graduated we started teaching the women and doing demonstrations and giving women special advice at mass meetings. I increased my support for the organisation and intensified my participation in the mass association and all the organisation's works. So I had to be more educated. Basically shig woyanits are chosen by the people; they choose those who are most active voluntarily among the people. The shig woyanits learn in different areas either around their villages or in a central place.

One of the most important things is mobilising the people altogether as a force towards achieving something for themselves, like road construction. I worked on that during my training, and at the moment in Sheraro we are working to construct an air raid shelter. We are mobilising the mass to dig the trenches. I always admire things like this.

A shig woyanit is the active ingredient in the mass and the one who has the ability to lead the mass in every area of activity, who can motivate and agitate the mass. It means 'a flaming torch for the revolution'. We work in coordination with the baito. The baito will give a proposal and plans and then we will work to mobilise the people. This is what happened with the air raid shelter. We were told about the work by the baito, and then organised the work according to the different sections of the association. Each was given an assignment. The chairs of the mass associations discuss the proposals with us, and get advice and suggestions. Then the people discuss it together independently, with the shig woyanit as an active member, but not necessarily as a leader. Then they divide up and do the work. We do the same thing in order to care for the family of a fighter, their land and problems.

My child does not limit me in any way. When you get more children you can feel tired and your participation gets less, but I prioritise my organisation, and will do my best to fulfill the organisation's demands. But even though I say it like this, the organisation will not impose on me if I get tired and unfit. There are many shig woyanits who manage to have families and who work for the revolution.

I have my own land, and have always ploughed it myself. I now have a child, and I will try to pay someone else to plough it for a while. I have no oxen but because my husband is a fighter, I got them from the people. My land is enough to support us and so as long as the rain is good, there will be a good harvest.

Knowledge is power: the women's schools

March on, March 8,
To celebrate
Our solidarity.
March on, March 8!

To recall our oppression,
And recount our suppression
We rally to remember
Working women everywhere.
To win equality and equal pay
This is our day.
March on and say
March 8, our holiday!

March on, March 8,
To celebrate
Our solidarity.
March on, March 8!

Tigrayan International Women's Day song

'Struggle' is the word you hear most often in Tigray. "The solution to all problems is *struggle*," I was told by women again and again. After talking to me about their experiences, they would often ask for information about the situation in Britain. How were women conducting their struggle here? What are our main problems? What success have we had in achieving equality? I felt that we had a lot to learn from Tigrayan women.

'Struggle' is a much broader concept than the military confrontation with the government. It is more a state of determination, a habit of mind which is aimed at change no matter what the short-term costs amount to. Of course the most important struggle of all is against the 'chains of the mind', as the women in Sheraro called them. The struggle is on many fronts – against malnutrition, disease, dependency on hand-outs, ignorance. Education underpins every one.

Before the revolution only about 5% of Tigrayan children had any schooling at all and these were in the towns. The situation was much worse in the countryside, where there was almost total illiteracy. Under a Swedish aid scheme a few rural schools were opened in the last years of Haile Selassie's reign, but the Derg closed all of them on the pretext that the teachers were TPLF sympathisers. The number of highly educated people before the revolution was appallingly low. Many of them fled to the West and only a small proportion have given their support to the revolution. There are still, for example, only six or seven doctors and surgeons, trained in the Western sense, serving the five million people in Tigray. However many of those who fled the Red Terror in the towns to become fighters had some schooling, some up to twelfth grade, and any education was to be an important asset to the revolution. Some of these were women, but on the whole women were discriminated against in education at every social level. I have talked with men educated at Addis Ababa University or in Moscow or the West, who have acknowledged that their sisters remained illiterate.

From 1979 the people asked TPLF to open schools for them and now there are more than three hundred schools in the rural area. TPLF trains the teachers and the *baitos* are responsible for building the schools and providing the teachers' necessities of life. By 1987, nine hundred teachers had been trained, half of them in a special teacher training institute. We visited several schools and, although the classes were sometimes huge with as many as a hundred students, it was inspiring to see their excitement, attention and motivation. We noticed at once how much older they seemed than school children in the West; in fact they were scarcely children at all. We learned that in 1986, after educating twenty-seven thousand children to sixth grade, the TPLF Education Department changed its policy from educating children to educating adults from fourteen to twenty-five. Poverty imposes bitter choices. The priority had to be the social and economic needs of the people. These couldn't be served by children, so it was necessary to educate a generation of adults who could themselves become teachers as soon as possible or go on to train as health workers, vets, pharmacists and so on. Meanwhile the children who were literate were engaged to help in the literacy scheme, which was mainly directed at women.

The mass associations are the basis of political education in Tigray, but there are also political schools for educating cadres and *shig woyenti*. There are special schools for fighters who can learn intensively all the year round, unlike the peasants who can only attend schools in the dry season in the lull of the agricultural year. There are also several technical schools for teaching woodwork, electrics, metal-work, mechanics, and tool-making. Women seemed to be between 30% and 40% of the student numbers at all the ones we visited. Recently courses have been set up for developing the skills of artisans and craft-workers.

We visited the two women's schools, Marta and March 8. They were founded to help women take advantage of the new opportunities of the revolution. March

8 is named after International Women's Day, celebrated on that date every year in Tigray, Britain and other countries. It was chosen by Clara Zetkin, a German Marxist, at the Second International in 1910 to commemorate a women garment workers' strike in the USA. Both these schools aim to make women familiar with the history of women's oppression and women's struggles internationally and in Tigray, to equip them to struggle for their own equality and to help other women to take part in this struggle – but they each do so in different ways. The students of March 8 School are drawn from both peasant women and women fighters; the curriculum is mostly political education about women. Marta School students on the other hand are all fighters. The curriculum also includes political education on women's issues, but their primary purpose is to learn skills, practical and theoretical, which they then pass on to peasant women in the communities after graduation.

We spent several days at Marta School. At that time it was in western Tigray, hidden from MiG surveillance in a tree-filled valley. The river had shrunk to a tumbling stream and the dried-up river bed served as class-room for the four classes we observed one afternoon. The school had only recently moved from another river-valley because of bombings by government planes, so the women students were still busy outside class times constructing their houses from wood and thatch. Two Wednesdays in each month are set aside for felling wood and gathering grasses for thatch and camouflage and for construction and maintenance activities. The school emphasises strength and fitness – its first principle is that women can do anything men can do and certainly everything for themselves. Their assembly hall was further up the valley. Camouflaged with black plastic and thatch, it could hold more than three hundred women.

Policies have to adapt constantly to the changing conditions brought about by the revolution. Literacy skills and basic education are now available generally in Tigray, so Marta School takes women after fifth grade and no longer teaches literacy. This means that it can produce many more skilled women in a much shorter time. The curriculum is directed to the demands of the pressures and conditions of life for Tigrayan women. The teaching is rational, objective and practical and in many ways the graduates become a vanguard in the villages against the taboos and superstitions which have traditionally oppressed women. They go on to teach village women how to plough if they want to, how to control and not be controlled by their biology, to be proud of menstruation instead of ashamed. They teach the nutritional value of vegetables and how to grow them and so overcome traditional conviction that vegetables are only fit for animal food.

I made a point on my recent visit of tracking down some ex-Marta students in the villages where they were now working. They were a team of three who by chance had all been students at the time of our first visit and remembered me. Their dry-season project had been to build and demonstrate a new design of cooking stove, remarkably efficient and economical of wood fuel. Its efficiency had already won over the suspicious peasants we talked to and the women were very interested in the prospect of having to spend less time cooking and, more important, fewer hours seeking scarce wood from the deforested hills. The rains were due and some families had already agreed to start a pilot horticultural project as soon as the first drops had fallen. On our first visit, the prejudices against eating vegetables other than pulses and onions seemed insurmountable, but two years later I noticed vegetables like chard, carrots and rocket available in some markets. Even cabbage and tomatoes play a part in the struggle.

Women and education

Román: In our struggle the main problem is that we have not been educated and this limits our contribution when we join the Front. For example, many peasants have joined the Front who are in the military, political and other departments. But, for some of them, if they had been educated their participation would have been much greater. This problem is found in every corner, even in the mass associations. Most of the leaders of the mass associations in TPLF know how to read and write – but a few of them still don't. Some women in the baitos can judge, can settle conflicts, but sometimes cannot write and read – and there lies the problem.

Another thing is, you know, our country is a backward country; even if we achieve something, there's always more to do in order to liberate the women. Even if a woman has got land, she has still got a problem because the material base is not changed and the kitchen is still backward, the labour of the kitchen is still loaded on her – like grinding, carrying water, bringing fuel from the forest. This is time-consuming and makes her very tired.

March 8 School

March 8 School was established in 1984 after the second Congress of the TPLF decided that positive measures must be taken to enable women to participate in the revolution. Marta School was founded for the same reason. The main aim of the school is to know the 'woman question' and to struggle for women's equality. There are women from the mass at the school and women fighters too. The policy is to have equal numbers from the mass and from the fighters; altogether we take several hundred each year.

In one teaching group, the women who are a little in advance of the mass in their consciousness, and the fighters who can equal them in their consciousness are together. We are forced to separate others into different groups because of the problem of the seasons. Education for fighters we can arrange at any time, but for the peasants it is difficult. At harvest time we can't teach them because they are occupied with the harvest. In the rainy season it is also impossible for them to come, because they have to prepare everything for the next year. Their

Chris Taylor / 3W1

Chris Taylor / 3W1

A meeting of the Women's Association, Sheraro

Jenny Hammond / 3W1

Kebbedesh and Genet, before Genet became a fighter

Jenny Hammond / 3W1

Sofia, driver for TPLF

Jenny Hammond / 3W1

Genet two years later ...

Jenny Hammond / 3W1

Yomar, Endaselassie

Jenny Hammond / 3W1

Marta School's improved stove, built by Neriya

Jenny Hammond / 3W1

Sesayt, shig woyanit, Sheraro

Ababa grinding – the demonstration stove was in her house near Adi Hageray

Askale, Makelle

Jessica Barry

Woman ploughing near Awhie, western Tigray

Jenny Hammond / 3W1

Kindehafte and Zafu, Adi Hageray Baito members

Jenny Hammond / 3W1

Medhin in Gedaref Workshop

Jenny Hammond / 3W1

Atsede 'armed with a bass guitar'

Jenny Hammond / 3W1

The coffee ceremony in Abrahet's house

education has to fit in with the agricultural year, and comes between harvest and sowing time.

March 8 and literacy

We have this special literacy programme for village women who come to March 8 School. They come for two to two and a half months, which is about the longest time they can be away from home. There are schools in the villages, but at home they have children, so although some of the women do go to school, they have to leave when their children are sick or something like that – so they come here to our school, and leave their domestic responsibilities behind. They follow for the whole two months and they learn how to read and write immediately, because they are not giving attention to their house. Their food, everything, is provided by the school, so they study very intensively.

The 'woman question' is the basis of the curriculum

Most of the curriculum is political education about women. We start with the theory and teach them the history of women's experience, starting with the primitive society and going on to the capitalist system and other kinds of society. We tell them about the slave society under the Axumites, the Romans, about the women in feudal society in Tigray, Turkey and India, and about capitalist society in Britain, America. We then teach them about the countries which have led revolutions before us, for example the struggle of the women in the democratic revolution of China, the good things, bad things, policies; about armed struggle, the experience of the Vietnamese struggle, the women of Vietnam. At the end, we return to our own experience, what has been achieved and what remains to be done.

We also do a little on health education. A Tigrayan woman doesn't know her nature and she is ashamed. So in order to make women know their nature and be proud of it, we teach them health education, including the reproductive system and their organs.

Teaching methods

When we teach, we divide the women into groups according to their level of political consciousness. We select the first group according to who has taken political education courses already with the men. Women who are baito members and association leaders must have that education and they are in the first group. The second group is drawn from the others who are better able to cope with education, then if necessary there is a third group and so on.

For example, if there are two groups, we teach them *Women in the capitalist system* in the morning according to the daily programme; in the afternoon they split into small groups to discuss all they have learned earlier. We give them questions for discussion. The teacher explains the topic she has been teaching. They listen – some of them, if they can, take notes – and in the afternoon, in one and a half hours, they discuss all the things they have learned earlier. Also they have activities to set off this education – for example, panel and debating, sports and a cultural group. Their songs supplement their education. And the panel is also like that. For example, if our topic is modern capitalism, their debate might be, 'Is capitalism useful for women or not?'. That would be additional to the teaching in the class.

We have a deep pool under the water-fall where we teach them to swim. Swimming makes the women a little bit freer, not only for crossing rivers when as fighters they have to travel across the country, but it is also one kind of sport that makes them relax and breathe.

Marta School

Saba: I became a fighter in 1976, one year after the revolution began. Two years after land reform there was a new law on marriage. This was the central aspect of women's oppression, and when this was changed I became very happy. I asked to come to Marta School, as I became more interested in the 'woman question', and I'm now director here.

Recently I have started to study the international women's movement. The heroic history of other women – Clara Zetkin, Rosa Luxemburg – I was encouraged by their movement and I began to admire their contribution to the international women's and workers' movements. After I knew about these things, there was a question which bothered me. Is there a women's movement still following in the footsteps of Clara and Rosa?

Throughout these years of struggle we have been putting our development to the test, especially through women's achievements, their participation in politics and their professional skills as doctors, teachers – which were never possible before the revolution. I became more concerned with the international women's movement, about women in other countries who are not able to achieve these freedoms. I began to hear there was a world women's movement and I came to understand more about it.

The history of Marta School

As Román has said, the school was founded in 1984, after the second Congress. The Congress had recognised that women were equal in law, but not in practice, and that they lacked education and skills. It decided they should have political education and skills training, and that there should be different sorts of schools; Marta School is for fighters only. Women fighters were nominated to the school and teachers were appointed. At the same time, it also decided women should be organised with their own organisation so it formed the Women Fighters Association of Tigray.

Who was Marta?

There are two Martas – the first Marta was at Addis Ababa University. She was a prominent member of the student movement. She was fighting in the Ethiopian revolution and the Tigrayan revolution. In 1972 she tried to hijack a plane with some other university students; they failed and were arrested by Haile Selassie's police. She was executed.

In 1974 when we started the revolution, the first woman fighter was called Kasu. The other fighters renamed her Marta in memory of the early comrade. She was a worker in a factory in Asmara, but came to join the revolution. When she arrived she was illiterate, but within one month she could read and write. In 1980 she was martyred. The school was named mainly for her but indirectly for the first Marta.

Student numbers

In September 1983 they collected women fighters from all over Tigray. We started with four hundred fighters, who were mostly illiterate. This was a problem – we could not give academic education, so we taught literacy first and then gave other lessons. The students were of mixed ability, and we taught them for four years. Ninety-two graduated to fifth or sixth grade in 1986; the others graduated in 1987.

The main change since then is the decision to take students who already have from fifth to sixth grade education. This is possible because now there is more general education available throughout the liberated area. First they are educated in other schools and then they come here. Now that they should have passed fifth grade before they come, we teach them for only one year.

"Women can do anything men can do"

As to the philosophy of the school, in our society women are said to be dependent on men. They cannot live without them; they don't participate in productive activity; they cannot leave the kitchen; they can only cook and look after children. Even the women believe this. The fighters, though, are free, but they come here to learn skills. Men believe that only they can build houses or do agriculture. So we teach the women that they *can* live without men – they can build, make tools. Women can do anything men can do. They see in practice that they can do this. Before, they learn this in theory, here we teach them in practice.

First of all, they make their own houses, kitchens, clinics and stores. Secondly, some students learn weaving. They weave the shawls for the other fighters. They make *kutas*. Others make clothes, or adjust them to fit or repair them. They embroider different things, like pillow cases.

The aims

Our main aim is to train women fighters in many skills, in order for them to work with women of the mass. Most of the women of the mass were severely dominated by feudalism, so they are still confined to the kitchen. They have come to know their oppression and to struggle, but they need skills: home economics, rural science, health care, mother and child care, agriculture, women's health. The second aim is to make women fighters more politically conscious, to understand their oppression and struggle consciously.

Health education

The first subject is health education. We teach women to know their bodies, menstruation, pregnancy and so on. In our culture men considered menstruation to be abnormal, and the women would try to hide it. We try to show that these things are normal; that they have something to be proud of because they are connected to the creation of society.

This subject includes sex education and how to control pregnancy. The students learn themselves and then go to the mass to teach the peasants scientifically about pregnancy and family planning – how to plan families according to economic capabilities, to space children by three or four years and how to build a healthy society. We teach the menstruation cycle and the 'safe period'. In addition they learn how to prevent diseases, especially through personal hygiene and social sanitation.

Rural science and home economics

The main aim of these subjects is to change rural life. For example to use tools and resources to build a new house, to have a bed and build a latrine or a shower, to plan and improve life based on the conditions and possibilities available. The conditions are different in different regions – in Afar or Agew country – so teaching must be based on cultural practice too.

The aim of the economics training is to teach peasants to manage the home based on their income. In our country there is a diversity of produce. One peasant can produce eggs, meat and grains, but they only eat *injera*. So we teach them about nutrition and how to use all their produce and cook these things. Also how to build a house economically, using their own labour.

Agriculture

Thirdly there is agriculture. The aim of this subject is to give women a knowledge of the garden. How to produce things, when to plant, how to grow vegetables using a small amount of water. Also we give lessons on soil and water conservation and terracing. Agriculture is mainly taught by the agriculture department, so our aim is to give a basic knowledge of it. Before, women had no right to land, so there are many young women or widows who do not know how to plough. They have to pay someone to plough for them. So we teach them how to plough. The women fighters learn how to plough and go to the women and encourage them to plough for themselves.

Handicrafts come under agriculture. Traditionally women do not become skilled artisans, like weavers or embroiderers. At home they make basic things, like pots and some clothes, but here we teach them to become more skilled. It's a great thing for women to plough or to weave, as the men have traditionally done it all in this culture.

Politics

Next there is politics. We give women a real sense of the 'woman question'. First they learn about the international women's movement. There are different examples from India, China, Arab countries and capitalist countries. We teach how they are oppressed. We also teach about African women, women in Ethiopia and women in Tigray. Human relations also comes under politics. We teach them to live with the people, how to relate to the mass, how to politicise the people and solve their difficulties. They need skill to solve conflicts among the peasants.

Language and literature

They also learn Tigrinya, including grammar, literature, poetry and so on. We want to make them competent in literature. Women are not active in literature, so we try to teach them to participate in this area, in poetry for example.

Other activities

We have gymnastics in the morning to build strength. The students carry grain sacks and collect wood. They play volleyball. In the future we hope to have tennis and basketball, but we don't yet have the equipment. We have cultural activities: drama, singing, music, literature, writing, and reading poetry, and we have a cultural group. This helps students to relax.

Teaching methods

We focus on theory and practice, in learning, for example, how to filter water or grow vegetables. On the old site before it was bombed, we had a demonstration field and had daily agriculture. We had cows, goats, hens and so on.

We have classes and divide students into small groups of ten to fifteen for discussions. We also have assemblies to discuss central issues. Our teaching aids include painted diagrams, for example, for health education. There are four groups. Each group does all six subjects each day. The classes are forty-five minutes long. There are four periods in the morning and two in the afternoon, except in the hot season when we start earlier in the morning. If it is hot we teach all six periods in the morning and rest in the afternoon.

The rainy season is usually a vacation. But sometimes there are exceptions. In

1987, bombardments forced us to move the school to a new site, so we started late and we continued through the rainy season.

When the students leave Marta School, like any other graduate, they feel mixed emotions. They are going to lose that feeling of collective comradeship, so they feel very sad. They even weep. On the other hand, when they leave for the mass, they are more self-reliant; they can understand their question, so they feel more comradeship between themselves; they are more conscious in their struggle. They realise they have skills and a task to teach the mass, so they ask, "Why are we weeping? We have a good future to work with the mass."

A Marta student at work

Neriya: My name is Neriya Wahabi, and I'm twenty-four. I come from Endabaguna. My father is a weaver and my mother is a housewife. I have been a fighter since 1980 when I was fifteen. I've never been married. I started at Marta School at the beginning of 1987 and graduated by the end of 1988. Before that I was a combat fighter. I faced a lot of battles and I was wounded in the shoulder.

I don't know why we were selected for Marta School but I think it was because I was already literate and they felt that I would have an ability to communicate what I had learned. Being at Marta School means that we have learned skills to spread amongst the people. We are agitating the people, and take as our starting points the people's own conditions of life and their economic problems.

Let me tell you, not just in Adi Hageray, but for the whole of Tigray the following are the main problems, because Tigray is one of the least developed countries. The women go great distances to fetch water and firewood and the tedious work in cooking takes a tremendous amount of time. One of our most important areas of development is around the stove. Here our stove facilities are very poor. They use a lot of firewood, and water is lost during the boiling process; much energy is wasted. This increases a woman's journeys for water and wood, and makes her exhausted before her time. This household problem affects women's participation; she is always stuck with the cooking! So it was important to make the stove more economical and to enable it to cook different things at the same time. In this area we have demonstration stoves in two tabias. When we started on stove-making, then women were very eager, and now every woman wants to join in.

We also work on hygiene. Since our society has an all-purpose house for sleeping and cooking with the cows and goats altogether, there's always a risk of getting ill and catching infections. We give women education, not about using soaps and detergent, but using ashes for washing or a plant called *shufti*, which is like soap.

We give advice about limiting the tedious labour in housework. Getting fuelwood takes a long time and uses a lot of energy, so we reserve fuelwood in a special local store. We are trying to encourage the growing of different foods which have a wider nutritional value, such as vegetables. We advise women on how to work with their husbands on agricultural activities, in weeding, or making a garden in their compound and rearing chickens.

All our activities are controlled by the local baito, and they coordinate our activities. There are three of us here from Marta School, and we talk with the committee and make a plan about how to approach the people. At first we faced great resistance from the men and women. But we had included that possibility in the Marta curriculum so we were prepared for this before we came. We knew that it would be a hard job! We first had joint meetings with the baito, making a good base for practical work through holding meetings with the people. We talked about our aims and then about the practical implementation with two selected women. We chose women who were more advanced in their activities, and whose homes were situated centrally. They've acted as models for the others, and demonstrated what we teach, because we can't train everyone at once. It takes a long time to show results in changing attitudes, but we find that once some women are successful, others will always follow.

Changing cultural attitudes

The clouds are covering the sun.
Let's work, my ox, work on
To finish ploughing the land
Before the rains come.
Go tell my woman what you've seen,
How hard we both have worked
Turning the hard and stony soil
Before we spread the seed.
Woman, let me plough the earth
While you pull out the weeds.
The rains will fall, the grain grow tall
And give us all we need.

Prerevolutionary ploughing song

'Culture' is a difficult concept because there is almost nothing it doesn't include. It is the total way of life of a society, but also the imaginative and creative expression of that way of life. A society's sense of identity is bound up in its culture, and language is fundamental to it. The colonial powers knew this well. The coloniser's first act is to separate a people from their language and culture. The Amhara rulers of Ethiopia, although a minority group, imposed Amharic as the national language, took steps to suppress the languages of other nationalities and repressed as far as they could their written expression and their national songs and dance. It is understandable therefore that the first act of resistance of an oppressed people should be to reclaim their language and culture. From the beginning TPLF has encouraged the growth of the people's confidence in themselves and the struggle by emphasising the importance of Tigrinya, of Tigrayan history and of celebrating the revolution in song and dance.

The paradox is that culture can work in two ways – both for oppression and for liberation. In Tigray therefore the revolution has had to reclaim and work through the culture while at the same time working for cultural change. Traditional feudal culture, as we have seen already, was especially oppressive of women. The women I spoke to in leadership positions were both proud of the achievements so far and yet aware of what remains to be done. They have expressed this forcefully in their testimonies. I met and interviewed Mahta in London, where she was one of the representatives of TPLF. She feels that living in Britain has deepened her understanding of the complex interrelation between different cultures and women's problems. Material wealth doesn't necessarily change the exploitative principles on which a society's attitudes towards women or other oppressed groups are based. Zafu and Abrehet are both still living in Britain and in the chapter *Beyond Tigray* they also make some interesting cross-references to their experience of British and other cultures as they perceive them affecting women.

Both women and men I talked to were aware that it takes time for cultural attitudes to change. Mahta refers to the prevalence of superstition and, on my recent visit, Iyassu, the head of TPLF Cultural Department, told me about types of sorcery and other cultural practices in Tigray before the revolution. Superstitious beliefs and activities flourish where people have no practical opportunity to improve their lives and, since the revolution gave the peasants access to land, education, decision-making and local judicial procedures, the power of these beliefs in Tigray appears to be fading. However it is difficult to see how they could disappear completely in the short time since 1975. For this reason, instead of relegating all these references to the chapter on *Women in feudal Tigray*, I have included some of Iyassu's information here to indicate the problems involved in changing cultural attitudes.

Different kinds of sorcery were practised in Muslim and Christian communities, often in the context of revenge for offences or injuries. Highly educated Muslim adepts can still be paid to harness the power of forces called *amderebi*. The *debteras* were Christian sorcerers, with a reputation for causing impotence at wedding times. But the references I heard most frequently in Tigray were to the *budda*, who were men or women with special powers, similar to the 'evil eye', which still retain some influence among the people. Many of them were blacksmiths and in fact all artisans, but especially blacksmiths and metal-workers, were feared by the peasant community. Many buddas came from the area around Axum, which, as the heart of the ancient Axumite civilisation, has been the centre of gold and metal-working skills over hundreds of years. Their power wounded the victim through the eye like an arrow. It took the form of possession and there are counter rituals for exorcism.

The *hamien* are another group with special powers. They form distinct communities in particular areas, from which they travel around the country. They earn a living by performing for weddings, fairs and feasts for those who can afford their services or by going from door to door. The men are dependent on the women, who are skilled at a particular form of poetry and song; the men play the *tchira wata*, the haunting single-stringed Tigrayan national instrument played with a bow. During festivals the woman goes alone from door to door earning money or grain with her complimentary poetry. When the household is generous, her words become evermore beautiful and flattering, but if she is sent away empty-handed, then they turn, within the terms of the culture, into extravagant and terrible insults. The *hamien* were a protected group, allowed to say whatever they liked, no matter how wealthy or important the person addressed. They could refer to things otherwise forbidden and break all cultural taboos without fear of reprisal and, because they were feared, people would be willing to buy their silence. The TPLF Cultural Department have collections of *hamien* poems. The ones reproduced later in this chapter were dramatised to me on my recent visit by a member of the cultural troupe who is a daughter of a *hamien* family.

The years since 1975 are too short a time to demand a fully-developed revolutionary culture in which women are equal in every way. Nevertheless, while I travelled in Tigray, I was looking for corroboration from people's behaviour of the declarations of intent about women's equality which I heard on every side. I was impressed that so much had already been achieved. In this as in most other things the fighters are a vanguard because their re-education is so much more intensive. The most visible changes are in women fighters, but many of the women in the rural areas who are participating in their associations and in local administration are not lagging behind. The example of these women and others who participate in a wide range of roles and jobs formerly the exclusive preserve of men must be an increasingly important influence.

I saw many signs of changing attitudes to men's and women's roles. When we were travelling through the country on our first visit, sleeping in the open and cooking where we rested, Berhanu, our guide, and Tetjanna, one of the guards – both men – did all the cooking as a matter of course. On many occasions male fighters took our clothes to wash, especially before we had developed the skills of washing on stones with little water. The women at Marta School on the other hand refused to let men do anything for them that required strength and fitness. In Sheraro a peasant woman proudly killed a chicken for a meal, a task women were formerly judged unfit for. We were present when a group of women fighters were challenging some men fighters on exploitative male attitudes to the recently relaxed laws on marriage for fighters. Women were not only present at *baito* meetings, but were speaking out. In Awhie I met Leteberhan, a calm, articulate *shig woyanit* of twenty-one who ploughed her own land, was active in her local community, and still chose to remain unmarried. Her mother, on the other hand, was too shy to speak and, although judging from her own likely marriage age and the ages of her ten children, she was probably only about forty, she looked about seventy to us. Such contrasts say a lot about the changing position of women.

Songs and poetry have always been an important part of Tigrayan culture, as the ploughing song at the beginning of this chapter indicates. Since the revolution, cultural activities have been an important means of changing attitudes. Every community and town have their own musicians, singers and regular festivals of song and dance. All the schools have song and dance as an important part of the curriculum. The TPLF Cultural Department has skilled cultural troupes who not only write and sing revolutionary plays, poems and songs, but

A Hamien woman's words

I salute you, my beautiful one!
Your teeth, gleaming and even,
Are set in lips like jewels.
When your husband rides your hips,
When your lips meet,
He loses his heart.
But the power of your mind
Draws everyone to you.
Your waist is slender.
Your hair is beautiful.
Your yard is full of lilies.
I salute you, madam, my beautiful one,
With your teeth, gleaming and even.
See the bread in your basket –
Let it come to us!
See the teff in your grain-store –
Share it, share it with us!

So she sends us away!
Did you hear? Did you hear her bark
Like a dog –
That one with a bad ass?
The one who never cleans her floor,
Whose piss is a lake,
Whose shit is a bog,
Who farts lightning amid storm clouds.
She doesn't wash her armpits –
A wanker, who doesn't wash her fingers
Even when they're used to feed her cunt.
No man would want her!
Her belongings reek and her mother
Never taught her to make love.
For she is the mate of horses and donkeys,
Desiring to be taken from behind.
May you be toothless
And your cattle dead of plague –
Both you and your cows only dried meat.

research traditional cultural practices and dances. New songs are written to celebrate victories against the Derg and important events, but they also reflect the importance of women in the struggle. On my recent visit I was part of the audience when hundreds of young fighters wept at a musical dramatisation of the kind of bitter exploitation their own families had suffered before land was distributed under the revolution. The woman singing at her grindstone became a poignant symbol of the oppression of the whole society. The drama went on to show how land redistribution followed the defeat of the feudals and ended with the same family harvesting their own produce and singing rousing songs which celebrated the revolution, TPLF and the liberation of women.

"The achievements themselves help to change their outlook"

Mahta: Since the revolution the most important economic and political changes have given women independence. Even if a woman is a wife or a daughter, she has her share of land from the age of fifteen. With her own land, she can choose when she marries or, if she is a widow, she is able to support herself and her children. Now she can participate in elections and in the administration of her neighbourhood through the people's councils. The councils have raised the legal age of marriage for women to fifteen, forbidden circumcision, abolished the concept of illegitimacy, and changed the law of rape so that a woman never has to prove herself innocent.

But it is not a simple matter to change traditional culture, even if it is oppressive. Early in the revolution, over 75% of women did not want women's associations. It took a long time for them to understand it. Women only began participating as they do now about seven or eight years ago. Nine years ago there were very few women in the TPLF. The main work was done in the mass associations, but before these were formed, women fighters would organise local meetings in which they could discuss women's oppression and listen to the women's problems. After one or two years of talking like this, women came to realise the importance of mass associations for themselves.

Superstitions were completely crushed in some areas by the TPLF within the first two years. There they talk about it now as past history although in the urban areas outside TPLF control it still exists. The problem is not completely solved. Priests' conferences are helping with the problems of Church attitudes to things like menstruation, but we cannot dictate to priests and Muslims – we work by argument and persuasion. Menstruation is still a big shame. Rural women have neither underwear nor tampons. Women still can't say they want sex, and divorce is still more of a problem for women than men. Among fighters, women can choose their husbands, express sexual interest, or finish a relationship. If she loves a man she can say 'I love you', like that! As most fighters are from the peasants, they are an important influence for changing attitudes.

Because of her economic dependence, divorce was not possible before the revolution. Women without husbands were considered rubbish and there was widespread rape and violence. Now, if she wants a divorce, everything is divided equally, including the dowry. If he wants a divorce, especially when she is pregnant or has a baby, he has to give something more than an equal share. This is the law now, under the TPLF. Before, the man kept everything including the dowry, except for a pittance, a few *birr*. Small children go with the mother, older children can choose who they go with.

The TPLF believes women have to be free, along with the whole of society. If women are not 'conscious', if women are not concerned about their question, if women are not involved in building society, the revolution will lose out, so if we want a free democratic society, women must participate equally with men. Therefore in the cadre schools, in women's associations, they discuss the woman question and its history. Traditionally, women were *economically* weak, because they couldn't own the means of production and because all production was in the hands of men. But are women *really* weak? Even the ordinary man from the mass associations, who doesn't want to act clearly or openly against women, has believed till now that, 'She is not equal like me.' These attitudes can't be changed in ten to twenty years. Women must participate in all spheres of society if that man is to change. But, even with the encouragement of the TPLF, even within the TPLF, women still don't participate as equals. But the TPLF must go on trying – in the two women's schools, in political cadre schools, in every place – the traditional division of labour must disappear and be replaced by a more equal division of labour.

But there are difficulties. In Tigray we can't rotate domestic jobs, as fighters do, because it takes maybe eight hours to grind the grain, to fetch wood or water, to prepare food, and therefore if we want a changed society in which men and women participate equally, we have to develop our country. To develop our country isn't going to solve our problem – look at the developed countries! – but you can socialise all tasks in time.

Traditional men don't accept that women must plough because they are equal. If we forced it on them they would be against the TPLF. Laws can change, but it doesn't mean that the outlook of society changes. Women can't in fact be equal in ploughing, although in law they are, because of their domestic obligations, therefore first we make general economic changes and change people's consciousness. I don't want to say that all Tigrayan women believe completely in the 'woman question'. They are still fighting just to change their own minds – but they at least don't openly declare the traditional attitudes. The achievements themselves help to change their outlook. But it takes a long time. We work gradually, in steps, in the ways we challenge everything. The women from Marta and March 8 women's schools spread out all over Tigray to improve women's capacity to take up the changes *in practice*. Every woman has to fight it, even in her own home. She has to understand her husband, what he thinks about her, what he understands of the 'woman question'. She has to change his mind. It is heavy to liberate just yourself, but to change your husband and the rest of society ..!

As for the future, I hope our revolution goes on in full consciousness. The TPLF has made many progressive steps in changing the culture towards women, but I think the 'woman question' will be solved by the TPLF and the resolute struggle of Tigrayan women. To solve the democratic question so the future will be good will be a big struggle. This revolutionary situation is not simple, but we are going in good condition, so I hope the future will solve many problems and the TPLF will achieve many things.

The situation is not good internationally – it is different from Tigray. You know the problem in Britain is bigger than the problem in Tigray. In Tigray, backwardness is a big contribution to the oppression of women and there is class oppression. But in Britain there is a big problem of violation of women and discrimination against women, especially violence against women and children. The big problem is getting unity. There is such an emphasis on individualism and women as a force for change are not united. Even under capitalism and even here in England under the Thatcher government something could be achieved, but not if women are divided. This is a big problem that only women can solve.

Whenever I see films or advertisements which are very sexy or when I hear about violence against women, I feel very bad. Then I appreciate my culture, even though it is technologically backward. It's all a consequence of capitalism in a bad condition.

"We must study housework and make it scientific and easy"

Aregash: It's tough to change the mentality of the male. They are used to working outside the house and to women working inside. Sharing work is important, but it doesn't solve the whole problem. Men work outside in society, so if we try to make men work in the house it will take time. The solution is to make housework easier to do than at present. If it could be done in a shorter time, women could work outside the house as well. So we aim to have meals that can be mechanically done so women don't have to grind corn which is so laborious, time-consuming and destroys women's health. They go for one or two hours to fetch water or wood. If they had a water supply in their village it would give them extra time. We must study housework and make it scientific and easy. If we can do this and it can also be shared, these two things could ease the problem. Of course men have to be taught to share cooking and child-care. We teach them to participate as much as possible and try to set an example.

We live among them as fighters, so they can take ideas from what we do. They see male fighters baking bread and doing all the tasks of the kitchen. Women traditionally have the skills of cooking. Men preferred to eat what we cooked, but we forced them to share the cooking. Now the fighters are having babies, the men share the child-care.

Remnants of the 'dirty society'

Román: In sexual matters, the boy or the man is free. He can do whatever he likes. He is not asked, but the girl is controlled by the family – her mother, father, brother all control her. Even if she is seen talking to a boy, as a girl with her family, whether she is a student or in the village, she is asked: "What is going on?"

Zafu: Normally our women can't express their sexual feelings. If a woman were to say she wants sex, her husband would think she was like a prostitute or maybe even having sex outside the house. So it is forbidden for her to say 'I love you'. She can't show she loves her husband. If she shows that she loves him, other people will think she is a prostitute. This is the feudal culture. If her husband is away from home for a long time, he cannot kiss her when he comes home because he can't show he loves her, even if he does inside.

Zodie: If he comes back and four other women are there with his wife, he can kiss them but not his wife in front of them. At a celebration they can't sit together. They have to sit in different places. This is still customary in the countryside, although not in the towns. Even in the villages things are beginning to change.

Berhan: As for menstruation, if women can get to the towns they usually buy pants, and place a cloth inside. In the country women use rags pinned to a cord around their waists. They fashion a pad out of cloth with a loop at each end and thread another strip of cloth through the loops and tie it around the waist. Others use nothing at all, but place a square of cloth underneath them when they sit down on a chair.

When women are out in the fields during the time of their periods, and if they are not wearing pads, they will squat in the usual way whilst working, with their skirts well spread out around them, and will then cover over any soiled patch of ground with a little earth when they get up. Normally women don't mention to anyone that they have their period, there being a lingering feeling amongst some rural communities that it is something shameful. In the real countryside a woman can't see her husband until she has finished. We are trying to change women's attitudes through health education classes in discussions about the menstrual cycle and pregnancy, but church and men's attitudes will take longer.

Zodie: She is not permitted to go near the church during her period. It is forbidden – it is a really bad sin. She doesn't want to, because she feels really dirty. It is the same for the first few weeks after she gives birth. This only applies to women in the orthodox church, not to Catholics. About Muslim women I'm not quite sure.

Zafu: Periods are natural for women. They are not a curse, but just part of the biological difference between men and women. The Orthodox church especially is very conservative and the priests keep all these beliefs going.

Zodie: Priests are everywhere, but in the towns TPLF have not been active until recently so they are more powerful in some ways.

Berhan: If a woman has a period she feels guilt, still, because of the old tradition. It is hard to change it straight away.

Zafu: If a woman has sex with her husband, she can't go into church. No one else knows, but she knows herself and feels dirty.

Berhan: This is a religious tradition. It takes time to change, but, to be honest, it is difficult to know how fast it is changing.

Zafu: The priests, even if they secretly believe that women who are menstruating should not go into the church, they can't say this aloud in the liberated area. There are some politically-conscious priests who would challenge them.

Zodie: If a woman were in labour, her husband would not enter her room. As soon as the waters break, he leaves and calls a woman to help her. He can't go and see her for about four or five hours after the birth, until women with her have put holy water in her room.

Berhan: If the baby is a girl she is baptised at eighty days, if a boy at forty days. For a boy the women ululate seven times, but for a girl only three. A newborn baby boy is laid in a sieve basket which has very fine mesh. This signifies he can keep a secret, that he is strong, that he doesn't show emotion and doesn't have to explain himself. The female baby is put in a sieve with big holes to show that she is weak emotionally and talks too much. This is still done in the countryside. The TPLF are trying to change all this, but it takes a long time.

Zafu: Prostitution? Well, we in TPLF believe that prostitution cannot survive if there is enough work or if they can help themselves. Most of them got married under age and had no idea what life was like or what marriage was about. Some have run away from the village to the town and became prostitutes to survive. Some never even got money – they were forced to have sex. They couldn't do anything about it.

The TPLF approach is that no one should be forced to have sex. We can't stop prostitution at this time because we don't have enough jobs for them. So as long as they want to, they can be prostitutes, but the men must pay them. If possible, though, instead of prostitution, they should work or be in trade.

Román: Fighters have achieved a little more sexual equality, but there are still problems because we have been in the dirty society. The remnants of all that... when we become fighters, we don't leave them behind! These things have marked our minds over a long period. Also the material base in Tigray has not yet changed. All these attitudes, for example inferiority in us and chauvinism in them, are to be expected.

Of course, men ought to be concerned about the children as well as women. This happens among the fighters. This is an important part of their political education. One of the recent issues of the magazine for fighters *Mekalih* has been about family planning, abortion, about organising women. It is a magazine for all fighters, both men and women. It comes out every six weeks or so. If you are going to do things only for us women, we will always be behind, so...

Laila: It requires a very long period to eliminate this idea of inequality. Even in the West it is a big problem and in our country maybe it's even worse because it is very backward society. It is very hard to understand the 'woman question', even to understand about our struggle, but it is easier for us, the women fighters, than for the women of the mass because we are living together all the time. We struggle political questions together. Then it's the practical work of our organisation to address every oppression, to give rights for every oppression. It is a big aim, so everyone fights to fulfil it. But half the struggle is believing in the process of gradual change. Every time a problem occurs, we discuss it. It is not like most societies, working with men, telling them, "Don't do that!" and expecting them to accept it and then ignoring the problem. Here, we tell him and we discuss it each time: "It is very bad to do that, to follow that idea." Or we discuss it all together, organisationally. If he believes in the struggle, he has to obey and the organisation's beliefs become his beliefs. So to say at this moment that now we are equal or that it is a simple thing or that now men are responding to every oppression of women is impossible for us. Now we are in mid-process.

Young men are organised in youth associations in their villages, so they know a bit when they come to be fighters. From knowing nothing, they know something. But they still have so much to learn, through observation or practical work all the time. Even more important is that in this organisation we are participating equally with them in every task. This helps them to understand.

Even as women, it is not possible to change ourselves all at once. We are not certain of all the answers. We are studying together with our comrades. We have to know it together, we have to struggle together. We are more concerned of course because, if we don't work with men for equality, we will be separated and alienated from society and we won't achieve anything at all. We have to know about the woman question ourselves and teach it to others. We, women and men, have to work together.

Marriage and friendship

Laila: The lowest marriageable age for women has been raised not by the TPLF but by the district councils, called baitos. Before, in our society, marriage was earlier, twelve, ten, without law, simply as parents decided. Now it is over fifteen for girls, over twenty-two for males. The people decided themselves because they had learned a lot from the organisation. They have their own meetings. Now we will continue stage by stage. It would have been hard to raise it straight off to eighteen or twenty. It has been hard, but we have improved a lot.

For a long time there was no marriage for fighters. It was first allowed in 1985. Now we are not sure about marriage. We know what it means in our society, but we want to improve our society, to found a new society, so we must fight for this together. There may be so many problems and yet we have to go on with the struggle. Slowly stage by stage, the more people know, the better society will be.

Zafu: In TPLF marriage was not allowed. In 1985 I was working in the Sudan. From there I went to the Field for the discussions about marriage for fighters. The women fighters especially were opposed to marriage. Most girls want to join the mobile forces, and we were afraid that if a woman had a child it would stop her being eligible to join. But we thought too narrowly. We are not separate from society, nor are we nuns! We were thinking emotionally. So we became convinced that marriage was a good thing. The women from the mobile forces were still strongly opposed to marriage and we discussed it in our association. We decided that as women we should expect to have a child and that in general marriage is right, but that a woman who does not want to be married will not be forced. Our people believe that because so many people have been killed by the Derg, we need to replace them for the future of our country. It should be a 'conscious' decision, not an emotional one.

You know, we teach our people to always have agreement to have sex. If a woman doesn't want it, her husband shouldn't force her. But if she is forced and doesn't speak about it, then there no way we can know. Of course we can't say this never happens because things are not yet completely changed. But when a woman does expose this, we teach that this is rape. Before the revolution, rape was not even a crime. Even young boys would try to rape, but this is completely changed – now it is a very big crime. There is a punishment and everyone hears about it. Now things are changing. Young people are choosing their husbands – and this is love. Before, if a girl was raped no-one wanted to marry her, or if a girl didn't want to marry, the mother and the father could arrange for a man to take her by force. They could say, "Before someone else takes her, you should."

Women in my country are very close and friendly with each other. They were not allowed to go out or speak in front of men. Mostly they sat at home and spoke to each other and shared their experiences. If a woman has problems she tells her best friend, whether she is a neighbour or a relative. We have a saying,"Your neighbour next door can help you more than family living a long way off."

Maybe the close relationships between women have come from these things. You know, most women in Tigray are more backward than men, because they don't have a wide view of life. They sit at home and think about their children and their husband; they care about them and they don't know about the world. So that they won't feel lonely they spend any time they can with each other, making tea, drinking coffee and cooking injera.

"Women will not be pushed back into the home"

Aregash: We are intending to have a strong hold. In the event of victory, and as the struggle continues and the general aim is upheld, we believe women will not be pushed back into the home but will come to the fore. It depends upon political organisation and the correct line. If struggle is led by a party out for its class interest, the women will be pushed into the home. But if we are led by a party which stands with all oppressed people, we won't face this problem. We plan to retain a voice. We have learnt from other women who have been sent back.

Laila: Sometimes, during struggles or during revolutions, organisations have encouraged women to participate so that they can win and after the revolution women are forgotten about and their priorities are lost. In Tigray we are confident because of our demand that our organisation, the TPLF, has as one of its responsibilities the organisation of women. If we understand these issues very widely and if we are struggling for them, even for ever, if they ignore us we will fight. Because we have known our oppression we have to fight. Those who don't know may be cheated by simple things, but we are supported by our organisation to know about the issues that most concern us as women. We ourselves want to struggle about these issues. We know that in the end our oppression will be abolished by ending class oppression. Our target is that we must go on till then. Until we achieve this we won't give up – we know that, they know that, our organisation knows. We'll fight and they will help us.

TPLF and the minority nationalities

The issue of the nationalities, which, suppressed or ignored, has blown Ethiopia apart over the last few decades, is also reflected within Tigray itself. The Tigrinya speakers are the majority nationality in Tigray, but there are four minority nationalities, the Afar, the Kunama, the Saho and the Agew. The dances of the Saho and the Agew are represented in all the cultural shows I have attended, but they seem to be more or less integrated with the majority culture. However, the distinctive cultures of the Afar and the Kunama people have been seen as problems in the past and the TPLF are putting a lot of energy into confronting issues of difference.

Differences of nationality overlap with differences of religion. Tigray is 70% Christian and 30% Muslim in broad terms. The nomadic Afar people who live in the eastern lowlands are Muslim, but there is also a non-Afar Muslim population distributed throughout the region. The majority religion is Orthodox Christianity, but there are a small number of Catholics in towns like Makelle and Adigrat where there were Catholic missions.

The Orthodox Church allied itself with the feudal power structure and the priests were powerful and oppressive landowners in their own right. Muslims were discriminated against in every way, but, most important, they had no rights to land. They became merchants and traders, but as they had no rights in law, they were a prime target for thieves and bandits. Yet Muslims and Christians have lived peaceably side by side in the communities and there has been a certain amount of intermarriage. Without any purposeful investigation, I came across families which contained both Christians and Muslims. I can't speculate on strains this might have caused in a discriminatory society, but in a recent conversation, a woman who was brought up a Catholic told me of the difficulties with her Orthodox grandmother: "When I went to see her with my brothers and sisters, she would cry because we were Catholics. Even the food she prepared for us she would not eat, although it was her own food." There is now complete freedom of religious observance. Muslims can now build mosques. Priests are free to carry out their religious duties as long as they do not work against the revolution and they have the same rights to land as anyone else.

What are the TPLF doing about long-term racism and discrimination against minority groups? First of all, they argue that, as the impetus for their own revolution was determination to end their national oppression by the Amhara, they must not allow themselves to oppress or exploit any nationality or minority within Tigray. The first priority is economic equality. All now have equal rights to land, unless they have alternative means of support, through trade, for example.

However neither the Afar nor the Kunama people are agriculturalists, so the problems of these peoples are not so simply solved. But the nomadic culture of the Afar, traditionally an efficient and ecological way of subsisting in semi-arid lands, has in recent decades made them particularly vulnerable to drought. The Kunama people have also had problems in subsisting through hunting on traditional lands in the north-west which have been steadily encroached upon by Tigrayan landowners under feudalism. In 1987 at the Baito Congress for redistribution of land, we heard the members debate the issue of Kunama land. It was decided that their territory had so shrunk under the raids of Tigrayan landlords that their land should be excluded from redistribution in reparation for past exploitation. However this land is still not sufficient to support a hunter-gatherer life-style. Since the revolution the TPLF have been encouraging both peoples to adopt agriculture as at least a partial solution to their problems.

The TPLF seem very conscious of the dangers of cultural erosion for the Kunama and Afar that increased participation in agriculture could bring about. We talked at length to Mulugeta, the head of the Institute of Nationalities, about his discussions with the Kunama chiefs and people about ways in which they can benefit from the revolution, establish a stable economic base and yet as far as possible retain their culture. These discussions are also going on in Afar areas. The problems come when traditional practice, in relation to marriage or women for example, is in itself oppressive. Among the Afar, the TPLF are encouraging discussion of female circumcision as disadvantageous from the man's as well as the woman's point of view. They trust in the slow evolution of change through discussion and persuasion. Banning traditional customs would only cause resentment and put back the pace of real change. When the people themselves decide to change the law in the baito, as with child marriage, it will stick.

The TPLF are fighting against racist and discriminatory attitudes in several ways. The most important is through the process of political education in the mass associations, where the oppressed minorities can gain an analysis of their situation and the confidence to challenge it, while the associations of the Tigrinya-speaking majority can develop a consciousness of their attitudes and the chance to criticise them. Other important means of encouraging mutual respect for different nationalities are the cultural troupes. Cultural shows give an important place to nationality songs and dances. Particularly popular are the Kunama dances, in which the energetic, even acrobatic, movements of the dancers get roars of applause.

I have not been able to visit either the Afar or the Kunama heartland. The eastern lowlands are inaccessible and hot and on our first visit military activity made them out of bounds. I interviewed the Afar fighter, Eysa, in the west. I only managed to get to the edge of Kunama land and to speak to Kunama women who had lived for a long time among Tigrayans in Sheraro. In the testimonies, there are some interesting contradictions between their comments on marriage and Román's – Román is Tigrayan, but because of her responsibility in the Mass Bureau, has worked with the different nationalities. Before the revolution some Kunama people had become semi-integrated into Tigrayan life-style and attitudes, and had dropped some of the more progressive aspects of their matriarchal culture in favour of the feudal practice of arranged marriage. The interview had the added difficulty that the women didn't speak Tigrinya, so we needed two interpreters, both of whom were men. When I tried to ask about circumcision and other aspects of the culture, the Kunama interpreter refused to translate. Yes, there was circumcision, he said, but he was too shy to ask about it.

Eysa's story

Eysa: My name is Eysa Mohammed. I am nineteen. My people are the Afar and I come from Endele in eastern Tigray.

I am the eldest daughter of four. My family is middle class. Their stand towards TPLF was ambivalent, especially because the TPLF were new in that area. They were not for or against TPLF. The TPLF used to come to Afar regions as long ago as 1974, but they only liberated my homeland in 1983.

When I first became a fighter I was not politically conscious. When I first saw fighters around my home I was surprised. When I saw women with the men fighters I was more surprised! I had never seen women fighters before. The fighters were not able to speak Afar so I can't say they gave us deep political education about their aim. But I understood their movement from things I saw. The women were equal with the men. The men cooked their food; the women cooked their food; men spoke at the associations and so did women, equally. The men had guns; so did the women fighters. I saw that they gained their equality through struggle. In fighting they affirmed their equality.

We Afar women were dominated in the extreme. In our land women were seen as half-human. We had not even the right to see our husbands fully; we had to cover our faces. When I saw women fighting for their liberation I felt inspired and I began to fight, not consciously at first, but to fight nonetheless. When we realised the nature of our oppression and saw these women had gained their equality through struggle, we decided we must struggle too and I became a fighter.

Two fighters who could talk our language, Iyassu and Adam, made contact with us. We discussed everything and they agreed that if we wanted to struggle we should. They said we would have to go that night. There were others there, so that night we got up silently and made it look as if someone was sleeping in our beds. Then we crept away.

I was thirteen when I left home in 1981. First of all, we went to Warey, central Tigray. We stayed there for some time, trying to learn Tigrinya, the language and the alphabet. It was very difficult, but we were only a few Afar surrounded by Tigrayans so we had to learn Tigrinya. Eventually we overcame the problems and became fluent Tigrinya speakers. Then, after two years in Warey, when we could read and write, we were sent to the training school. After nine months training there, I was sent to the political department in Warey to work, where I learned politics and academic education, and when I'd finished that they sent me here to Marta School in 1984.

The conditions for women in Afar culture give them many problems. When we are children they sew our labia together and then tie our legs together with a rope. This happens when we are seven or eight days old or, if the girl is very small, after forty days. One important thing is the culture of marriage. Most Afar women marry between eleven and fourteen. If someone wants to marry they have to give money to the woman's family. We women are treated like commodities – they buy us with money and they also have to buy jewellery and clothes for the bride.

Before the wedding time the bride is forced to enter a room full of smoke. She cannot breathe but she has to sit there because it is meant to make her beautiful. They leave her there for a month continually and this makes her very thin and pale. Her bones become frail. She sits there for a month without moving, allowed only to go to the latrine. She cannot even use her hands to eat, someone has to feed her with a spoon. Her nails grow very long – this is thought to be a sign of beauty.

Our dark night begins on the wedding night. It's very difficult for us to talk about it. They decorate our nails with a kind of ring which goes round the nails in a spiral. When we fight with our husbands on the wedding night we are afraid our nails will be broken and we will lose our beauty. So we submit. Also the smoke makes the bride very weak and unable to fight. It is very hard for the men too; if they cannot penetrate they are ridiculed. It may take a month and all this time is torture for the girls; all this time they fight. They don't know anything about sex, why this is happening to them.

Another thing is wealth building. Women have to play the major role in creating the family wealth. We have to carry water on our backs for very long distances. In our village it may take four hours, on average, to get water. We have to go to market to buy everything, even our husband's cigarettes! Most of the markets are in the central highlands so we have to travel one or two days.

There is a house we use called *senan ari* made of mud. Women have to make these houses. Men don't do any labour. They just come at ten for a cup of tea, then at lunch and again at tea. We look after the cattle, fetch water, cook food. The men just comb their hair, clean their teeth and wear good clothes. They do not work at all.

The wealth of the household is built by the women. But women have no right to divorce. Only the husband, or occasionally the bride's family, can call for divorce. If the two families quarrel, they may make the couple divorce, whether they want to or not. At the time of divorce, a woman can take only her clothes and the goat or cow her father gave her on her wedding night. The father gives her husband double the amount of cattle at the wedding time, but even if they breed she can take only the same number she herself was given. Her husband gives her only fifteen birr.

Another thing is eating. The woman has no right even to drink water in front of her husband. If they go to a wedding ceremony she cannot eat or drink while he is there. If he leaves, she tries to eat while he's gone. Even in her own home she has to cover her face with a shawl when she takes him food or pours him water to wash his hands. If he wants, he can leave her some food. If not, he finishes it all up. She cannot eat alone, so if she is hungry she has to go to a neighbour's or invite a neighbour to her house to eat.

Before the revolution young women discussed these things, especially about marriage and the wedding night. They had some idea about this and the problems in the house, overwork and so on. Some of them tried to escape to foreign countries, like Saudi Arabia, or join the ELF (Eritrean Liberation Front). Some committed suicide even before they were married. Others decided never to marry, but they were forced.

A middle-aged woman is in a very bad situation. Whenever she bears a child, it makes her vagina wider and it has to be stitched again each time. They discuss these things, but they have no political analysis; they only see it as natural. Old women accept it as cultural law and as legal. If they hear younger women complaining they say, "Why are you complaining? We've been through this, and so must you."

One reason we joined TPLF was because of this. On the one hand we saw that there was equality in TPLF, that both sexes had guns and both cooked, on the other hand we were afraid of marriage. We realised we would have to face the same things as our sisters and mothers. We thought that male supremacy was only present in Afar country. We expected the men and women in TPLF to be equal so we were never afraid of them.

I feel happy and proud because I am a fighter. I have gained so many changes in my beliefs. At first I joined simply because I was afraid of marriage and because I saw men and women were equal in TPLF. But since then I have come to know what equality really is in a scientific way. Before, I thought only of the Afar women, because I was not able to see more than that, but now I understand the domination of women in Tigray, in Ethiopia and throughout the world. I feel proud that I am fighting for total emancipation, that I am a model from the Afar women. I am struggling for the total people's liberation. This also makes me happy.

It would be interesting to return to my homeland, to see the Afar women liberating themselves. But I cannot decide for myself. I am willing to work in any way or any place that the organisation sends me.

The Afar nationality

Román: The main problem of the Afar is that their culture is harmful for women. In particular I'm talking about pharaonic, or total circumcision. When a girl is born, her vagina has to be sewn up. This is to control her when she goes to tend the cattle when she is a kid, in order to avoid problems like kidnapping or rape, although it does not really control these things. When they marry, the man is forced to tear the sewed part. It is a problem for men too, but their culture teaches that it shows the man is strong. They accept it and even the women see it as a good thing. After marriage, when a woman is pregnant and gives birth she has more problems, because even after her marriage she has to be sewn up again and when she gives birth it is going to be torn again. Some of the Afar girl children suffer from infections, some of them die from infections.

In fact clitoral circumcision has been practised throughout Tigray. In some areas they still do it. Of course we are trying to put a stop to that practice for women. It is in order to control the women, that they should not be sexy or something like that. It is condemned in the baito constitution, but we have not yet set any punishment. We are trying to change attitudes through education, not through compulsion. Conscious people are no longer doing it.

It's a problem to gather women together to teach them about circumcision, and other aspects of their culture. First we must agitate the people in general about our aim and our intention towards the Afar. After that the men know, if the women are separately organised, they will refuse to be oppressed by them any more. So they are doubtful. Because of this, we cannot say, "We are going to reorganise women to do such and such." We say that our aim is to work, to distribute the land. Then, they realise that we are something positive. Only after that will the women, following the example of the fighters, want to go and discuss their problems.

Now we are at the stage when we can gather women together separately and teach them something in general about society. We've got a constitution. People set the constitution at their conferences or in their meetings and then they condemn infibulation and circumcision. In fact it's not practised now by most of the Afar people. But some of them, especially the older women, are not accustomed to go without sewing their vagina. They feel something is wrong with them, but this is becoming rare.

Because there is a constitution which condemns this circumcision, if the old women do have these attitudes, if they are seen to be trying to get their grandchildren circumcised, they can be exposed and given education. If they are going to do it, they will do it in secret. But the attitudes of most of the people are changing. The men said at the conference that it was a real problem for them, the fear that penetration might take three days or longer – it was very hard for them too.

When the Afar men first saw women fighters, they were afraid that we would say something to their women or that the women would come to us. But we have never acted like that. We just give our programme, our aims, distribute the land. And they make their own judgements. When they see all this, they think more favourably of us. Even sending their women to a meeting shows some confidence in us.

Some of the women hadn't considered going to meetings to discuss their culture or their society. They assume they are not included. But the majority, almost all, are attracted by women fighters. They see she has got land by the struggle, she has got some freedom, especially these meetings, the age of marriage – these things attract them.

The age of marriage before was nine or ten. First it was raised to twelve and now it's fifteen, as in the rest of Tigray. And there was money to be paid – almost like buying a woman in the market. The money was too much – one thousand birr or something like that. But now it has decreased. This is an improvement, because we can't say, "Stop all this completely!" Before, it was not easy to divorce. A man could have seven wives. A woman was still tied by the economy and she didn't have the right to divorce. When an Afar woman wanted to divorce or when the husband wanted to send her away, he used to give her only a token of fifteen birr. But now she can divorce and she can take a hundred and fifty birr.

Of course it's shameful for a woman to be divorced and be sent home, but she goes to her parents all the same. She doesn't have any other place to go, unless she migrates to a neighbouring country – Saudi or somewhere like that – but this is rare. She can remarry, if she has money; if she hasn't, she won't.

On the Kunama nationality

Medhin: My name is Medhin Komo. I am twenty-one and a Kunama fighter. The Kunama people are different from the Tigrayans. They have their own culture, language, territory and history. Before the revolution we were severely oppressed by the landlords. They saw us as animals. They repressed our beliefs and culture and we faced many problems. Our land was taken by the landlords, so we had no land to farm and had to eat roots and plants. We tried to grow some food, but we only had primitive tools and we weren't accustomed to agriculture.

At first when TPLF started to agitate us we didn't believe they were any better than our previous exploiters. Recently we have come to know TPLF supports the people, knows their needs and is struggling for the people, so we have come to accept them.

Before I became a fighter I was living with my family. We are peasants. After TPLF politicised us, I began to realise how Kunama were oppressed and how to struggle to be free, so when I was seventeen I became a fighter. Although no family wants to be broken up, my family understood my point of view and they support the struggle.

Kunama women had many oppressions. If a woman was divorced she got nothing. I want to see an equal society with no oppression of women. Secondly, our people weren't used to agriculture. Recently our people have been growing crops, but then they sold them and migrated to somewhere else. Then they came back for the rains. As a fighter and a Kunama I would like to see a developed society for Kunama within Tigray, a settled society with a developed agriculture to raise the standard of living, to improve housing and service. We have to fight all chauvinism to retain our culture and history. We want to build schools and publish in our own language and to build a strong identity within a free Ethiopia.

Román: The Kunama people have still got remnants of the primitive society in their culture and their marriage customs. It's different from the highland culture of the Tigrayans. For example, the Kunama don't mind if they give birth to a boy or a girl. They see both of them equally. But among the Tigrinya speakers, if the baby is a girl, they knew they would have to give a dowry when she got married. They assumed her to be a problem before the revolution and we still have remnants of this attitude now.

The age of marriage among Tigrinya-speaking people before the revolution was eight or nine, but among the Kunama it was different. If a girl was fifteen or had started menstruating, the mother built her a house in their compound, meaning that she was an adult, that she could stand by herself. So, after the appearance of menstruation, the girl went to her house, and youngsters – young men, came and danced there every night. After the dancing she could choose one of them to stay with her. If she wanted to marry him, for it to last, the boy would stay till early in the morning. If, when the mother went to check, she found someone there, she knew her daughter had chosen a partner. If she didn't want him, she would send him away early in the morning before the mother came. This is very different from the custom of Tigrinya speakers.

"We are starting to feel equal as human beings"

Letemariam: There are maybe eight hundred Kunama people mostly living to the west and around Sheraro. We've always lived around here.

Letentiay: We are not of the same family though maybe we are distantly related. Letemariam is fifty, and I am thirty-five.

Letemariam: I was married at fifteen and have three children, the oldest is thirty-one and the youngest is ten.

Letentiay: And I got married at thirteen, and have two chidren. In the Kunama nationality, we do not depend on a trade. Our economic situation is based on agriculture and hunting. If we lose these two we have no means of life. Before we developed agriculture we were a hunting people – hunting mostly from December until June, when we weren't farming, but we also hunted in the rainy season. Hunting is now decreasing, because every family is now fully dependent on agriculture.

We don't have an organised administration, but culturally we have a chief.

When he is about to die his responsibilities are transferred to the chief's sister's son. If there is no sister, or if she has no son, then the chief can choose his successor.

Before the revolution we had a lot of oppression. As women we shared the agricultural work equally with men, and also in the house. The only difference between us was in hunting, and in this the men were seen as superior. This made him superior in all activities, and the cultural oppression was high. If a woman wanted to divorce her husband, she had to leave all the wealth behind and go empty-handed, except for the clothes she had on, a water container and all the children.

The choosing of a wife depends on the man. When a man wants to marry a girl, he tells his father and mother and they go to the girl's family and ask if their son can marry the daughter. If the girl's mother says no, then the girl won't marry. If she agrees there is a sign for a positive reply. There will be a presentation to the girl of a *mashingla*, the special water container, and a special shoe made out of leather, and a piece of cloth measuring two metres will be given to the girl.

Before the revolution we didn't know any way of life except the traditional way. We didn't know ways to practise agriculture and we didn't know how to communicate outside the Kunama people. We were a degraded people and very isolated. When I realised this it seemed really a darkness, but now we are catching up with the daylight.

As I have told you, even in our internal condition we oppress each other, the women by the men and other backwardness. We were also oppressed by Tigrayans, who degraded our culture and insulted our language, even our physical appearance. Economically we were heavily taxed and when employed in Tigrayan houses we were the lowest paid, and the hardest workers. We were not even given enough to fill our stomachs. They always shouted at us and frightened us.

Letemariam: The problems are slowly being solved. For example, let's take marriage. Before the revolution marriage was based on the parents and the groom, and didn't include the interests of the bride. Now if young people want to marry it only depends on their own will; they discuss it together and the parents have no power over the decision. In divorce also we share out our property between us, keeping all rights not to be insulted or beaten.

As for development, before the revolution we didn't have any services like clinics. We only had inadequate healing systems. Now our organisation has introduced a health clinic to look after our needs. Let me give an example; before the revolution many pregnant women suffered a lot giving birth and many died. Now the women give birth in clinics and the mortality rate is decreasing compared with the past.

These are the most important things, for example education. We haven't conducted a literacy programme yet. We still need a bigger clinic, and more ploughshares. We need help with transportation like more carts and wheelbarrows. Our rights are now respected, but we shall deepen them. Our rights should be our culture. So to make this happen, it needs struggle, and hard work, but we have to grow from the grass roots level. That's why we said we are struggling to get full daylight.

Letentiay: As for a measure of self determination, we have our own language, our norms and cultural practices and we do have the right to be independent and to work with our Tigrayan comrades. Most importantly as a small clan we don't have any intention to establish a separate state or infrastructure. We do have separate baitos. We choose to be hand in hand and at the same time to keep our language and some traditional ways and culture. We participate in the revolution to ensure this. We have sent many young people to the TPLF and this shows that we want to live with our brothers. We see the fruits of our struggle and we are starting to feel equal as human beings, and as an oppressed people. But the problem we have faced is the language, at meetings and at cultural shows. The organisation is obliged to prepare material in different languges, including the other nationalities. But what we are now doing is translating the policies, aims and agendas and whatever we're going to discuss into the Kunama language. The TPLF send bilingual Kunama fighters to do it with us.

"They weren't even thought of as human"

Zafu: Black people in Ethiopia were formerly the slave class and before the revolution they were called *barya* or 'slave'. They weren't treated like human beings or even thought of as human. They could only be servants, doing all the heavy work of grinding or carrying water and things like that. They were the poorest people, without even one goat. The Kunama could be treated like this, or people from southern Ethiopia. They and their children could be sold like cattle and when a son or a daughter was married, a *barya* could be given to them like a cow or an ox. Black people are still called *barya*, but now they have land like anyone else; they can express their views in baitos and participate in the constitution. Sometimes you hear *barya* used as as an insult or a reference to a dark complexion, but under TPLF these attitudes are changing because of education.

The land is ours!

O God, where are you now?
Where is the land you gave me?
This land is rich
But where is mine?

If you were mine, my ox,
I could fill all my house
With the fruits
Of this harvest.

Your work in the fields
Brings grain, my ox.
The grain gives bread.
The milk from your mother
Brings butter, my ox.
Where are they now?

In the weeding and the ploughing,
In the sowing and the harvest,
I labour in the fields
With you my ox.
In the threshing field
You go round and round,
Yet I am not allowed
To taste the grain
I get from my labour.
Yet it is the straw
That comes to us
And the grain to the feudals.
Let us go and be hermits,
My ox, you and I together.
This land is not our land.

Prerevolutionary harvesting song

Tigray was startlingly different from what I expected. We had travelled from the Saharan landscape of Sudan on the huge trucks of a night convoy for twelve hours. Perhaps because so much emphasis had been placed on the problems of aridity and land degradation, I was unprepared for waking up among magnificent trees, to the rush of water in a great river nearby, to the flutesongs of brilliant birds and the rustle of dried grasses over six foot high. It was halfway through the dry season but there were still waterfalls and streams tumbling over the rocky water courses. The underpopulated west still has plenty of tree cover, but I was to discover later that the highlands in the centre of Tigray are virtually treeless. Without tree roots to hold the fragile fertile soils, the torrential rains of July and August wash them down the mountain slopes and into the rivers, where they end by silting up the Nile in Egypt. Deep gullies fissure even the flat fields of the high plateaux in the centre.

Yet few people know that Ethiopia is in fact one of the great world centres of plant diversity, often called Vavilov Centres. Virtually everything we eat can be traced back to fewer than a dozen centres of extreme genetic diversity, named after the Russian botanist, N.I.Vavilov who first identified them in the 1920s. Since the ice ages brought plant evolution to a stop in the northern countries, these areas were responsible for proliferating plant varieties throughout the world, and now, through contributions of germ plasm, for maintaining plant health. Ethiopia is the original home of bread wheat, sorghum, finger millet, pearl millet, pigeon pea, black-eyed pea, okra, garden cress, cantaloupe, watermelon and coffee. This puts a different perspective on food aid!

So what has happened to this once abundant and fertile land? In fact land degradation is comparatively recent. Henry Salt in 1813 writes of an Ethiopia of trees and water and abundant game. Earlier, between 1769 and 1773, James Bruce had travelled in Ethiopia and described the forests and rivers, the fertility of the soil and the profusion of birds and animals. I contrasted the towns he describes as having so many trees "that at a distance they appear so many woods", with the relatively treeless towns I had recently visited. "At Adowa and all the neighbourhood they have three harvests annually," he tells us, and goes on to describe the successive sowing times for wheat, teff, barley, other grains and pulses. But on the same page he also reveals the human degradation, the systematic exploitation which, with no inputs or development from the landowners, was to lead inevitably to land degradation:

> "With all these advantages of triple harvests, which cost no fallowing, weeding, manure or other expensive processes, the farmer in Abyssinia is always poor and miserable...the land is set to the highest bidder yearly... the landlord furnishes the seed under condition to receive half the produce; but I am told he is a very indulgent master that does not take another quarter for the risk he has run; so that the quantity that comes to the share of the husbandman is not more than sufficient to afford sustenance to his wretched family."

But the peasants themselves were not a homogenous group. They were differentiated into rich, middle and poor peasants according to the kind of land rights they had and the number of oxen they owned. The vast majority were landless peasants handing over most of their yields to those who held the land rights and with so little margin that disruption of war or failure of rains could make the difference between bare survival and starvation. Every peasant we spoke to cited land as the primary benefit of the revolution. The first action of TPLF after an area was liberated was to settle disputes over land tenure and to distribute the land. In fact the practice of land tenure was by no means uniform throughout Tigray and in this, as in so many of their land policies, they took the best model available and built on it. In at least two districts, Hamasien and Wajerat, there was a centuries old tradition of land distribution every seven years known as *des-aa*. If an outsider came to the area during the seven-year cycle he could appeal to the elders for a share of the land. The community, like the *baito* now, was the divider of land.

The greatest beneficiaries of land reform have been women. Women on their own now have means of support, but even young women of marriageable age living within the parental family have their own share of land and so can choose to get married or not on other than economic grounds. How many women in the West have their own economic base from the age of fifteen? Land distribution was only the beginning, however. Traditional taboos against women ploughing had to be overcome, including resistance in women themselves. The testimonies that follow show an interesting development in attitudes towards women ploughing since the revolution. Because ploughing has added so much to women's burden of labour, TPLF have since rethought this policy and now encourage only women who particularly want to learn, until some of the problems of women's work have been reduced.

The first land distribution in the early years of the revolution was antifeudal; the second in 1987 was to build a war economy and illustrates the TPLF policy of giving responsibility to the people. Agricultural self-reliance is fundamental to the conduct of the revolution. Belay, head of the Tekezze agricultural project said:

> "When we talk about a 'war economy', we mean that it is a people's war. The people have to feed themselves. They must not rely on TPLF or foreign aid. We must teach them to plough and increase productivity through scientific agriculture. Most of the people able to produce have joined the revolution. Many sons and daughters are fighters. This lowers production, so we compensate by helping the people's agriculture."

We saw several projects through which TPLF is supporting the people's agriculture. Tsebri farm is a huge agricultural project in the fertile western lowlands where the TPLF agricultural department have been developing drought resistant strains of white sorghum. We were there after the harvest, but in time to see the seed being threshed and bagged up for distribution to farmers all over Tigray. Belay again:

> "Our main aim is to help the people develop their agriculture. Our main strategy is to give everything to the people. We teach and train and then give everything to the people. We offered them this project (Tsebri farm), but they were not ready yet – it is too far from the town."

At the TPLF horticultural project we saw not only hectars of tree seedlings for reafforestation, but also fields of chard, tomatoes, peppers, courgettes, onions and groves of lemons, grapefruit, papaya, and banana for distribution as seed and seedlings to farmers as part of the campaign to increase nutrition by gradually overcoming peasant resistance to eating vegetables. The link between nutrition from vegetables and health is made at every opportunity. At the regional hospital in the west, we were given a tour round the fruit and vegetable garden, planted to feed staff and patients.

The TPLF's priorities are to develop agricultural methods which farmers can understand, participate in and take responsibility for. These are not always the same priorities as those of aid-givers. TPLF acknowledge that they have made mistakes in the past and one example is the Shawata agricultural project, financed by Western agencies. This project involved complicated terracing over a whole valley to conserve annual rainfall and succeeded in getting yields of three crops a year. Within its own terms it was successful, but not for TPLF. The project, while enriching local peasants at the expense of their revolutionary consciousness, was beyond the capacity of the average peasant to imitate. The TPLF prefers the patient and realistic policy of *standardisation*, whereby the agricultural cadres use the achievements and most successful techniques of local farmers – in terracing, soil and water conservation, production levels, for example – as models for their community. Every dry season the cadres and the communities work together to terrace selected farms so the number of improved plots is steadily increasing.

The people's agriculture is of course undertaken by peasant farmers, but administered and overseen by the baitos, which are elected bodies of the people and responsible for every aspect of administration. We coincided in 1987 with the second land redistribution and attended a *Baito Congress* which was establishing the new laws for land redistribution, and, a few days later, a meeting of a local baito where the members were discussing how to implement these laws. At both these baitos, about a third of the members were women, several of whom we heard contributing to the discussion. The laws include provision of land for cattle pasture and for reafforestation, and land cannot be sold, mortgaged or rented. I was impressed by their humane and practical detail. Peasant fighters don't lose their stake in land for their share is given to their families. Land is also given for Tigrayan students in Derg towns, to people coming from Derg areas, to those in prison, and to the families of 'martyred comrades and peasants'. Only those who have alternative means of support for more than twelve months do not get a share of land.

Two years later, during my journey through the central highlands, I was able to see the beginnings of a few reafforestation projects on the higher slopes, but the millions of seedlings which would make reafforestation effective are out of reach of TPLF's slender resources. A higher priority therefore has been given to natural regeneration of forest cover, and the effect of the baitos' prohibition of all felling and cutting of trees without permission, is everywhere visible and in some areas even striking. It will take a long time and with every year that passes the rivers will run red in the rains with precious topsoil.

'Land to the tiller'

Besserat: The most important thing in the early years of the revolution was to declare that land must be given to the tiller. The tiller did not mean just the peasant men, but the women as well. We had to break the law that women couldn't own land. We said: "If you want to hold on to your land, then you have to defend it. To defend it, you have to be organised." Men and women are equal human beings. They need their land equally as they have all the same needs, as everyone living. So we organised, and, as women, we organised separately because we had to struggle against our backward culture, that kept women so subdued, so submissive and with inferiority complexes. We started to teach them that they were human beings like everybody else; that they had needs, they had power, they had brains, they had everything. We are only different physically from men, as they are also different from us!

It wasn't easy. In the second year, land was given according to participation and people were elected to distribute land by measurement. The first problem was that men tended to be elected, and the women found out that all the poor land was given to them. They said, "Something is wrong here. By what accident is it that we get all the land with poor soil, and the land with rich soil is given to the men?" We reorganised the whole land distribution. Then the men, who invariably did these things, said, "Women never had land before. Now you give a woman an inch and she takes a metre!" That's how they saw women, you know. If you give women a chance they'll grab everything. But then we explained, through political education and agitation, our ideas of justice and democracy. They were criticised in their associations and were put aside, and others were elected to distribute the land. We divided the land into three parts, the rich soil land, the medium soil land and the poor soil land. A man and a woman would then get equally from the three types, which makes it a more democratic process. But they would complain: "In all our long history, women never had land. Now the TPLF comes along and says 'Land to the women and land to the men'. All right, we agreed because we understand this justice. But now they want land of the same type. Now women are getting too much!"

But eventually they saw that there was injustice in the kind of manoeuvres that some of the men made. This is how women came to political power, by the organisational power they had – all the women in the liberated areas are organised. *All* women. There isn't a woman who is not organised, because their being organised is linked to their rights, and no one would not want their rights – their rights and their duties and their political work are all linked up together. So their right to their land, their right to education, their right to medical facilities are all arranged through their associations and any complaints they might have are brought to their associations.

Belaynesh's story

Belaynesh: I'm sixty-three years old and the oldest woman fighter. There aren't many of us old fighters left now!

A long time ago, before the revolution, my husband and I were farming another person's land and taking some of the production. I was sharing in the agricultural work, although I was not allowed to plough. I did the weeding by hand like most women in our country. After that, when my husband died, we moved to a town, Adi Nibried, and started selling local beer.

In 1977 I became an underground member of TPLF in Adi Nibried. I started to work in different ways for TPLF, sending messages, carrying information. This town was under the control of the EDU. In 1978 the EDU were pushed westward from Adi Hageray and Adi Nibried was liberated. I was also a member of the people's militia with a carbine gun for seven or eight years. After that there was the revolution. and then I had my own land, which I ploughed and I also continued to sell local beer.

To struggle is not a new thing for us. During the *First Woyane* in southern Tigray, there were sisters the same age as I am, fighting against the Amhara rulers as women fighters. As I learned more about this and as I was working underground, I began to feel I was fighting more and more. I became more and more conscious of the oppression and more interested in being a fighter myself. Living in a town could not give me full satisfaction, so when I realised my sons and daughters were fighting and sacrificing everything for the revolution, I said, "Why am I not fighting too and contributing to the revolution also?"

So I went to the Public Relations office to say I wanted to be a fighter. At first they refused, saying, "You are already contributing to the revolution. It is better that you stay here." But I refused and came here to Tsebri and started a new life as a fighter. I decided to work by any ability that I have and to participate in anything the revolution asked me to do. Because I took a course in agriculture, I am involved in agricultural work here.

Women and ploughing

Aregash: The original policy for women ploughing was not to involve everyone, but only those who were capable of bearing the burden of ploughing on top of house activities as well. But the policy was not guided properly. We tried to involve all women interested in learning to plough and very willing to learn. The emotional response and sympathy we got from them pushed us to involve more and more women, but as we progressed problems began to appear. We found that women were just becoming even more burdened by work.

So we decided to check the movement in order to handle the conditions properly. We made it clear that too many women cannot be involved in ploughing at this time because it is an addition to their work-load, which is hard enough already. We have to find the means to facilitate household activities so that women can be released from work around the house to participate not only in ploughing but in other activities of society. We have tried to simplify the life of the village and the house. For example women spend too much time bringing water from distant places. This harms their health. Every morning they stand and bend and grind, as well as lifting the heavy water pot and the baby.

We are trying to ease this way of life in cooperation with some development organisations by building wells nearer the village. We are also trying to do research into making easier work of the grinding with simple powered mills, like the ones used in India. In some of the towns, Sheraro, Adi Daro, Adi Nibried, there are grinding mills, but they don't solve the problem of most of the villages which are far from towns, where most women do all the grinding themselves. Grinding facilities would relieve the women, save their time and improve their health condition.

There is a problem of shortage of fuelwood. We are using dried dung now and eventually reafforestation will supply our needs. The new stoves we are introducing save fuel and worktime. We are also trying to teach the women about agricultural activities around their houses, without going too far. Marta School students are trying to involve themselves in this work. The main job of the students is to organise the women to do tasks around the house, and give them time to do other activities, agricultural as well political. One new development is to implement the original policy – that is, the selection of women who are capable of ploughing in addition to their household activities – in a planned and guided manner. Women who want to learn can get training, and women are still ploughing, particularly the cadres, and women on their own, such as widows.

If the people know their interest and their needs and can get their needs through struggle, if they are sure something is beneficial to them, they can break out of their old-style sentiment and spirit. So it's a matter of teaching them, of politicising them, and of their seeing the benefit in front of them. If they see that, they will try and involve themselves to change their own situation. It is not necessarily a matter of evolving through generations. It will demand a great effort from those who are affected by their background, but for those who are active by nature, the demand will be less as they will easily be politicised.

"In practice there were a lot of problems about women ploughing"

Geday: My name is Geday Legesse and I'm twenty-six years old. My home is in Adi Daro, and I come from a farming family. I didn't go to school because I lived in a village outside Adi Daro and I was an only child so I had to help in the house. I was expected to help in all the tasks of the house from the age of seven.

I was married when I was nine years old. I only stayed two months, and then I ran away because I didn't like him. I ran home to my parents and stayed there two years. Then I married Esmellesh and later I had a baby. When our son was forty days old his father went off to join the struggle. We were living with his parents before that so then I went back to live with my own parents. They weren't happy about it, but there were not too many problems. I had two oxen which I used as a livelihood, hiring them out for a share of the produce. When my husband joined the struggle I had no idea what it was all about. My people were not conscious about politics.

He left in June or July in 1979 and early in the following year TPLF started to organise the people in Adi Daro. I joined the youth organisation. I met the fighters and they started giving us training. I knew some women fighters from my own village, and they talked to us about women's equality in the struggle and we were convinced and wanted to join them. We had a great deal of interest, and my ambition was to be a fighter myself, but I wasn't allowed to join because I had a baby.

The fighters set up local committees and asked us to elect leaders and choose members of the community to be cadres. Then we had a series of meetings to do the usual baito things. In January 1980 we had land reform and I was given a piece of land for myself, but not for my son because he was not yet three years old. If nothing else, the revolution has shown me my rights, especially my rights to land, and that I have equal rights with everyone else.

Two years later I went on an agricultural course to learn how to plough. I trained as an agricultural cadre and after that my duty was to train the women in the village so that they could plough themselves. In fact in practice there were a lot of problems about women ploughing. There are not so many women ploughing these days because it really just adds to the hardships of our lives. Of course there are lots of reasons for the heaviness of womens's lives, in childbearing, cooking, getting water, grinding and the problems of the monthly period. There have been no studies on the effects of the additional labour of ploughing, of supporting the yoke when you're pregnant, for example. Also there wasn't enough political work done in the beginning to convince the people that women should plough so it wasn't universally accepted. There has to be a lot of change in men's ideas, as well as in the women's; there were a lot of problems not taken into consideration. TPLF are rethinking the policy and what can be done about it. In general they have stopped training women how to plough, although if a woman wants to learn, she can get training. Those who already know how to plough can still do it; no-one will stop them.

But in certain areas women have actually been ploughing and harvesting since the revolution. At the beginning there was muttering from the men, and even the women weren't all for it, but it went through quite successfully. The final order to stop came from TPLF and the people who objected didn't do much to oppose it. Some will plough because they have to, and we'll wait and see what changes the organisation will bring for the others, otherwise I see little prospect of a way forward at present. I don't see anything that has been developed yet that can bring about much change in the area of women's work. Obviously there's a war on at the moment, but in the new Tigray after peace I just hope a lot can be done to improve the situation.

"It's a chauvinistic outlook that a woman can't plough and produce for herself"

Kindehafte: My name is Kindehafte Gebremedhin, and I live in Adi Hageray, but was born in Makelle. I am thirty-one and I have two children, a son of eleven and a son of six months. My husband became a fighter in 1980. I am a member of the baito and an agricultural cadre although I am on the trade committee of the baito as well. I trained to be a production cadre in 1982 at Asregar. The training was for one and a half months, and I left my son with his aunt because my husband was not here to look after him. I first had my own land in 1976. At first my husband ploughed our land, but after he became a fighter I was engaged in small scale trading in addition to my farmland, since the fighters' land is ploughed through the people's participation, by the mass, to help the fighters go to fight.

In our agricultural training we were learning how to plough, how to conserve water and soil and a little about how to terrace our land. At the same time we took part in the literacy campaign. I haven't done any training since because of the Derg's offensives. After training I was ploughing my land, making little terraces and passing on what I had learned on soil and water conservation to the other people in the tabia. I did this in demonstrations and at meetings when we were given time to talk about what we had learned. At the moment I'm not working as an agricultural cadre because since I became pregnant I have been unwell.

There was resistance when we first started, but in general we were successful. We argued with the resistant ones and they came to see that they were wrong. Mostly the resistance was to women ploughing; I can tell you that it's a chauvinistic outlook that a woman can't plough and produce for herself. I think that women can do whatever men can do. In our tabia there are still two women ploughing. I am one of them, and the other is Wihebet. Her husband is away as a fighter. Women on their own were given priority in training the first time, but by the fourth training even women who had husbands went. The others don't plough now for many reasons. I did hear about the policy change to discontinue ploughing training for women until the overall problems of women's work are solved. But women can still plough if they want to even though the policy says that women need not be involved in such tedious work.

I think there will be development in agricultural production. For instance, in soil and water conservation some farmers have already begun to show results in increased production. It is obvious that in a mountainous country like ours that it is very easy for floods to wash away the soil, and with it the cereal crops. It is necessary to conserve soil and water by terracing and through reafforestation. These take time. It's a gradual process but some farmers have now successfully started. There's been some success in stopping erosion, and I'm hopeful. The baito is conserving woodland but we cannot replant because it demands extra resources, but we are encouraging individuals to replant and some have been successful. They can get hold of seedlings through the TPLF, and the baito controls how the seedlings are growing up.

Famine and migration

*I will go back to my home
And grow wheat.
Another's country will never be
As your country.
Another soil will never be
As your soil.
Famine has parted me from my country
For too long.
How can you spend your life
In another's homeland?
How can you, sound of body,
Be a parasite?
We are forced to live against our will
By another person's gift.
Famine has confused the intelligent
And made blind those who can see.*

Repatriation song

Most people in the West have only heard about Ethiopia in the context of famine, which they have been encouraged to think is a 'natural' disaster caused by drought. But there is a distinction to be made between drought and famine. Recurrent droughts have always been a factor in the Sahel and Horn of Africa; for this reason, under the farming systems in many of these areas, before they were interfered with by colonialism, the farmers always stored their grain for two to three years as a margin against drought. Even drought has an element of human agency. Besserat, later in this chapter, refers to the interrelation between forest cover and climate. Trees take up and retain rainfall, preventing the erosion of topsoil, and then transpire it gradually to maintain a moist micro-climate. In Ethiopia gross oppression and impoverishment by governments have driven the peasants to deforest their mountainsides.

It takes politics to turn a drought into famine. Besserat points out that most of the bad famines since the nineteenth century have been 'green' famines, caused by war not drought. Amartya Sen's work on famine has shown that in many famines, including the terrible famine in northern Ethiopia in the early 1970s, the overall food-production hardly decreased. The problem was one of distribution and lack of political will. In the well-publicised famine of 1984-5 drought was not uniform and the problem was once again one of distribution, not only of home-produced grain, but also of relief aid.

In fact, food restriction has been used relentlessly by the Ethiopian government in the hope that it will demoralise or starve the opposition groups into submission or kill them off altogether. It is difficult to believe the Derg's protestations that it wants to feed the people, when bombing raids by MiGs at harvest and sowing times have been routine in most years. All convoys over the border from Sudan have to be made at night because by day they have been bombed by MiGs and strafed by helicopter gunships. In 1987, Dawit Wolde Giorgis, the former head of Ethiopia's relief agency, the Relief and Rehabilitation Commission (RRC), who had claimed political asylum in the USA, gave several interviews on the conduct of the famine. He said in *The Guardian* on July 2nd:

> "Hunger and war were intertwined, and the most seriously affected areas were Eritrea, Tigray, and Wollo – the areas where the major insurgent movements operate. There was an understanding among the hardline elements, including Mengistu, to let nature take its toll and deprive these areas of food and other assistance, starving the guerrillas out, punishing the people and depopulating the area."

The famine only led to an intensification of this policy. Little of the food aid donated to the government reached the people in the most-affected areas in Tigray and Eritrea, so that the REST convoys were the only life-line for those who could not get to the refugee camps in the Sudan. The Derg policy of setting up feeding camps was itself misguided, forcing already starving and weakened people to walk long distances, many of them dying on the way. During the food shortages in 1987, access to food at Derg camps like Korem depended on peasants having identity papers from their government-sponsored peasant associations. Those without could immediately be identified and persecuted as Tigrayans from TPLF areas, which, once the news spread, deterred the majority from making the journey. Moreover, these camps were used as rounding-up points for forced deportation to resettlement camps in the south, purportedly to move peasants from eroded to fertile land as a solution to famine, but in fact a plan for undermining by dispersal the TPLF war effort. Dawit Wolde Giorgis said in *The Times* in October 1986:

> "Thousands had perished before reaching shelters and distribution centres,"Mengistu wanted to take political advantage of this situation and launched a massive resettlement programme involving 1.5 million people. He believed that this was an opportune moment to establish a model collective farming system and it was easier to expedite this policy with helpless people who were in no situation to put up any resistance. There were many volunteers in the initial phase, but their number was no way near the target that Mengistu has established. Therefore force had to be used..."

Forced deportation was carried out at gunpoint in market places and feeding camps, mostly in disaffected areas. According to testimony gathered by *Survival International*, some peasants were sent in unpressurised planes and many were dead on arrival. Many, as Lemlem Hagos explains in her testimony, were moved into areas in the south and west, given a little grain and little support and told to settle in a region different in climate, vegetation, culture and health risks from the cool highlands of Tigray. But the land was not empty. It was the land of other peoples including the Oromo people, who were also disaffected by long-term Amhara colonisation and fighting a liberation struggle of their own. It seems likely that resettlement has the dual purpose of setting Tigrayan against Oromo, so undermining both struggles. Another example of social engineering is the government's villagisation policy, affecting Oromo people in certain areas and some of the deportees from the north. Designed to facilitate both social control and the collectivisation of agriculture, people are moved into 'villages' markedly different from the scattered thatched settlements of their traditional culture, with huts symmetrically laid out in straight rows. Berhan's work experience for the Derg brought her into contact with this programme.

Many Western commentators believe that massive support from the EEC and Western agencies during the famine helped to fund the Derg military campaign against the people of Tigray, Eritrea and Oromia. There is strong evidence that much of the food aid was sent to the garrisons to feed the Derg armies. Dawit Giorgis again:

> *"Ironically, the Western humanitarian assistance not only saved millions of starving people, but it also saved Mengistu and his regime. There is no doubt in my mind that without this help, there would have been a bloody chaos that would have resulted in the removal of Mengistu and his henchmen."*

In fact there is nothing wrong with the principle of resettlement as long as it is voluntary. TPLF encouraged it in the early eighties from the overcrowded central highlands to the underpopulated and fertile western lowlands. I interviewed several resettled families in Awhie and it seemed to be successful – they talk about it later in this chapter. But the support and services which REST provided to make it successful proved so expensive that for the time being they have not been able to continue it.

Not until I spoke to families about their experience of the 1984-5 famine did I realise that the exodus to the Sudan was not a spontaneous flight by starving people, as suggested by Western journalists, but a highly organised operation by TPLF and REST to save the people. The same degree of organisation and attention to detail went into the repatriation programme two years later. Our journey out of Tigray in March 1987 coincided with the last wave of repatriated refugees travelling home from the Sudan. There were about eighteen hundred men, women and children resting in the shade of trees. They were well-organised by REST in groups from the same district and, within these, in smaller groups of forty, each with a leader to check numbers, food provision and health, with fighters for support and security, and with REST representatives with medical supplies. They walked for two days and rested for two days, so that at the camp each group was given four days provisions. They were worn with experiences and bereavements, tired from walking, some sick, but still overjoyed. "I feel reborn now I am going home – it's a new life," said one peasant we talked to. Another said, "When we came inside and joined our organisation, she gave us everything she had. Now I am happy."

In 1984 reactionary priests blamed the drought on women. They said God was angry because women had broken the prohibition against ploughing. On the other side, we heard so often of the cooperation and help given by friends and neighbours to each other. "Our friends saved us," says one of the women from Edaga Hiberet in this chapter. In some ways the famine has been a leveller of wealth, but not always. Many richer peasants lost many or all their animals and, after the famine was over, TPLF gave money for seed and for a share in an ox to all poor farmers. Despite this level of support, farmers had many problems the following year and even in Tigray those with more are able to exploit the situation. The problems, even with this level of support, of a farmer called Deste Welde in Edaga Hiberet help to explain the problems faced by TPLF in their programme of agricultural reconstruction. Deste told us in 1987:

Because TPLF gave us fifty birr, I spent it all on seed without putting any aside. Fortunately I got a good crop. I had to borrow one hundred and seventy-five birr to rent an ox to plough my land. Then TPLF gave me one hundred and seventy-five birr to buy a half-share in an ox, but I had to use it to pay back the loan. The price of grain is very low now, so we can't get enough from selling the surplus to buy an ox because the price has gone up. If we could take the crop to a Derg town, there the price is high, but we are too far away. But maybe this year or next we will be able to buy an ox.

"Droughts only become famines because of the political reasons behind them"

Besserat: There are three important reasons for the recent famines. First, there's our own backwardness. Our agricultural implements, our knowledge of agricultural science are so backward, that when nature is cruel we can't cope. This is because we were a feudal society, and we didn't know until recently how to conserve water and how to use the soil in a proper manner or how to use our forests to our advantage and not destroy them.

The second reason is drought. Drought cannot mean famine in a highly technologically developed society, because if it meant that, then in Britain you would have gone hungry a few years ago, or Australia too.

But the most important reason has nothing to do with so-called natural causes. It lies in the fact that our peasants have not been able to produce what they need in peace. Since 1975 the Ethiopian government has seen to it that there has been a military campaign in the sowing and the harvest seasons; bombardment of villages and farmland. In that time, we've had eight or nine huge campaigns where a quarter of a million soldiers were deployed in Tigray alone. Incessant bombardment has meant that the peasants have not been able to work their land for seven months. For six months they have to work really hard if they are to produce anything.

Mind you, there is a just war and an unjust war. The war you carry out against injustice is just in itself. We don't believe in giving one cheek when the other is slapped, because we have to survive. For a hundred years we have been struggling in many ways, but this is the time when we are organised under a political slogan, under the leadership of an organisation. The Ethiopian government cannot crush us. It has not been able to crush us so far, and it will not crush us ever.

In the last hundred years we've had sixteen great famines in Tigray, and most of them were not caused by lack of rain. The first great famine was at the end of the nineteenth century. This was at the time when Menelik, the central king, brought us under his domination, and destabilised our society. This started one of the biggest famines when two hundred thousand Tigrayans died, and in all the seven years that we starved there was always rain. In the Italian war against Ethiopia in 1943 there was a huge famine again and another quarter of a million people died. Again there was no drought then.

In 1973 there was another big famine, but again this was not the result of drought at all; it was the result of Selassie's efficient, systematic way of underdeveloping us. Another quarter of a million people died. During the famine of 1984 the Ethiopian government burned fifteen thousand tonnes of food in western Tigray alone which is where most of the reserve surplus food for the central highlands is grown. So you see, droughts only become famines because of the political reasons behind them.

In the last hundred years, we've lost 85% of our forests, 90% of our wildlife, and almost 98% of the rivers have dried up because the forests have been felled. In the nineteenth century travellers such as Salt, Pierce and Augustus Wild told of the fruit trees, the forests, the elephants, the lions, the leopards, the huge farmlands, all the great rivers – we don't have them today. This shows what systematic oppression can do to people in a hundred years. Some reports by the UN indicate that with a proper afforestation programme in Tigray, most of the rivers can start to flow within fifteen to twenty years.

We believe in long-term projects. First and foremost, we believe that we can only prosper and take care of our needs under a system of justice. We are changing the economic system, the political and social systems and the culture. We are learning how to conserve the water and soil, we are introducing reafforestation, we have to industrialise our society, we have to tap our natural resources. We have lots of minerals – iron, zinc, mica, potash, sulphur, copper and so on.

In the field of agriculture, there will be short and long-term programmes. In Tigray in the last few years, we have demonstrated that, with only as little as ten days real downpour, through conserving this downpour and conserving the soil with the systematic use of terraces, we were able to provide two harvests. The first was durum wheat and the second was chickpeas. If we can produce such a fantastic result, we should be able to take care of ourselves in the short-term. But we do need to support the peasants during this time; they need tools, and oxen to replace those who have died in drought or through bombardments; they need grain if they have lost crops through the war or locusts. In the long-term we have to industrialise, to bring science and technology into our agricultural work, and the kind of economic system we have should be geared to the needs of the whole society.

We need the help of Western agencies, but they must realise that the Tigrayan people cannot live forever on handouts. Their demand is that they should be helped to help themselves. The projects and the kind of relief aid that we need must be long-term programmes of development. Of course it is necessary to relieve the pain and starvation of the people, but there should also be real development projects that would enable the peasants to learn new techniques of agriculture, to be involved in other areas of economic life and industrial development, because we are living in the twentieth century. I don't mean to say that all technology is important for us – there's some that we don't need at all and which the world would be better off without, but I mean industrial projects that would be to the advantage of ordinary people. The mining and meat industries could be developed. Our water resources could be improved. We could get help to build roads through our very difficult mountainous terrain.

Aid agencies must give us a hand to stand on our own; even if the whole world contributed money, you can't feed five million people every day – it's impossible! Whatever aid is given to the Tigrayan people, we make sure that it will regenerate itself. We believe in Tigray that famine and malnutrition are not only our problem, but the problem of the whole world, for the simple reason that we belong to this world and we have a right to demand that we should not perish. It is the peripheries that are dying and you can't afford to let that happen. We don't see it as charity, we don't see it as anything to be ashamed of – to help is the duty of the developed world and also our right, because it is the overall system all over the world, the huge injustice, that has caused this disaster.

But there is competition between the Americans, who helped Selassie, and the Russians, who are helping the Derg, the Ethiopian regime which is bombarding us, destroying us, our crops, our farmlands. The Derg is supported economically by the USA and Western Europe and militarily by the Soviet Union. We, as Tigrayans have refused to bend our will for survival under such tremendous powers against us. We want people to know about the fundamental changes we have brought into effect – changes in the lives of women, women who were prostitutes, beggars, farmhands, maids. Now they are leaders of society. People must understand this message. We have suffered, our kids have died and our women have died in famine and war. Despite this, Tigray is not a land of tears and crying, it's a land of hope and that's the vision and message we want to project to the world.

Famine and resettlement:
"The famine in 1985 is terrible to describe"

Rishan: We come from Igela, near Adua, in the highlands. Land was scarce and there was no rain, so the TPLF fighters told us it was better to move to the west where there was better farmland and the chance of an improved way of life. REST was responsible for overseeing and supporting the resettlement programme. No-one was refused permission who wanted to move, although some families who were advised to leave refused and remained behind and faced terrible problems. That season was the worst and the next year they were forced to move anyway.

The first group registered and moved in May 1982. In that way they were settled and able to reap a harvest that same season. We also registered in 1982, but we didn't move until the second group left, in November. We stayed in Igela through the rainy season, although in fact there was no rain. Many families moved with us, so we knew other families here. But, although we moved by choice, we felt very sad, very unhappy, when we left our homeland. We were expecting something bad even here. We were suspicious. We didn't have very much information about Awhie – we came on trust, acting on just general information.

Transport was a problem. We had to leave everything behind, bringing only our children and food for the journey. We have seven children; the oldest is twenty-two, and the youngest is only two. We were in a group of about five families, all on foot. First the fathers, the heads of families, were directed here and given land; then they returned for their families. When we arrived the only shelter was an awning erected by the family heads. The journey took about a week. It was very tiring, but we rested and only a few got sick.

When we arrived, we first had an awning and then a simple house. For the first year the TPLF lent us grain, one quintal (one hundred kilos) of sorghum. After that there was good rain and so we grew our own crops and repaid the grain in kind. But the TPLF *gave* aid in the form of farm implements, household materials, all necessities.

The famine in 1985 is terrible to describe. There was great danger. We thought we would never survive. Before the drought we had four oxen, five goats and one donkey. One ox and the donkey starved to death. We sold the goats and three oxen survived. Our son of seventeen died of cholera in an outbreak produced by the famine. After TPLF explained that we could go to the refugee camps in the Sudan, we felt happier, but we did not go to Sudan in the end. We were better situated than many other peasants, with more grain. There was also grain from aid and we sold our cattle.

There were good rains after that, so we were able to recover. The TPLF gave us fifty birr for seed and it was a very good season, so we had increased production of sorghum and sesame and a surplus to sell. The market is a day's walk away at Edaga Adidaro. We go there every one or two months. We feel good about living here now, but there are still many problems in the highlands.

There are difficulties facing a new community. At first there was so much mutual distrust. People asking, "Who are they?", "What are their characters?"

We solved it in different ways – first, through our holidays, when we had parties with local beer and music. Then we had meetings together to discuss our difficulties and our hopes, and so we got to know each other. Thirdly, our sons and daughters were exchanged in marriage, although after the baito was set up in 1984, we decided that marriage should be determined only by the agreement of the two people involved.

I go to the women's association meetings which are very near. Generally our lives are tied to the revolution. My husband is a member of the executive of the baito. He puts his own interests second to the revolution. I remember once he went on a course of political education and stayed there rather than doing the ploughing. We are attached to the revolution because it has liberated us from our problems.

"The Derg received much aid, but used it to feed the soldiers"

Leteberhan: I'm twenty-one, and there are twelve of us children altogether, three sons and seven daughters. We also used to live in Igela in the central highlands. We liked our life there. We were happy, but there was a terrible drought and we lost all possibility of feeding ourselves. Because it was impossible to live there any more we decided to move in 1981, one year before the resettlement move. We had relatives who had come earlier, so we sent our animals to them, and they were saved. We came independently without registering and therefore without the help of TPLF or REST.

The land was not cultivated and there were no buildings, but because we had been in the area a year already, we knew the conditions beforehand. At first there were one or two problems, but nothing much because we expected it. In the first year most of the people came with food for one season and those who had none were helped by the TPLF. The best thing was the good rains that year. We built our houses and had a good harvest.

Before the drought our life was good. We had enough production to last easily for twelve months with a surplus to sell. We had fifteen cattle including calves, twenty-five goats, twenty sheep and four donkeys. Now, since the drought, we have ten cows, including calves, fifteen goats, ten sheep, and one donkey.

In fact it really was a problem at first to get to know each other, to make a community out of strangers, even these neighbours. It took us more than a year. After a while we came to know each other. First we got to know people from the same *woreda* and then after two years or so we began to mix and form a new community. Now we have no more problems. We come together on saints' days, taking turns each month for a *tsebel* (party) – Mariam Tsebel or Gebriel Tsebel. Our family is preparing for one in September. According to their wealth, families invite others every three or four months. We have a system of weddings to tie the community together, although children are no longer promised in infancy. It is the best way to have a strong community. Another good way of getting to know the community is to do political work and to go to meetings.

The 1985 drought was so bad; it's very hard to express. It was caused by lack of water and strong winds. The war made things difficult too. Of course we know about the Derg. They sell vegetables to other countries and buy weapons. The Derg received much aid, but used it to feed the soldiers. They didn't give us a single grain, when more than a thousand were dying a day. Yes, we know this! From this village, forty-five people went to the Sudan. Compared to other settlers we were better off, but some of our animals died. Others we sold and we also sold our goods to survive. We all had help from the TPLF, some grain and flour and fifty birr for seed. That would buy enough sorghum seed, which is cheaper than teff or wheat, to last through to the next season. The following year we had a very good season and so we recovered.

We are quite well off now. In a good year we can grow a surplus over a year's supply of crops. We are more related to the community and really we are beginning to feel this country is like our homeland. Of course we miss our own land because everyone likes to be where they belong. But we had problems there and we know we cannot live there.

Our revolution has brought many changes. If you take women, women were oppressed and dominated by class and sex. No woman could manage even her own life – it was under somebody else's control. But today, all this has been got rid of. We women are equal with our brothers. We can be elected in any administration and have any political power. We can go to any meeting and make any suggestions. All this was forbidden before.

Although my family do not participate in the revolution, I am a shig woyanit. I have my own land. After redistribution, I will still have my land, although because I am unmarried, it will stay the same portion.

Repatriation by REST and TPLF

Kiros Gebru: We left Bora in Raya Azabo in 1985. There was very serious drought and famine and pests had finished all our crops. There was nothing to eat. TPLF called us together to take us to a transit centre – at first I went alone, leaving my father and mother. They followed later to Sudan, but they died in the Wadel Colbi Camp. [near to tears] I was in another camp called Canedeba.

When I reached Canedeba, they gave me a tent, food and medical treatment. We were treated as well was possible. REST took us to a camp in Sudan and then handed us over to the Sudan High Commission for refugees and foreign aid agencies.

I am very glad to return home, but I'm not really fit enough for the journey. I feel very weak, especially because I am carrying my baby on my back, but really I have never been so happy in my life. My revolution is like honey, she gets sweeter all the time.

"Our friends saved us!"

Beriha Medhin: We are all from Edaga Hiberet. I am forty-six, Beriha is twenty-three and Aregawit is seventeen. Under Haile Selassie we lived by farming – but our produce was taken by the landlord. Beside this we had to pay various taxes to the government. Every landlord and government official took from us in kind or in tax. Life was very bitter. When the season was good and there was rain, we had more produce. There was enough for all the year. If the harvest was bad we still had to pay the same, so there was not enough left over to feed us. It varied from year to year. After Haile Selassie fell, we passed only a year under the Derg. But this was still as bad.

Beriha Egzigre: The main change brought by liberation was that for the first time land was given equally to everyone.

Beriha M: Land distribution was not the only change. Women got the same right to land as men. We got equal land and we got our rights. Before liberation we couldn't even move one kilometre because of the bandits. They would take everything we had or rape us. Now we can move wherever and as far as we like. No-one can take our money or our dignity. Now a woman can plough, can own her own land and have her own produce.

Beriha E: To express the changes from the revolution would take a long time. But briefly, we have our own administration in the baito. Before, officials governed us, now we can administer ourselves. Also we have a court set up to judge and punish wrong-doers. We have a health centre and a school for our area.

There was an literacy campaign two years ago, so the three of us can read and write. There are different courses, especially in health and agriculture. We have only just learned to read and write, so we haven't yet had a chance to learn these other things. There is a shortage of teachers.

Beriha M: Before the famine I had two children to look after alone as I am a widow. I had sixteen goats but no cattle. I arranged to hire an ox, paying in kind out of my production. I grew sorghum, teff, maize, sesame, and beans.

Aregawit Teklemariam: I live with my father and mother and three other children. Before the famine we had enough to feed our family from what we grew. We had seven cattle and twenty four goats.

Above all, our development is poor and we have no modern technology. Also we have no forests for people needed wood for buildings or tools. Some farmers cleared the forest because they wanted new land. Then wood is used for fires and cooking. They were damaged, so the rainfall decreased. This was before land distribution. Landlords and rich peasants could take any land they wanted. They destroyed the forests and exposed our soil to wind and flood.

Beriha E: The famine was a bad time. Our crops were bare stalks in the field, with no fruit. So we sent the cattle to eat the stalks. Then we started to sell cattle to survive. We sold half of them and half died. We were in a very dangerous state.

Beriha M: It was bad. Our crops were useless and were eaten by the animals. I started to sell my goats. The price of goats was low and the price of grain was high. For one goat I only got two to three cups of grain!

Aregawit: It is hard to talk about it. At that time there was no food to eat. People ate roots and leaves they had never eaten before. Some of these things were poisonous and some people died this way.

Beriha E: The main problem was communication. Transport was impossible so aid couldn't be brought here. Some people brought flour on their donkeys. Others could only bring a little. But they shared it out or gave some of their own crops. Our friends saved us. They gave us flour or maize. At that time any plans for improving our lives disappeared, especially health care, schools, and the mass associations. Most of the organisers went to the Sudan. Only a few stayed to administrate. The famine was totally disruptive.

One thing I remember is the Derg destroying our houses. It was the rainy season. Many people had no shelter. Rain was falling on them. Then the TPLF and peasants were organised to build new houses and the TPLF gave us seed and money for oxen. Now I have three cattle.

Beriha G: We are full of hope that things will improve now. We were told by the baito not to cut any trees and to plant new ones, and to make terraces.

Beriha E: We want to contribute a lot to the revolution. We are active in women's associations and took lessons in March 8 School and we are in the cultural group.

The Derg's forced resettlement and villagisation programmes

Askale: I'll never forget some of the worst things about the famine of 1984. The poor were very emaciated, going all over the place for food. Although the world community gave a lot of aid, the Derg officials never gave it to the people. They lured the poor with food and when the people were gathered together, they were then encircled by the soldiers and taken forcibly by plane for resettlement. The aid materials were then sold on the open market. The officials responsible for the distribution were improving their lives in a comfortable way. The Relief and Rehabilitation Commission was managed by the Party committee who shared out the aid and the higher proportion was taken by the Party. I remember I volunteered for work with an Italian medical team during the drought time and we were helping the drought affected people and some in Makelle. The manager of this team asked the government to expand the hospital, but the government refused.

Berhan Hailu: I worked for the Derg's agricultural department for a year in 1981 and was posted to the south of Ethiopia, to Oromia. I can't say much about their culture because I was only there for a year, but this much I do know. Oromia is very fertile, and they grow coffee, bananas and papayas. The people are scattered over very wide distances, so bringing them together in villagisation makes it easier to supply health centres and water, but when you see what it does to them and their culture you can't support it. Those who are kicked out of their lands and those who are resettled have no choice at all. They are taken from their houses and their land against their will.

When I was there villagisation was just being started, and they were building rows of identical huts. There were three phases: first of all you had to provide your own tools, but you worked together. In the second phase you had your own bit of garden but everything else was jointly owned, and lastly everything was held in common. It only works as a system becuase it is compulsory. If you refuse to do it, you are seen as anti the revolution and you are arrested and perhaps killed. People will work for themselves, even for a twenty-four hour day. It's not the same when you're working for the association because it's not based on their own interest; even their share of the produce is often not enough to last them the whole year.

"Derg soldiers came and herded everyone into some waiting lorries"

Lemlem: My name is Lemlem Hagos. I am twenty-five years old and I come from Wojarat. I am married and have two children.

One day in June 1985 I went to the market in Raya with my husband, leaving my children at home with my sister. The way was long, and the market was already busy when we arrived. Almost immediately after we got there, Derg soldiers came and herded everyone into some waiting lorries. I was too frightened to really understand what was going on. All I could think about was my children.

We were driven to Makelle, and put in a huge tent. We stayed there for one month without ever being allowed to go outside except to the latrine, and even then we were followed by guards. We lived on *ketcha*, a kind of unleavened bread.

While we were there, more and more people arrived. Some of them tried to escape, but were always caught. When this happened our guards were doubled. After one month we were taken by plane to Gambella in south west Ethiopia and put in a resettlement camp. My husband and I were assigned to a grass hut. We were given fifty kilos of flour and some salt. This was supposed to last eight people for a month. To make the food more palatable, we bought pepper with the money which we had taken with us to the market, and which the soldiers had never taken away from us after our capture.

The place where we were living was surrounded by jungle; there weren't even any visible paths. At night we weren't guarded – presumably because the soldiers never thought we would be able to run away. But after two weeks six hundred and fifty of us escaped after dark, and began to make our way back to Tigray. We had no idea which direction to take, so we just watched the sky. We ate fruits and leaves and kept going in this way for several days.

After a month or so we were captured by some local people and taken to a village, and made to work for the people there. We stayed in the village for three years, by which time we had learnt to speak their language. One day we overheard one of the men saying that on the far side of the mountain which we could see on the horizon, 'brown' people were living. It was then that we decided to try and escape.

We made for the mountain, and after travelling for two days we reached a road - the first we had seen since leaving Makelle. A car came along and stopped. The man looked very surprised to see us, especially as we were not wearing any clothes, and started to speak to us in Oromo. We replied in Tigrinya, and immediately he said, in our own language, "What are you doing here?" When we told him what had happened his eyes filled with tears. "Hurry up and get in the car" he said, and he took us to an OLF camp where we were given soap, food and clothes. We were taken to Khartoum the following day. The Sudanese authorities took charge of us and after a further eight days, we were visited by the TPLF and went to stay with them until we had recovered from our ordeal.

We are now working for Sudanese families in their homes, but I am hoping to go back to Tigray shortly to find my children. Perhaps my husband will be there too.

'Women can do anything men can do'

*The mountains scrape the sky
But we can climb them.
The rivers boil in flood
But we can cross them.
Our strength is in our people and our politics
And we will not submit.*

TPLF song

What have women in Tigray achieved so far? It seems useful, though difficult, to make some sort of assessment. Equality is not an absolute. If we want to ask how equal women are under the revolution, then we have to ask first: What do we mean by equality? How do we measure it? How equal can we expect women to be at this stage? As Aregash says in her opening words: "We have to be flexible and understanding about the pace at which women can absorb changes which contradict the habits of so many years." Women from any culture know the gap between the rhetoric of equal opportunity and the provision of relevant education and confidence-building conditions which will enable them to claim their rights for themselves.

We have seen already how in Tigray separate organisation in mass associations and special educational provision have accelerated women's capacity to take advantage of the revolution. We know they have equal rights to land with men and that therefore they have their own economic base from the age of fifteen, whether married or unmarried. We know the baitos have changed the minimum age of marriage and also the laws on rape and illegitimacy. Women are now equal before the law. These are issues which touch women deeply and represent real achievements. Neither should we let the differences in material standards of living between the West and Tigray obscure the fact that this political thinking is way in advance of the West.

Women are also participating in the broader life of their society. There are now women physicians (dressers), pharmacists, teachers, vets, laboratory technicians, mechanics, drivers, electricians, agricultural cadres. Most important of all, women are now sharing in decision-making, not only as members of the baitos, but on the executive as committee members or as chairpersons, like Zafu and Kindehafte in Adi Hageray or Medhin Gebrehiwot in Sheraro. Many of the women interviewed hold positions of high responsibility. Román is in the Mass Bureau and secretary of the Women Fighters' Association. Saba is director of Marta School. Laila works in the Information Bureau. Harnet is a newscaster in the radio station. Besserat is now working for TPLF in California. Kassech is in Washington, Zafu in London, Mahta in Sudan. I met many more, such as Kudusan, TPLF secretary for Adi Abo zone, or Azeb Gola, who is in charge of book production for the Information Bureau.

The context for the increasing participation of women is a society which under revolution has been tasting democracy for the first time. Participation in the administration of their communities through the baito or in national policy-making through the TPLF Congress is a new experience for men too. The baitos are independent of TPLF. Only they can implement changes in the law, and, in the new participative democratic structures set up by TPLF, this happens only after extensive discussion and debate. There is therefore little chance of a semi-professional executive passing measures inadequately understood or supported by a passive majority. Communication is a problem in a society slowly emerging from illiteracy as well as repression, if the people are going to share in determining their own future, but it is a problem consciously and effectively addressed by TPLF. Suggestions for change are circulated in draft in the mass associations for discussion, modification or rejection so that by the time they go to the baito the terms and the implications are understood. This is where the real debate takes place. I have witnessed heated debates, for example on the details of land distribution and was impressed by the time and patience spent on one dissenter by other members in setting out the arguments for respecting Kunama land.

In the chapters *On the frontline* and *Our land is ours!*, you will have noticed the changed policies over two years on women ploughing and women as combat fighters. What effects will these changes have on women's equality? I can understand the changed approach to women ploughing. Perhaps in the early days after the revolution, what was important was the symbolism of breaking the taboo against women ploughing, their invasion of a totally male preserve, and the revolutionary impetus and confidence this gave to women. As I grew more familiar with the problems of rural women's work, the difficulties of adding a whole new agricultural role to the burden of their work certainly crossed my mind. Nevertheless, I was relieved to see on my recent visit that some women are still ploughing, thereby preventing it from reverting to gender-determined work.

I still find difficulty, however, in adjusting to the withdrawal of women fighters from a combat role in favour of socially useful work. At the second Women Fighters' Congress in November 1987 it was hotly debated and there was great resistance. This decision and the change of policy in 1986 allowing fighters to marry and have children have been the two decisions causing most anxiety to women fighters about their equality. "Before, we used our full capacity," says Lichy (*On the frontline*), "but giving birth has reduced us to a very limited capacity." Later she adds, "Personally, I don't want to have children, because I believe that it hinders my activity." These are the difficult choices that face women in every society. A part of the dilemma is how society evaluates different activities – in Tigray, the activities of combat, of socially useful work, and of childbirth. TPLF is seeking to give high status to childcare; not, they say, to keep women imprisoned in the home, but to give credit to a vital and arduous role, which with education men can share. It is a fine line between the two!

In the West the issue of genuine equality for women has never been seriously addressed. In Tigray, women are 'half the struggle'; their equality is a fundamental tenet of the revolution. Nevertheless there is a long way to go. Women are not yet equal. Yes, there are women at all levels of decision-making, but at every level there are many more men and the higher the level the fewer the women. Aregash is still the only woman on Central Committee. This is only to be expected after so few years, when war and limited resources constrain development and educational policies in so many ways, but it will be interesting to see whether the proportion of women in decision-making roles changes with time.

"It's a new thing for a Tigrayan woman to go to a council meeting"

Aregash: We have to be flexible and understanding about the pace at which women can absorb changes which contradict the habits of so many years. It's a new thing for Tigrayan women to go to a council meeting and talk about politics or even about their oppression. Through their associations, they have come to recognise their oppression, that they can be liberated through struggle and increasingly through the actual practice of participating.

The Central Committee of the TPLF has one woman member. We feel women should participate in all areas and we try hard. Of course, we feel there should be more women on the Central Committee.

In the baitos they share the activities on an equal basis with men. Their number is more than 30% overall. This is good, considering the backwardness of the culture.

Román: Before, women were forbidden by law from taking part in any kind of political organisation. Of course the number must be raised higher than this, but it is an achievement in a short time.

Besserat: Today we have about sixty woreda baitos, self-administering districts, what you would call in Britain counties, which cover most of Tigray. Under these are many more *tabia* baitos, and making up these are *kushette* baitos at the most local level. And in all these people's councils, about a third of the political leaders are women. Some of the chairpersons are women. Remember that women were prostitutes fifteen years ago, women were farmhands, women were maids. These today are the political leaders of the districts of Tigray, and I think it's a wonderful achievement for a poor and backward society.

That's why when the TPLF came, women were the biggest force to stand behind it, because we said, from the beginning, that all this had to change. We were tired of oppression, not only from the Amharas, but from our own people too. So we had our priorities, our ideas, our own ideological stands, which were geared towards equality and justice towards all human beings.

THE STRUCTURE OF BAITOS

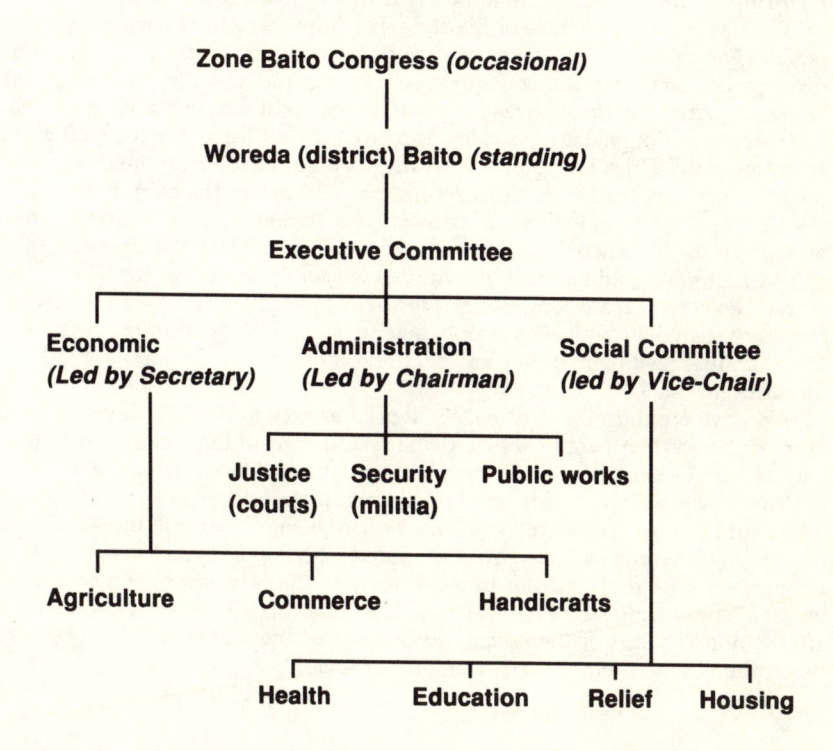

Zone Baito Congress *(occasional)*

Woreda (district) Baito *(standing)*

Executive Committee

- **Economic** *(Led by Secretary)*
- **Administration** *(Led by Chairman)*
- **Social Committee** *(led by Vice-Chair)*

Under Administration:
- **Justice** (courts)
- **Security** (militia)
- **Public works**

Under Economic:
- **Agriculture**
- **Commerce**
- **Handicrafts**

Under Social Committee:
- **Health**
- **Education**
- **Relief**
- **Housing**

"...Determining with their brothers the form of society"

Zafu: My name is Zafu Tsehaige. I have always lived in Adi Hageray. I am thirty-six and married to a farmer, with two teenage sons and a daughter of three. Adi Hageray has been liberated for twelve years and it was one of the first areas to support the TPLF. It has had a baito since May 1984.

I have been a member of the baito from its founding. I have been a council member since 1984 and when the baitos were re-established in 1988, I was elected as chair of the tabia level baito. There are now five women out of sixteen on the Adi Hageray Baito Committee, as ordinary committee members.

At that time the main changes in baito law were that elections should take place every three years, and that whereas before the baitos were only at woreda level, now they are at tabia level. There have been more recent changes which have not yet been implemented. Now baitos have been extended to kushette level as well and representatives will be elected by the people and assigned to the tabia baito. It helps the tabia because it is even more grassroots than before. There are so many kushettes that before it was difficult to administer them.

The baito is the structure of the state. It administers all the activities of the people. For example, let's take the case of handicrafts; recently we have sent people who can learn handicrafts to have training, and now they have returned. We have got four workshops ready and soon they will start work. We hope they will produce ploughshares, sickles and axes. In addition we look after the activities of the clinic. We control what the people contribute for medicines, and see that they get proper services. As for law and order, the baito has its own regulations so we refer to them for crimes. For different crimes we have different punishments. If someone hits somebody else we look at the case carefully according to the guidelines. If it's murder we send the case to the TPLF or to woreda level after examining it ourselves. We have a jail here if necessary for the crimes we can deal with. The people take turns in looking after the prisoners. Their families feed them if they are local, and if not, either the baito or the TPLF provides it.

We have regular meetings and we work out how to fit baito duties around other duties. When people are particularly attached to their housework, they stick to that. Of course it affects the time I spend, but if I look at it as revolutionary work I see it as temporary and I can sort it out. Sometimes women help each other but I live with relatives who can look after the children. I think it's very important for women to take part. Compared with the past years of oppression, women are now participating tremendously in the revolution. Some of them become baito members which was not seen before. They are involved in social affairs, not only out of the house, but as part of the whole society. They are determining with their brothers the form of society.

Participation: "The main problem was, they were not men!"

Belaynesh: Before the revolution – it's never nice remembering those hard times – women were so oppressed by the landlords, they had no rights in the home, in land, even in their children. The main problem was, they were not men. Women had not the right to go out of the house, to the meeting-place, to speak out their feelings, to administer themselves. Women were secondary in our society.

After the revolution, because we women struggled for our liberation, because we struggled strongly, we now have the right to be elected to the baito, in a mass association. Women are organised in the women's associations.

Women are now trained in different professions, as medical workers, as teachers, as women farmers, able to plough, buy oxen – women from the peasants. Especially now, women are struggling alongside men to bring down all reactionary forces.

"I am armed with a bass guitar!"

Atsede: I am Atsede Teklai and I'm a bass guitar player in the cultural troupe. I'm twenty-two and I come from Adua Awaraja town in Edaga Arabi. My family was very poor, and my grandparents too. When I was born we had nothing to eat or drink so at the age of five I was hired out to a feudal's house, to keep goats and sheep for him. While I was working I had to look after my little sister, carrying her on my back. Because I was the first child of my parents, I was very loved – and I loved my family too.

At the age of ten I was engaged. Though we were very poor, according to the culture we were from a feudal line, so the man I was engaged to was very rich, but he was old enough to be my father, not my husband. This was the time when the revolution was happening. I did not want to get married, to have a child and to look after a house.

The TPLF fighters used to come to our house to rest during their work. There was a fighter called Hassan, who was responsible for our village. When I look back with my present priorities I see he was a very special political figure; he was like a child with the children and an old man with the old people. At that time there were shepherds, flute and chamboka players among our neighbours, and I was very interested to hear these instruments played by the fighters.

Then the land distribution of the TPLF started and I came to see the real changes of life for my family. The area I lived in was a notorious feudal area and when the TPLF distributed land to us and gave grain, the feudals sent a band of thugs to our house and burned all the grain, and all the buildings to the ground. Because they liked my father the villagers helped us a lot, because he always spoke the truth. He always spoke out against the feudals. My mother became very attached to the revolution. In fact she was more political than my father. She was the one who would have fights with the feudals in the baito, for he was a very gentle man. He never spoke much and thought the little he said was too long.

So when I was a child I was more interested in the TPLF than marriage, and ten years ago I went to a TPLF camp and began making tea for them. I was in a hurry to be armed and fight against the enemy. After three years of training I was accepted in TPLF. My brigade was organising a cultural troupe and I was assigned to that. I started to sing for the first time openly in front of the brigade. It was a song I made up about my AK 47. "You have thirty children to fight with you!" – the AK 47 has thirty bullets. Then I started acting in cultural dramas. As you know there are many possible roles, but I decided to be a peasant child, because that's what I knew most about.

A friend who was a player began to teach me the bass guitar. It was the policy to have more women instrument players, so a plastic guitar was brought for me from Addis. It was destroyed in an air raid after three months, and that was the first time I'd ever cried as a fighter. Anyway I didn't lose hope but wrote to the Cultural Arts Department to try and get another guitar. Then, understanding my problems, they assigned me and another fighter a guitar and we started to learn it properly. I played the bass guitar because there was another woman playing the guitar. I was very pleased about this, because I was the first student to play it. The first time I played, the people really accepted me, and clapped. Fortunately there was a foreigner there, so I have photos of me playing!

Although I play the bass guitar I never go to see the musical dramas. Whenever I see the plays about the old farmer, I always think about my family. Whenever I hear the music, I cry, because I think of my old house and my family and the country. One song, 'Embelay' is about saying, 'No, no, no to the feudals' and it makes me remember my father because he was always against the feudals. When the words are very powerful I can't help the tears coming out. The part played by Ganno, the child of the family, was the part I was interested in ten years ago. So the whole of the musical drama is connected to me and to all the fighters.

Some sad things happened in my family. We were six children. Three of them died in the Sephawa refugee camp during the famine. My mother was with them, and when my father in Tigray heard about the deaths, he travelled all the way to Sephawa and tragically died of starvation himself. When I recently went there with the cultural group I tried to see the graves of my father, and my brother and sisters, but they were not marked.

I am married now, to a man of my own choice; he is an Amhara, formerly a PoW. He is from Gonder, so we are from two different regions, but of course we are from the same country, Ethiopia. We have the same political aim, and most importantly we love each other. Our main problem was one of language. When he wrote to me I was forced to show these personal letters to someone to read because they were in Amharic! By now we have got over all these differences. The most interesting thing for me is that he loves my mother and my family too. One thing about my mother is that she is always asking me to have a child. She would like me to have a daughter, and I would like to have a girl too. We are not in a hurry to have a child yet; not even my husband! We want to serve the revolution first and have a child next.

Lastly I'd like to tell you two things. I am very pleased to be a women musician in the revolution. I write songs and I act in dramas. I write and read poems and I compose music – very easy cultural songs. Secondly, I know I am armed with a bass guitar and am serving the revolution as much as the comrades on the war front with their bullets. I know that art is war by itself.

"Women involved in driving is a new thing for us"

Sofia: I'm Sofia and I'm twenty-three, and I've been a fighter since 1981. Before I was a driver I was a combat fighter, and then they chose me to train for driving. There were criteria for choosing drivers. The first was self-discipline, the second, ability to learn new skills and the third a strong belief in the revolution. There were forty-five of us trained together, back in 1982.

We were trained in Eritrea, although there were also training programmes in Tigray, for at that time we were in friendship with the EPLF and some of our brigades were fighting there in the Red Star campaign. We learned on small vehicles like Toyotas, and then we came back to Tigray to learn about driving trucks. I had two months in Eritrea and two months in Tigray. For about six months I was driving big trucks but then because there were not enough people to drive the small vehicles I went over to the Toyotas.

I have also trained as a mechanic, but there are big problems with spare parts, so our training is about prevention. If it is a minor breakdown I can repair it. Since our roads are very bad and bumpy, after a trip the vehicle's screws might be loosened. So between each trip I tighten these and check everything else like batteries and electrical connections and I always keep my vehicle clean and oiled.

Because I'm a fighter, I have an aim and to fulfill this aim I decided to work at any job, and I'm assigned to be a driver. Since my society is backward, it does not realise that a woman can be involved in work such as driving, so women driving is a new thing for us. The organisation gives us responsibility and skills to enable us to take part in every field. So this work makes me love my organisation and the job itself. The nature of the job is very pressurising. We always travel over great distances, from, for example, Makelle to Endaselassie, and then from there to Tembien. On long trips we get exhausted, so we stop and rest.

We are often attacked on the ground and from overhead by MiGs. It is too dangerous to drive in the daytime because we would be exposed to MiGs and bombs. So to secure our vehicles we are obliged to drive at night. We use several kinds of camouflage in case we are caught out in the open during the daytime. We stop in a safe place, where we can hide under trees or in a little gorge. But if we are caught in an exposed area and a MiG comes, the only thing to do is for the passengers to scatter and then I drive as fast as I can to avoid bombardment until I think it is safe.

"I love my job, because I have these skills"

Abeba: My name is Abeba Negash, and I'm twenty. I have been in the struggle for five years. I am a *hakim*, a medical worker, for the TPLF. I'm a laboratory technician in Dejenna. Altogether I have been a *hakim* for three years. In the beginning I was a combat fighter, and in several battles with the enemy in different places. I was wounded in my left arm.

It was not my choice to be a hakim; the organisation selected me. But I love my job because I have these skills. When I serve my people and the fighters, I am glad and have full confidence. The Dejenna clinic is three years old. It looks after the fighters, but there are also mass clinics here, and we get patients transferred to us. We accept and treat them, so we treat the mass through referral. In my clinic we have twelve hakims. The most well trained are the two nurses, then we have three advanced dressers, five first aid dressers, one laboratory technician and one pharmacist.

The most important thing in health is preventive care, to keep the body and the house clean, to wash clothes, and pay attention to food preparation. We give education on these things to all fighters. The main health problems are TB and malaria. Dejenna is in the highlands so it is relatively healthy and there's no anthrax here although there is some in the lowland areas. TB is not widespread, but it takes between one and three years to treat, so we send them to the hospital, first treating them here for a while once we've diagnosed the disease through laboratory work. I am responsible for diagnosis.

This clinic was established for the fighters, as well as for referrals from the mass. We also treat the war wounded. The clinic is divided into two parts, the medical and the surgical. At the time of the battle of Dejenna in July 1988 one group treated the TPLF fighters and another group the Derg soldiers. We treated them exactly the same, but organised ourselves to do the work most effectively. The army also had its own medical and surgical units too, so we weren't the only clinic. We gave initial treatment but seven cases were sent to the regional centre. We also care for, when necessary, pregnancy and childbirth in women fighters. We cooperate with the people's clinic but in our clinic there are no mass health workers.

"I am happiest working on engines!"

Medhin: My name is Medhin Gerzgiher, and I'm twenty-three. I've been a fighter for eight years. I come from Igela, west of Adua, which was liberated eleven years ago. When the TPLF came to our area I emotionally wanted to be a fighter even though I wasn't conscious. I realised that TPLF was very democratic and I wanted to spend my life working with them. My parents are peasants so they have benefited from the revolution and support it. I have two brothers who are fighters, and my sister is a member of the baito. My other brothers and sisters are in the youth association serving the revolution through that.

When I first finished training I joined the combat forces, but because I was very young I went to school for a year to learn academic subjects. I'd only got up to grade two before I became a fighter. After that one year I became a mechanic. During my year at school I studied metal work, electronics and mechanics and I wanted to continue in this line. We had to choose which to specialise in and I chose mechanics. During this year there were forty who trained with me, including nine women. The year after there were sixty trained and there were thirty women. Many women prefer being auto-electricians and mechanics. Women are also volunteering for metal work.

There are ten women here now, excluding three who are giving training courses in Tigray. A third of our workers are women. They're in all the sections; transport, repairing, the warehouse and woodworkshop. Altogether we have about five hundred workers, including drivers and their assistants. Some are seasonal, for during the rainy season our work stops almost completely, so workers rest or help their families on the land. I am a specialist in mechanics, and I can do a job on any vehicle, whether it's a Fiat, Toyota or a Mercedes truck. Although I am prepared to do anything mechanical, I am happiest working on engines.

There is constant travelling and exchange between all the workshops to keep a balance of skills. This is the major garage in the liberated area, and is also a referral centre. It's also where the convoys leave for Tigray so it is very important. All the worst cases are referred here for specialist repairs. We have a machine which can grind certain parts, and we can make our own nuts and bolts. Also in our machine shop we have a lathe for smoothing distorted metal parts. We have all sorts of machines for repairing and making spare parts, including ones for soldering. If we cannot make spare parts ourselves we order them from other countries. We have a store here for our own use and a large warehouse that distributes spare parts. There is one general store and one garage store. The general store serves us in this workshop as well as those all over the Field. There is also a woodwork shop which makes tables, cupboards, blackboards and shelves for schools in the liberated area. The schools order them from us, and then they are made up and sent.

We work in a group system, where each group has four mechanics. When a truck comes in for repair, the driver reports to the administrator and the fault is diagnosed. When they know what's wrong members of a team are set to work on the problem. Skills and abilities are mixed in a team, and we swop teams regularly to make sure that each one is balanced.

I can drive myself. All mechanics should be able to drive, even if it is not their job. When I've finished a job, I have to test the vehicle, so it's essential to be able to drive.

Liberating the towns

"Makelle has been like an egg; the shell has been so hard to break through, but there is life inside"

Words of a TPLF supporter in Makelle, on its liberation

In February 1989 the remaining towns, including the capital Makelle, fell into the hands of the TPLF. The whole of Tigray was now liberated. Two years before, we had been able to travel only in the liberated rural area, which in fact included 90% of the population. The larger towns, strung out like beads on Tigray's only all-weather roads, connecting Asmara in Eritrea to the north with Gonder and Addis in the south, were still garrison towns of the Derg. These came under increasing pressure as TPLF gained control of the roads between the towns, so that the Derg was forced to fly in all supplies by air. Then in early 1988 a series of assaults gained TPLF control of all the towns except Makelle, although they later withdrew to protect the people from bombardments. The Derg prepared a series of huge offensives to regain control of the province. In July they advanced on the TPLF base area in the west, but were convincingly defeated and, after the battle of Endaselassie in February 1989, were so crushed and dispersed that they evacuated the remaining garrisons of Adigrat and Makelle, leaving the entire province in the hands of the TPLF for the first time since the revolution began.

Visiting the towns was a very different experience from the liberated rural area. We had returned to England in 1987 with much of our ingrained scepticism overcome by the enthusiastic support for and participation in the revolution which we everywhere witnessed. We were inspired also by the evidence of real transformation in the lives of the peasants. Visiting the newly liberated towns was a more complicated and painful experience. On the one hand, there was massive support for the TPLF and the liberation of the whole province represented a dramatic advance in the process towards eventual victory throughout

Ethiopia; on the other, the politicisation and mobilisation of the people had only just started. There were severe economic problems and every interview spoke of the bitter experiences of occupation.

As the towns became islands of Derg rule within a TPLF-held province, cut off from the surrounding countryside, the natural economy, which depended on marketing, trading and transport links between towns and country areas, was destroyed. Instead, a false economy, totally dependent on the garrisons, grew up. Only Derg soldiers and officials, civil servants and offices workers had salaries to spend. Services dependent on these mushroomed – like restaurants, bars, small shops and hotels. Food and supplies had to be brought in from outside. With the departure of the military, this dependent economy has collapsed and a reconstructed natural economy will take time to establish. I travelled for part of the time with a Tigrayan who had not been in Tigray since 1971. His despondency at the decay and stagnation compared even with the time of Haile Selassie, made me aware of the effects of fifteen years of total lack of development. He saw the neglected and unpainted houses, the people only gradually recovering from demoralisation and apathy, everywhere evidence of, as the people say, a 'dependent mentality'.

People were keen to tell me what life was like under occupation. Husbands, sons and daughters had escaped to fight with TPLF, and their families, particularly, lived in fear, but the arbitrary paranoia of Mengistu's dictatorship has left few people unscarred. I lost count of those imprisoned, accused often unjustly of supporting TPLF. Askale, in her testimony, tells how she listened to TPLF radio secretly on headphones in Makelle, and the owner of a hotel in Endaselassie said he was so afraid of arrest he wouldn't have a radio on the premises. To listen to the TPLF radio station, to have contacts with TPLF, to work in the TPLF underground, risked imprisonment, torture and death.

The Derg military inflicted maximum damage on the towns before they left, destroying the electricity-generating and water-pumping stations. In Adigrat they set fire to the clinic. In Endaselassie they destroyed an ammunition store next to a clinic full of their own wounded soldiers. I spent a miserable morning shuffling through the tangled remnants of grenades, shells, ammunition cases, anti-aircraft rockets and thousands of bullets to get to the remains of the clinic and to the mass graves dug by TPLF. Burned and blood-stained mattresses and sheets still littered the blackened rooms, while the scorch-marks around the outside of windows testified to the deliberate use of fire-bombs within. I visited Makelle hospital, reserved before February 1989 for the Derg military, and now limping along with inadequate refrigeration for drugs and shortages of all equipment, but opened to the people. I saw children whose limbs had been blown off by mines laid indiscriminately on farming land in rings around the towns by successive Derg brigades. In Makelle also I toured the infamous prison. Now it is empty, but the cells were still filled with the filth and detritus of the miserable lives spent there and the walls were lined with greasy shadows where countless prisoners had leaned. I wondered which was Berhanu's, our guide who had been imprisoned there for six years, until released by TPLF in the Agazi operation.

Perhaps the worst effects of Derg occupation, however, were on women. Their experiences of living for fourteen years under the Derg make a mockery of Chairman Mengistu's address to the first congress of the Revolutionary Ethiopian Women's Association in 1980:

Neither genuine social justice nor the attainment of the ultimate goals of the revolution can be assured without the full participation of women in the country's social and political endeavours...Women should participate fully in the efforts to overcome backwardness and build a socialist economic order, free from any kind of exploitation and backwardness.

As the Derg came under pressure and its military position weakened in 1988, there was a marked escalation in violence towards women in Adigrat and Endaselassie, the two towns reoccupied by government soldiers. This in itself is an indicator that the kind of rape and assault we hear described on the following pages has everything to do with the abuse of power. Women have always been the most vulnerable to the violence of war and occupation. Rape and violence forced women into prostitution; the numbers of women working as prostitutes increased massively in all the towns. In Endaselassie, the largest garrison town, the problem was particularly acute. Women whose husbands were absent, as TPLF fighters or even as Derg soldiers, were particular targets, but, according to the stories I heard, no woman or girl was safe. Many women had acquiesced in order to secure the release from prison of family members, after which threats of rearrest were used to ensure their continued compliance. Under traditional prerevolutionary Tigrayan culture, any woman who is sexually interfered with, even involuntarily, is rejected by her husband and the community. Prostitution, along with selling local beer (*sewa*), is then the only way for her to support herself and her children.

How were prostitutes to live after the departure of the garrisons? Not only had most of their patrons departed, but salaries could no longer be paid to workers who stayed behind. Some women work in bars and hotels. Some sell honey mead and sewa in their homes. They live in groups, giving each other support and help with child-care. Women I spoke to were reluctant to admit they were prostitutes, although very critical and angry about the bitter experiences of women. This made interviewing difficult. Yomar and Rahma were so definite that their stories did not apply to them, that I began to be doubtful, but when Yomar returned for a photograph with her friends, their appearance, behaviour and life-style suggested that they too were working as prostitutes.

The interview with Abrahet was particularly interesting. She asked me to her home for the 'coffee ceremony', an elaborate ritual of roasting and preparing coffee for guests, fundamental to women's culture. On the walls were heart-shaped photographs of men and proverbs like 'Love is the salt of life' on banners in Tigrinya and English, which would never be seen in conventional households. The second half of her testimony contradicts the first. At first, she implies she is waiting as a loyal wife for her husband to return from PoW camp; then, as she recalls the behaviour of Derg soldiers, she begins to get angrier and angrier. She acknowledges her own experience: "This happened to all of us," she cries. "This happened to me."

The women's testimonies cover a range of responses and a range of solutions to impossible dilemmas. Abrahet's way of surviving was to have only two officers. Lemlem's solution, not very different after all, was to have three husbands. Aster had to choose between accompanying her husband to Addis and staying behind, which meant losing two of her four children. She stayed. In Adi Hageray I talked to three young Eritrean women who were fleeing from Asmara in Eritrea and wanted TPLF assistance to go to Sudan. They described life in Asmara, the nightly curfew, the poverty of their families, the impossibility of surviving on their wage of under two birr a day from full-time work in a textile factory, their strategems for escape. "We heard that the TPLF allows you to go wherever you like," one of them told me, "so we came here. We don't have any political stand. We just work in a factory and go home again." Yet the powerful impact they made on me would not translate into print. They were too distrustful to give their names; their silences were more eloquent than their words and their tears brought the conversation to a close; but they trusted TPLF and just wanted to be helped out of Ethiopia to Sudan.

Yet people in the Tigrayan towns are optimistic and prepared to put up with any difficulties in return for freedom from the Derg. When the TPLF took control, they gave people the choice to follow the departing military to Derg towns outside Tigray if they wished. Some left, but most remained. TPLF too are optimistic, although the short-term problems are severe. Aregash, on TPLF Central Committee, outlines the strategy for solving the towns' economic problems. The dependent population has to be fed and looked after until an alternative economy gets going and while I was there REST workers were assessing needs. Axum and Adua have been in TPLF hands for more than a year, but in Makelle, Adigrat and Endaselassie, which have only been liberated since February, already the people seem to be responding. When I arrived in Makelle, there was a meeting in which the country people, who have the more highly-developed political consciousness, were challenging the more sophisticated-looking townsfolk to pull themselves together and start to struggle if they wanted to solve their problems.

Derg towns and TPLF

Aregash: The economic life of the towns is very different from the rural areas. The liberated rural areas depend on farming, whilst in the towns trade is the major activity of the people. Under the Derg the economic relationship between the peasants and the towns was almost completely broken down. Life for the people was very tortuous in the Derg's time. People were restricted in their movements from place to place and they couldn't see their relatives. They had no right of protest nor any other democratic right.

Many people were employees of the state, and since the Derg has left, there are no longer any salaried jobs. Some people have gone to the Derg area because they can't live without salaries. The state intentionally made the people very dependent and detached them from actual production activities. Since the Derg left these dependent people have had many difficulties.

There are also many prostitutes. In general terms prostitution occurs because of economic reasons. We are not trying to discourage it; our approach is a political not a moral one. Basically prostitution cannot be solved administratively. Women use it as a solution to not having any job or income. The long term solution is to involve them in productive activity, as part of the economic development of the whole society. Production is at a rudimentary level at present, and it's obviously difficult to involve these women in agricultural work, for example. Meanwhile we have to make do with temporary solutions, and at this stage we are encouraging them to understand the cause of their problems, to identify their enemy, and to help them find their own solutions, in for instance, setting up small businesses selling sewa.

The electricity and water supply are not functioning properly because the generators and pumping stations were destroyed by the Derg before they left. Absence of electricity has made problems for grinding mills and bakeries, although we've managed to get the water supply working again. It's difficult to maintain a central electricity supply, because we have a shortage of appropriate technical skills. In addition the Derg could easily put it out of action again. So we are encouraging the merchants to buy generators and to use them in their locality. We have technicians who can maintain these, and spare parts are provided by the merchants.

We are trying to handle all these problems by mobilising the people themselves. We are, for example, trying to encourage the merchants to use their capital. We've had to organise them to put their capital into different areas of trading, and now the problem of shortage of supply is somewhat improved. They are trying to establish some activities which were banned by the Derg. For example, the hotels and restaurants were used only by Derg bureaucrats, but now the main customers are the people passing through and peasants coming in for market. They are trying to transfer their capital to buy materials from Sudan, and to have restaurants for the townspeople and the peasants.

At the moment we have to give many people aid to minimise their problems – relief aid and rehabilitation to support some levels of activity in groups. They can trade, they can involve themselves in democratic activities which will bring them money. The peasants have started to use the town as a market again, and the town to have freedom of movement outside. One consequence has been that the prices of foods have gone down which has helped. Anyone who wants can travel and sell to the peasants, who are now spending money on beer and food in the towns and giving an income. Things produced locally are cheaper now.

The people hate the enemy; their desire was to be liberated from the enemy, no matter what the consequent problems might be. They want a peaceful and democratic life. They say they can tolerate the existing social and economic problems if the Derg is destroyed as soon as is possible. They also want to know how they can help and everyone wants to be involved. But they don't know how to do it and are demanding direction from us.

The conditions of the towns are different now we are there. Everyone is free; they can speak out and say what they want. They are seen as human beings and not just political pawns; they have a say in their daily life and they can discuss what the future holds. This is very different from the days of the Derg.

We are handling it in a planned way. In the rural areas we have already reached a certain stage, but we know we are starting from scratch in the towns. We'll try and continue with the demands of the revolution at the level at which it has been developed in the liberated areas, and also see to the needs of the towns.

Endaselassie: "It happened to me!"

Abrahet: I am Abrahet Teklemuze, and I'm twenty. I have always lived in Endaselassie and my family are here too. I was married in 1985 and have a daughter called Rosina. My husband was a Derg soldier, and he is now a prisoner of war, captured by the TPLF in Endaselassie last year. When he is released I know he will come back here, and I'm still waiting for him.

I have been working for one month at this hotel, selling beer. I work for eight hours a day, seven days a week. I have no alternative to this work, for since my husband left I've had no means of support. I get thirty-five birr a month. This is additional to what I make here at home selling alcohol and sewa. My mother looks after Rosina for most of the time.

Last year I was selling drinks so I had no economic problems, because there were a lot of soldiers, but life under the Derg was very difficult. You wouldn't believe the number of prostitutes increased when the Derg occupied Endaselassie; the soldiers' behaviour was even more ugly during the second occupation. The young girls were searched forcibly by the soldiers and whenever they saw a girl, they immediately asked for her, without knowing if she was married or not. In the street they insulted us, and if we answered back they started beating us, and following us to where we were going. The proportion of men to women was unbalanced, and every girl was approached by many men.

This happened to all of us. This happened to me. I agreed to go with one soldier to save myself from violence. Even then I was beaten many times. I gave many excuses, but still they beat me without accepting the reasons. The worst thing was that even if you said OK, after they had finished the intercourse, often they didn't give us any money, but beat us up instead.

To avoid all this the only thing to do was to have the higher ranks of soldiers. I had two officers at the same time. These officers protected us from the violence of the ordinary soldiers, because they were afraid of them and obeyed them. The officers' protocol forbade them to fight or be violent to us. I don't know where one is now, but the other went to Makelle before the battle here.

I wanted to leave with the Derg but my family is here. My life has not changed since the Derg left. It's all the same to me, because there's nothing I miss. I still manage; it's all one. My mother especially is stongly against me doing this, but what else is there to do? It is the best way to get money. But I can compare life under the TPLF – it is the mental restfulness. Before I earned a lot of money, now only a little. Too much money is not safe. I suffered mentally and felt uneasy. Now although I can only earn a little, it is peaceful and free. But still I am not controlling my life. I am dependent. I am aiming to establish my own self-reliance at any cost, either selling drinks and perhaps in marriage as well. If my husband comes, that's OK, but if not I'd like to have one man only.

"If you refused, they took out their pistols"

Yomar: I am sixteen years old. I was married at thirteen, although I live with my family. My husband lives in Addis, where he is a teacher. It's my choice to stay in Endaselassie with my family, for I don't want go to Addis. I have one baby daughter of three years.

Rahma: I am twenty years old, and I married seven years ago. I left him after two years because I didn't love him. I have one child who is now six. I am living with my family. My father is a tailor. Before I was married I got up to seventh grade, and completed twelfth grade during my marriage. I learned with the help of my family because my husband didn't want to teach me. That was one reason why I left him just over a year ago.

Under the Derg, especially in Muslim culture, families arrange a marriage without asking the girl. They choose someone they want, and she doesn't know him, nor he her. Thirteen's too young to get married. When I asked my family to let me know who my husband was, they wouldn't tell me. This is not a good culture for women. But I've heard that in the rural areas controlled by the TPLF, Muslim girls can choose their own husbands. Under the Derg this did not happen; all my life has been decided by my family.

Yomar: Life under the Derg was very hard, because they did what they liked. They took the girls by force, even married women. If you refused they took out their pistols. They would arrest your brother, and when you went to visit him in prison they would ask you to sleep with them. In order to get your brother released or to stop his murder you had to choose whether or not to give your body. They even used to come to your home and take what they wanted by force. They did terrible things; my friend was selling sewa one day. A soldier came over and asked her to meet him. She refused, so he returned later and threw a grenade into the house. She was killed and her mother was wounded. Here's another example: one day a soldier came to a woman's house and asked her to spend the night with him. He gave her twenty birr, so she slept with him. After that he gagged her mouth and shot her with his pistol, and took her tape recorder and jewellery.

We were very oppressed by the Derg. So when the Derg was destroyed – what can I say? – we were very happy.

Rahma: We were not dependent on the Derg, but on our families. But those who were dependent on them are in trouble. This was the Derg's trick; they want us to be beggars, and not to work for ourselves or help each other. This is causing problems. Most people know this now, and those few who didn't realise left the town with the Derg. Some have come back now, because the Derg would not help them.

TPLF encourages us to be self-reliant, so we are all working together. Everyone says that, with peace, we can solve it for ourselves. We're both members of the mass association here. When we look at women fighters we are happy to see what women can do, and basically we feel that we can get our equality through struggle.

TPLF fighters in Endaselassie

Besserat: The Amhara government is very reactionary for the Tigrayan people, so since I became a fighter ten years ago, I've been fighting to throw this government out. Secondly I'm fighting for the equality of women.

Elem: The people of this town don't share the consciousness with the rural people. These people have been under the Derg before we controlled this town. So many people worked for salaries for the Derg and when the Derg left, they had no means of supporting themselves. But they like the revolution and TPLF; we teach them to solve the problems for themselves and they accept what we say to them. They say, "Our problems will be solved one day." It's an economic problem, not a political one.

Besserat: These people love the revolution because it's their own. Every home has sent its sons and brothers to be fighters so every family has connections with it. Purposely the Derg wanted to exploit the people and make them dependent and not self-sufficient, and therefore gave out wheat and salaries so that everyone had something from the Derg.

With so many soldiers here there were lots of prostitutes. Now that the soldiers have been destroyed they have no means of support. This is now a big problem in the town. The revolution will solve it step by step but it's not possible to solve it quickly. These women support the revolution, but for their short term survival, they raise this question, "How can we live?"

Elem: We both work in the mass association to teach the women. This is done not only by the Mass Bureau but by all of us women fighters.

Besserat: We organise them to know their interest. Their consciousness is only just beginning, but if they are struggling and fighting they can get what they want. Their problem will be solved when the revolution is won. We teach them to share in the revolution along with the women fighters, therefore they must organise and struggle in any way they can – there is no revolution without women.

We make our teaching very concrete. For example, we say that a woman will be the leader of her baito, and that she will own land. This is all in her interest. So it's not all talk, but actually doing something. So when they see this they want to follow and want to fight more.

Elem: It will be a long process to solve this problem so they can't accept it easily. They're also of the town, which has its own culture. At the moment it's only a few of them who can accept, and it'll take a while for others to understand. Because there's enough land, especially in western Tigray, the best way is to give land to women, at this time.

Axum: "I had to get married because of my poverty"

Lemlem: My name is Lemlem Mahmas. I am twenty-eight and I went to school up to tenth grade. When I was a student I was married, but my husband went to the Field twelve years ago. Before that I had one child.

After three years I married another man who worked in the agricultural office with the Derg. After we lived together for three years he transferred from Axum to Makelle. There was disagreement between us, because I didn't want to go to Makelle. After he went to Makelle he became a member of the Derg's Party. I had one child from him. Now my oldest is twelve years old, and the second, a boy, is eight.

After that, while I was living in the town I had no means of support, so I married a third time. I had to get married because of my poverty. He was a member of the Derg militia, and I had two more children. After that he went to fight against the EPLF in Eritrea.

I can tell you a lot about life for women under the Derg. It was very bad. There are many women who are educated here, but they never gave us any jobs. There were so many women's associations in this town, but at meetings the soldiers used to come in and molest us. They gave us no help against poverty, just hand-outs of wheat and flour from foreign places. The people were heavily taxed. Because of this we could not build houses or improve our homes or living standards. So there was much poverty under the Derg. There was no money, no consciousness, everyone dependent on the wheat of the Derg and a few salaries.

The greatest problem we face now is the dependency of the people. Many have no means of support, and although we have our organisation, how can we live? The TPLF is taking this step by step. Traders are beginning to travel from town to town. There were workers under the Derg, teachers and hospital workers. Now they have nothing. TPLF gives them pass papers for pensions. Anyone who wants to leave for the Derg can go, but TPLF are trying to help all who stay.

As for myself, my parents are in a rural area and bring me grain. I still sell sewa. There's been great change in my life. Of course I have many problems, but now I am free. My parents are near the town, but during the Derg's time I didn't see them for fourteen years. Now I can go where I like. I can say what I want. There are no spies now. I am the leader of the women's association in this town, and secretary of the town baito. So I will gain my equality through the struggle, and my money problems feel only temporary. My children are very young so I want to look after them first; the last thing I want is another husband at the moment!

Adigrat: "Now we women have a chance to come to the stage..."

Radiet: My name is Radiet Gebretensai, and I'm forty years old, with five children. When my husband joined the TPLF in 1978, people informed the cadres of the Derg and I was arrested. The Derg soldiers came to my house and encircled it. They began firing – seven bullets in all. Six missed but the seventh injured my one year old granddaughter. She was hit in her head, and the bullet entered her skull, but I couldn't afford to send her to the clinic so begged the community to help. They contributed about three hundred birr, so then I took my granddaughter to the hospital. She is much better now, although she is still brain-damaged.

After the Derg evacuation of Adigrat, TPLF came and started to agitate the people and I became a strong supporter of TPLF and began actively participating in stirring up the people. I was elected as a temporary administrator. Then the TPLF had to evacuate the town to avoid loss of life because the Derg was approaching again. When the Derg came, they told the people that TPLF were just bandits and not for the people. They told people like me to stop TPLF work and start Derg facilities going again so taxes could be collected. So the people started to oppose them openly. I remember people saying, "You are always taking our money by ever increasing taxation and last year you tried to burn the generating station but we stopped you. So how can we give you money? We are poor. We don't believe you will use the money for our needs, for our facilities." The one who spoke like this was supported by the whole town in a big meeting. Several students and merchants spoke out, but they were put in prison. All this time I kept on trying to influence the people against the Derg.

After the successful battle by the TPLF at Endaselassie, the Derg started to flee and evacuated from Adigrat again on February 16th 1989. I remember this date with great joy. I heard that the Derg left agents after the first evacuation and they burned the clinic. The so-called people's army left a powerful agent who was able to destroy the clinic with explosives. There were no deaths but one patient was caught in the blaze.

Under TPLF the most important thing I have observed is that the rural area and the towns have become interconnected again. Before, the rural people had a problem. If they came here they were always questioned by the soldiers when they tried to enter the town. If they didn't have pass papers they were often arrested and imprisoned. So the relation between town and rural areas became very distant. Now we are closer. Relatives visit each other, and country people come to bring their produce to sell in the market. We are creating a hand to hand movement between the towns and the villages.

Administration under the Derg was simply for getting high taxes out of us, and for conscripting soldiers. The TPLF said this, in comparing its success in alleviating the problems, "TPLF is not well-off. All we've got is gained through sacrifice and bloodshed, but that is not enough to establish electricity, watersupplies and hospitals for you. But we will help you democratically to start and you will continue." So I feel that this is much better than the Derg organisation, since it is freer. The only thing that we have contributed since the TPLF came has been a voluntary contribution of only twenty-five cents.

Another important thing is the women's activity. Women under the Derg were used just for sexual purposes. Now we have a chance to come to the stage and talk not just about our own problems but also those of society. We discuss things with our brothers and find the solutions.

Makelle : "The politics of TPLF seem cleaner and better"

Aster: My name is Aster Fitiwy. I am thirty-two years old and I've always lived in Makelle. I trained as a teacher; after that I took part in the Zemacha Campaign in 1975, but I didn't like it. At that time I didn't know anything about the campaign itself, but there was conflict between the students.

After I'd been teaching here in this Derg town for a while, I got involved in local politics, and ended up as vice-chair of the Worker's Association. But the people in charge, in the Derg hierarchy, put pressure on me to be dishonest and get someone else elected illegally. Despite protests from the members, I went ahead and did it; otherwise the government might have imprisoned or killed me. I knew people who had opposed things had been killed, so I was too frightened to disobey their orders. But they put it on my record against me anyway.

I knew nothing about TPLF at that time, but in 1984 a lot of Tigrayans were being sent to prison, because they were suspected of being TPLF members. I was scared about what would happen to me. The officials suspected the Tigrayans of resisting the rest of the party so they arrested them as the best solution.

Then the Youth Association chair was arrested and tortured; they told him to tell them the names of the TPLF members. "I know Aster. She is a member of the TPLF. She is contributing five birr a month to the TPLF." But it wasn't true. They called me and accused me, "Are you a member of the TPLF?" Then when I said no, they never believed me. They beat me and kicked me cruelly. They tied my hands and my legs and put sticks under my knees and hung me upside down. So I confessed to being a member of the TPLF because I could not bear their cruelty.

"Yes, you are controlling other TPLF members. Tell us their names." But I didn't, because I didn't know them. They tortured me continually for four days, and my right hand was paralysed for two to three months afterwards. I felt pain around my womb, so I was admitted to hospital and then they sent me to the main prison.

I was in Makelle prison for about two years and seven months. While I was there I worked teaching the illiterate prisoners. I was there during the Agazi operation, but refused to go with the people who released the prisoners, because I didn't know anything about them and I thought they would kill me. At first we didn't know that the TPLF was releasing the prisoners. We thought it was the state taking us to be killed. Even when we did realise we thought that because we were in Derg organisations, the TPLF would kill us. We turned off the light and hid. But the government believed that because we didn't go with the guerrillas we should be released, so we were let go after four months. But they put us under surveillance and were always watching and following us after that. Since the TPLF success last year in 1988, the government suspected that we were giving information about our work and meeting them.

I returned to being a teacher when I was released. The teachers who were with me at first were now getting a higher salary, but because I had been in prison for two years, I didn't get the same salary. That was demotion, because the time in prison was not counted for my service. Before my time in prison I was paid three hundred birr, and afterwards only two hundred and forty-seven birr. My friends were on three hundred and five birr by then.

After I was released I hated politics intensely. I didn't want to be involved in any political affairs. There was a study group in our school for the Party, but I never went there. Since politics were the cause of my being in prison, I wouldn't go any more. They continued watching me.

At the time of the Derg's departure, no one except the key persons in their organisation knew they were leaving. It was a miracle for us. The Party members were running around the town and the people were shocked and asking what they were doing. They never said whether the guerrillas were coming or not. Everyone who was not in the know was being mentally tortured. They saw them streaming to the airport by car and on foot. Some other members of the Party left their children and their homes and went alone to the airport, crying and very frightened; they thought that the TPLF would kill them if they stayed behind. They went to the airport, some holding suitcases, some holding their children's hands; some children were even left behind.

Even now the Derg won't leave us alone; jets come and bomb the towns, and kill many people, who are running here and there to escape the bombs. Then we have to leave our homes and when we come back our food and other things have been stolen. Now the TPLF is controlling that. In Makelle there have been three air raids, all around the airport. Even if they just fly over, the people suffer with terror.

One of the worst things about the Derg was what happened to some of the women and girls. If a girl was raped or taken by force, the families were in sorrow. Some ladies never told their husbands, because of fear of divorce. Or the men, they had to leave the town because the rapists might have killed or arrested them. Then they could do whatever they liked with that woman. Since she never did it voluntarily, she lives in sadness all the time. The only alternative if a woman was raped was to become a prostitute. After that the children sometimes hate and insult her. They became motherless and fatherless and street girls and boys. So these Derg soldiers destroyed the life of the whole family.

There were women whose husbands were killed, and who lived all the time in terror. After their husbands died they used to marry the security officials. They never loved them, but said, "Since they have killed our husbands, they may kill us." Many of these men left their wives behind when they left because they were not Amhara. But the women were happy. The TPLF said nothing to them and neither did the people. But now they have no means of support and this is one of TPLF's problems. They are listing the names of anyone who has difficulties and are giving help to those who have no means of income.

Before I never knew the politics of the TPLF, because I was involved in the politics of the Derg. After Agazi, I got a little bit of information on the TPLF, but not much. Then little by little I got to have some idea. When the Derg left Makelle, I decided not to go with the Derg but to stay with the TPLF. Even now hatred for politics never leaves my head, but the politics of the TPLF seems cleaner and better.

The Derg said that there was democracy for the people, but there is no democracy. They cannot meet together as they like, they can't speak as they like. Now I have seen the TPLF democracy and I like it. People can go where they like, talk as they like. If you can't write what you like, is that democracy? Living with the Derg is suffering, living with the Derg means crying all the time. The people have become very happy, because before there was no peace, no safety. When the Derg left, for a very short time there was firing, but when the guerrilla members came, they said "Just stay at home and be calm, do not worry. It is better that they leave the country and do not come again." The people want to live tight and together with the TPLF, who want the people to participate in everything.

I am married with four chidren. Two are with me, and two are with their father in Addis. We married fifteen years ago, between Haile Selassie and the Derg. He left with the Derg, but I refused to go with him. I had to decide whether to live with the Derg or to let those two children go. Even loving your family doesn't compare with hating the Derg.

"I will not kneel down"

Askale: My name is Askale. I used to be a state worker employed in journal keeping in the main bank in Makelle. It was a good job, but with bad pay. At first I was employed in Addis, but that branch wanted to employ only Amharas. I was paid two hundred fifty-five birr at first, but then the state reduced it to one hundred and eighty-two a month.

I am married with two children of eight and four. My husband is in Asmara.

He has been there for seven years, serving in the Derg army. Since the Derg left there is no work and also now I can't get any money from my husband. He joined the military to save his life; even though he was part of the state he didn't accept it. Although he did not oppose it outwardly, he was against the state privately and we often discussed the cruel acts of the government.

Under the Derg we had so many associations for women. But this made it easy for the officials to get their hands on the girls. They were always organising us to do things for the association away from our homes, so we were exposed to whatever they wanted to do. They would arrest women as well as men, but instead of taking us to the prison, they used to take us to their homes and rape us. The girls were forced against their will, and suffered great distress; some became affected mentally, some took to working as prostitutes or selling alcohol. Others left the country.

I remember when the Derg was introducing a constitution for the people. It said that equality, already formally declared, would be put into practice. But the constitution was read only by the person who presented it, with no discussion with the people. They simply announced it, although they presented it as the will of the people.

Before the Red Terror I was working with the TPLF as an underground member, but afterwards the cell started to deteriorate, because some of us had been killed and there were so many spies. I believed in TPLF's politics, but I had to keep it very secret. Although my behaviour was very restricted, I tried my best. The Derg was propagandising about the TPLF, "If you fall into their hands they will torture you, they will cut off your hands and they will brand you with a hot iron." I did not believe them, and I chose as my friends people who were likely to be sympathetic with TPLF in order to reject Derg propaganda.

I'll tell you about what happened this year, in February 1989. There was heavy combat in Endaselassie and the TPLF won the battle and destroyed the huge army collected from all over Tigray, including Makelle. So the soldiers were decreased in number. I really hoped that there would be an attack on Makelle, and I followed the news about the battle on TPLF radio and in articles about the TPLF. I listened secretly, using headphones. If I had been discovered listening to TPLF radio I would automatically have been arrested and perhaps inflicted with terrible punishment.

The Derg soldiers were nervous and tense, so everyone in Makelle suspected that the TPLF would attack and easily get control of the town. Let me start from my office. We were told that this battle might be conducted at very short notice and that we should save the money in the bank. All the money and workers would be transferred to Addis. This was a secret. No one should know about it or it would create chaos. They told us this on the Saturday and gave us an appointment for Monday at eight in the morning. They cheated us; they all left on Sunday, so this meant that many workers who were told that they would be able to leave, couldn't leave. Everyone wanted to go to Addis, especially the Amharas, but on Sunday no one left, because they thought they'd leave on Monday. Then the Amharas went on foot to Desse, Asmara and Addis, but all the Tigrayan workers refused to go. Actually it wasn't state money but that of the SOS

Orphanage, the Ethiopian Orthodox Church, the Ethiopian Evangelical Church, merchants, and the Ethiopian Catholic Secretariat, as well as the private money of workers. I myself had three hundred birr in that bank.

They had buried mines around the town during their occupation, and so many people and children have been killed, or have had to have limbs amputated. There were many prisoners in Makelle prison, and they were freed, but they were murderers or robbers, not political prisoners. These people are now causing chaos. Besides this, the Derg left propaganda with agents who had a secret mission to cause unrest by provoking trouble, by spreading lies.

The Derg left at ten in the morning and, when they had all left, one tank came and destroyed the electricity station, which also controlled the water supply.

After six hours the TPLF came. First of all I couldn't find the words to express it – they came through the castle at about six in the evening in a single line. The light was getting dim. Everybody came out of their houses and showed their joy, and they were ululating. From that instant we believed that TPLF could destroy the thieves and agents, and build up the towns again. They came down, men and women fighters together, and went off to different parts of the town. "Everyone be calm. Be settled. We are here now. Be glad."

TPLF organisation here in Makelle happens in two ways. Firstly the people here are dependent on food sources, from sales, or food for work or some handouts. So to avoid this dependency, TPLF helps us to help ourselves to strong organisation and unity. This is happening for the first time. We are deciding how to elect our leaders in order to solve our problems. Secondly, because of the deteriorated economy, TPLF is working to give aid for relief materials, and is registering those in need. I have already registered.

The important difference between the Derg and the TPLF soldiers is that the TPLF are politically oriented. They are from the people and serve the people. They know why they are fighting, what is their aim, from their political consciousness. The Derg doesn't stand for the people, and only thinks about sustaining its power. It brings forcible recruits to the army. Especially when the war intensifies, conscription increases. The conscripted soldier has no aim and no benefit from his experience. They are not the people's soldiers.

Even though I have two children, even though I have no income, even though I have many problems, still I support the TPLF. But these problems are temporary; I will not kneel down under them. I have mental satisfactions, mental resistance. There could not be anything more than this.

Beyond Tigray

Fly, my bird, fly.
Bear my words,
Carry my beliefs.
And sing everywhere
Our bright message.
Fly, my bird, fly.
Over the high mountains,
Above the wide oceans,
Across the land you fly.
Flap your wings and
Show us your red banner.
Fly, my bird, fly.

TPLF song

There are three regions in Tigray. Region One is the western lowlands of Wolkeit and Shire, Region Two is the central highlands where most of the population live, and Region Three is the eastern lowlands beyond Makelle. Region Four is not in Tigray at all – it designates the operation of TPLF in Sudan, Saudi Arabia, Europe and the USA – in other words, where there are Tigrayans to support as refugees, to organise in mass associations, to inform about the progress of the struggle and from whom to get financial and practical support. At a rough estimate there are slightly over a hundred thousand Tigrayan refugees worldwide. Sudan is the most important area in Region Four both because there are more Tigrayans there as refugees than anywhere else outside Tigray, about eighty thousand, and because the importance of the cross-border operation to the survival of the revolution makes diplomatic relations with the Sudanese particularly important. The Relief Society of Tigray (REST), a Tigrayan organisation providing humanitarian and development aid, also operates in Region Four independently of TPLF.

The contributors each have a different relationship to the revolution. Kassech and Zafu are fighters working for TPLF. Abrehet is a representative of the women's mass association in London. Her testimony gives a poignant insight into the kinds of experiences that led her and her husband to apply for refugee status in Britain. Presumably other refugees have similar stories to tell, like Berhan, now working for REST in Sudan, whose story vividly conveys the pressures of working under the Derg in Addis. The numbers of Ethiopian refugees in Africa, Saudi and the West, perhaps testify more than anything else to the problems of survival under the Ethiopian government. Genet's testimony in *On the frontline* shows the not untypical progression from unpoliticised girl to Derg prisoner to refugee in Region Four. She was in the Mass Association in Italy, began to work with TPLF and returned to become a fighter. The work of Abrehet, Genet and all the Tigrayans in different countries is of crucial importance, in raising not just funds, but awareness of the struggle.

TPLF Information Office, London, Britain: Zafu's story

Zafu: I came to London in September 1986 to work with REST as an accountant. I hadn't learned accountancy in Tigray. My subjects were science, biology and chemistry. So I was studying part-time, working in REST and in the Mass Association meetings. But I found it very hard outside the Field, especially when I was in Italy. When we were organising in Italy to celebrate March 8th, some feminist women rejected men from the celebration. They had slogans that men should be killed, that we should have an all-women society and all-women government. I was not interested in that approach. Also they were badly organised, except for temporary things such as specific events. For example I never came across study-groups in Italy.

When I came here I felt very alienated. Especially it was not easy to make friends here or to talk about politics. But after a few months I went to the *Women in Struggle* conference organised by Third World First in November 1986. This was my first chance to participate in a women's meeting. I was glad to be able to talk about my country. One of the discussions I took part in was not about the workers or about how women can solve their problems, but about wages for housework. That is not the solution for women's oppression, but it is encouraged by capitalists to prevent a strong relationship with the workers and to concentrate on minor things. They didn't ask me about the general struggle. They only wanted to concentrate on women. In my country they think the woman question cannot be solved in isolation, but even close English friends say, "The men only want to use you." But other friends have understood that it's good that we have land, that we participate in the administration. They have been there and have contributed much about Tigray through talks and activities.

It is very hard here, but if you are in TPLF you have to serve your people anywhere, in the Field, anywhere else. I must respect it, because I am working for my people. For my own interest I would like to be working in Tigray.

There are three regions in Tigray itself. Region Four is the Mass Association of all Tigrayans outside Tigray, especially the Sudan, the USA and Europe. The UK Support Committee of REST was started in 1983. Habtom and I opened the European office in 1986. TPLF set up an office in 1984. We have different departments here, such as the Information Centre and the Mass Association. The mass associations are important because the Tigrayan people living outside should be linked to the people inside.

All over the world Tigrayan people should be organised to know their country's oppression and to struggle against the enemy, to expose the Derg, to have links with workers, with democratic organisations, communicate what is happening. The finance comes both from outside Tigray, from our people's contributions, and from the organisation, which is partly financed from inside Tigray itself. The mass associations here have monthly contributions and if they have any extra money they can contribute it to TPLF. They sell T-shirts, postcards, pens and pencils and they hold lotteries. In the USA, in Britain, in Saudi Arabia, the associations do the same, in addition to their personal contributions. Sudan especially is the largest contributor in Region Four. In Tigray, before the 1984–5 famine, the people made contributions to TPLF through selling surplus crops or weaving, as well as the help through REST, but now it is different – there is not enough.

It is hard to convince even Tigrayan and Ethiopian people here of the nature of what they think is a free democracy. Last year I went to demonstrate with women against the Alton Bill, which wanted to restrict abortion. The police would not let us get further than Westminster Bridge. Bourgeois democracy makes them all think they are free but they are not at all. The people who live in Tigray are much stronger. It is not easy to break imperialist and capitalist ideology. It should not be done by us, but by the people who live here, and the struggle should not be narrowed down to women's problems, but widened out to international issues and the larger problems of poverty and work. The Tigrayan people here are affected by bourgeois democratic values too. The priority for them is their private life. They want to study, to have money, to get on.

But we do have some successes. We have a lot of friends who support our struggle, like the Tigray Solidarity Campaign, Third World First, African movements like BALSA (Black Action for the Liberation of South Africa) and the Black Consciousness Movement of Azania. So our achievement is not strong, but we achieve something. It is not what I expected. I expected more help from the workers here. People only know about us because of the famine, but there has been some development of interest in our struggle itself. We have been told in my country that imperialism and capitalism are bad, but when I see it in practice...! It is a very good education for me, because I never grew up in a capitalist country. Now I have seen what a bourgeois democracy is like!

Of course the position of women is much better than in feudal countries, because they can be educated, they can work and be independent. But in another way they are oppressed. There's a lot of male chauvinism and they're not treated equally. They had a lot of achievements, but since then little progress has been made. There is a lot of rape and sexual harassment. At work women have to keep their bosses happy – this is part of the class nature of capitalism. There will never be a solution unless they can understand the source of their oppression.

The other way is feminism. Just to think about being unequal, badly treated, raped, makes women aggressive, and working on those issues makes them appear strong, but it is dangerous too. Working class women are confused because feminism is a very middle-class movement. They don't see who is their real enemy. They see their enemy as the man, but they don't see that men are oppressed too, don't get properly paid for their work. The workers work to give profit to capitalists who exploit them. The top class should be destroyed. Women should organise with workers, women and men together. In that way they can work with men to overthrow their male chauvinism. They don't realise why male chauvinism recurs and recurs, never stops. The system makes women separate from each other, so that they don't share the same ideology. The bourgeois don't want women to know the main source of oppression.

In general in imperialist countries making the people understand is very different from Tigray. The government doesn't want them to concentrate on the big issues. It works to divide movements, because united they could overthrow the reactionary government. But even the Labour government in Britain did not support the workers strongly enough. The workers can't mobilise. Even Neil Kinnock isn't for a real Labour Party. He isn't able to communicate to the workers. He is competing with Mrs Thatcher. The workers have no strong organisers. If they were strongly organised, then the woman question would be solved. If women's organisation is in total isolation from men how can change ever come about?

Mass Association member, London: Abrehet Teklu's story

Abrehet: I have been in England for two years and three months. I was born in Axum and I lived in Axum until 1979. After that I went to Addis Ababa for seven years, leaving my father and other relatives in Axum. My mother and sister had come to Addis five years earlier. In Axum I had been to school until tenth grade, so in Addis I completed eleventh and twelfth grades. I did science first, then changed to accountancy, following a three year course leading to a diploma.

After I finished my studies I was without a job for a year – it is very difficult to get a job in Addis unless you come from a rich family. Otherwise, it's very hard for a Tigrayan to get a job, because the government does not accept us. In England I am regarded as a foreign student but in Addis, because of the political situation, I was regarded as the same. Most Tigrayan students have that problem.

After seven years I decided to go back to my father in Axum. I had been working as a TPLF member in Addis and several students who worked with me had been arrested in 1984 by the government. After my brother's death I wanted to go to the Field, but it was also terrible in the Field. I couldn't get out of Axum because it was controlled by the Derg cadres.

I was twenty-four. It was the beginning of 1985 during the drought time and the eighth offensive of the Derg. I stayed only ten days in Axum with my father. I escaped with someone my father knew to about ten miles away from the town, nearly to the Field. There we met fifteen Derg cadres. They asked where I was going, but I was too frightened to say anything. My companion said, "She is mad, crazy – I am taking her to see her uncle." I stayed silent. They asked me for my identity card, but all I had was two kinds of medicine, tetracycline and panadol, and a little money given me by my sister. They made a circle all round me and asked me over and over again, but I didn't answer and they let us go on.

Eventually we met three fighters. I went into Adete with them, when it was liberated. While I was there I met some peasants. They told me all about the atrocities of the Derg, but also how to handle the Derg and how to fight them. "Before the Derg reached Adete," a woman told me, "all the members of the TPLF got out of the town." I asked why she hadn't stayed. She replied that if she had, she would have been asked to reveal who was in the TPLF and where they were. She didn't want to be forced to tell and she didn't want to be raped so she escaped.

One of the things the people showed me was their cooking pots that had been used by the soldiers for shit. This was when there was very little to eat. They also grow different kinds of crops for sale, but the Derg harassed them all the time, raping the women, stealing the grain, shitting in the food, mixing the different crops together, pulling out the maize and sorghum to destroy it. They stole the honey from merchants and split the sacks. But after a short time the people lost their fear – they knew what to expect and they knew how to fight.

I was interested in becoming a fighter. I was sick at that time because of my brother's death. I had no resistance to anything, with constant headaches and bleeding. Although I was interested in fighting, I was very depressed, crying. The only alternative was to leave altogether. I travelled to Khartoum with a Canadian, because he had papers and white men weren't stopped. I rested at the TPLF house in Khartoum and after four months I felt better. I spent all my time in the TPLF office and sometimes I had meetings and told my experiences.

In Khartoum, the Tigrayan people were very strong supporters of the TPLF, especially the women. They made bread, drinks and even collected water to sell to make money for the TPLF. When a woman from TPLF is sick or in labour, the women all bring food and drink. For example, when a woman is in labour they ignore the husband and family – one brings food, another brings drinks and some look after the other children. If a woman was getting married, we would all form a group to help her. I shared in all this. I am interested in women and how we all can help each other. When you're coming from the Field from other directions, if you've got any problems, of not speaking Arabic, of not having anywhere to live, or it's too expensive, they will help you or find you another cheaper house.

I stayed four months like this with members of TPLF and the mass association. They wanted to know all about the situation in the Field, not just about their relatives in the Field, but how to support the struggle, and every detail of the Derg's operations and the TPLF actions. When I lived in the Derg-controlled areas I was very worried about the TPLF. Because of the Derg propaganda, I thought the TPLF was defeated. I could hardly eat or drink because of the lies of the Derg: "We have destroyed TPLF. There are no fighters left in the whole area." But when I went to the Field on a visit I found that they were not destroyed at all – I was astonished!

In December 1986 I went to Saudi Arabia to join my husband who sent me a visa. It's a very terrible country, especially for women.

My husband and I had been friends at school. He was a supporter and active member of TPLF. When I went to Addis Ababa he went to Saudi to work for seven years. We were not married then, but he was very worried about me and wrote letters every month. We got married and I stayed eight months in Saudi Arabia. While I was there I couldn't work and didn't feel too well because of the hot climate and my bad health.

As a woman, if you live in Saudi Arabia, you are still in prison. According to their religion, a woman must live with her husband. She can't even go out without her husband. She sees nobody without covering her face with black. Women don't know about money or family. Her husband knows everything. Saudi Arabia is the worst place for women to be, but they don't know how to change it. Without a husband, a woman cannot live. In fact many Tigrayan and Eritrean women live in Saudi without a husband, but they can't go outside the house. The soldiers even stop the taxis and ask for identity cards. Not all women have identity cards and if they are caught they are put in prison or sent back to Khartoum. It's illegal for a woman to buy a car and if you are stopped by soldiers even with an identity card, then you will be sent to prison. If you are accompanied by your husband you are all right, but if the man is a politician or a friend then they assume you are a prostitute.

I stayed four months inside the house. After I was married I wanted to go shopping, but I couldn't. It was like a prison. I couldn't get out to work in the TPLF office – I had plenty of time but I didn't have the papers. Also I was still very sick, constantly bleeding from my nose. I wanted to go to Khartoum, because there I could work for TPLF. In Khartoum there are problems with papers, but not so bad as in Saudi. In the end I decided to come to London.

I came to London with my husband in August 1986. I asked for political asylum here, but the Home Office hasn't made a decision yet. I started to study, but the courses were in Southall, very far from where we were living. I was still sick. My husband did an Access course in electrical engineering and has done very well.

Sometimes I miss my family, I miss my brother. Sometimes I am very depressed and find it hard to go on studying.

As soon as I came I participated in TPLF and the Mass Association. Last year I started a women's association with four women, Zafu, Mahta, Mulu and myself. Now there are eight of us and I hope we can continue. Our meetings are about how to achieve the TPLF revolution, how to get freedom, how to struggle, why should women organise separately – the basic struggle.

Although Western countries are developed economically there are things that are very bad. Western development hasn't solved the basic problems of women's rights, even if things are changed physically. Women are not paid equally – they have to work very hard for not enough money.

Western countries control all the main resources of underdeveloped countries and dictate to them by force in some countries. They say they help us, but they don't. They take everything from us for profit. In Tigray there are so many terrible diseases and droughts. Why do the Western countries only help the Derg? If you want to help and you can solve a problem, then do it. If you can't solve it, keep quiet. Why do you spread all the bad propaganda and talk about being humanitarian – all over the world, not just Ethiopia? How are Western people to believe TPLF fighters or TPLF's principles? In general I don't think the West is interested in helping Third World countries.

In the mass media, some papers report more accurately than others. Some months ago I saw on TV that the TPLF 'rebels' had bombed a UN convoy. It was all lies, but it was on the BBC, on TV and in all the newspapers. In general, the West doesn't care about people, but only about competition with Russia. In Britain humanitarianism is all a pretence – it's all about capitalism and the system of profit. Britain doesn't want to help Ethiopian peoples. The mass media gets all its information from the Derg through Addis Ababa, but it's the *people* who are important. I want to struggle with TPLF every moment of my life.

TPLF Mass Bureau, Washington DC, USA:

Kassech Asfaw: I am from Adigrat in Tigray. I have been in the Field eleven years since March 1978 and before that, I was an underground member of TPLF in the town for two years. Tigray is one of the oppressed nations in Ethiopia – I had that feeling from very early on, because I learnt from what my family said and from being asked in high school. I was always eager to fight and I was one of the first students to join the underground soon afer the beginning of the TPLF.

When the Red Terror started I was one of those suspected so I had to go to the Field. One hundred and fifty of us went at first. My friends, cousins, all of us, went to the Front at the same time. Zafu went to the Front at the same time as me. Although there were many hardships, I didn't notice them. I was always happy.

Now I am working in Washington DC in the USA. I am a member of the Mass Bureau. In the United States and Canada we have a Tigrayan Mass Association, called UTNA (Union of Tigrayans in North America). It is a TPLF association like those in the Field. I am working with this association, representing TPLF. We do propaganda work and it supports TPLF economically. The main office of UTNA is in Washington, but it has different chapters in different states in the USA and Canada. We have one in Toronto too which works with the Washington office. They send all the reports of their work to the offices in California, New York, Philadelphia and so on. In Europe as well there is the Union of Tigrayans in Europe and the Union of Tigrayan Women in Europe.

Region Four is very important to the revolution. The Tigrayans are supporting the revolution by organising themselves and their associations. The diplomatic work in the Foreign Bureau is also very important; we have links with the

Oromo and other Ethiopian peoples, as well as the Eritreans. We criticise each other and explain our programmes. REST also operates in Region Four and its main office is in Khartoum. It is an independent organisation with its own social programmes, but it also works closely with TPLF and the mass associations inside and outside Tigray. REST is helping to bring development aid to the people in the liberated areas.

In the USA we have very little contact with Americans, or with American women. When it's March 8th, we celebrate it with other Tigrayan mass associations. Once a group of us went to a women's group in Washington to celebrate with them. We had a discussion, but on the whole, you know, March 8th is not known in the USA as it is in Europe. There doesn't seem to be as much consciousness among women. In Europe, you see lots of women marching in the streets, but in the States you don't see this. We discussed this with them: "Why in Africa? Why in Europe? Why not in the USA?" A Black woman told us,"If they hear about Marxism here, it is something very bad to them. They hate it irrationally." She said,"They don't know what it is or anything about it, and we have to tell them about it without mentioning the word."

I was expecting some support from the Blacks and from the workers, but everyone is just working for a higher standard of living for themselves. You know, I'm very interested to get to know and to work with women's groups, especially Black women and poor women. If I had a chance to get in touch with compatible study groups, I would.

REST Office, Khartoum, Sudan

Berhan Hailu: I work here in REST in Khartoum as an information officer. I've been here for six months. We gather information from REST in the Field and we have an update every fortnight and a bulletin every two months. We distribute these to relevant organisations in Khartoum, and telex a copy to London. From there it is distributed round the rest of the world. If anyone comes to REST, and if anyone wants to go to the Field, REST provides all the information.

REST is the only organisation which helps in activities and projects in Tigray. We even provide food sometimes for short term survival. In the newly liberated towns it would be difficult for the people to survive now without REST. When the Derg left the towns, they took all the money from the banks and destroyed the electricity, water and health facilities. Many people in the towns were civil servants, on government salaries. Even in the rural areas there are projects which expand each year.

In Shoan towns outside the region of Tigray there are factories producing soft drinks, beer, cement, sugar, tractors, clothes and so on, but in Tigray, even in the capital Makelle, the Derg has made no attempt at development at all. Axum was the earliest area to be civilised, but now Axum is a poor town in the middle of Tigray, the poorest country in the world.

My family come from Adigrat. My mother is still there, but my father is in

Addis. I have one brother and two sisters. My sisters are still in Adigrat. I went to school in Makelle where my uncle lived. When my uncle moved to Addis I went with him and completed my tenth grade.

I then worked for the Ministry of Agriculture for a year in another district, but left when they tried to make me take on too much responsibility. I then spent three years at the university in Addis studying social work, but then I couldn't continue because I was pregnant and also I had to help my husband earn an income. I got a job and started in the Ministry of Information as a radio journalist. I worked there for two years but I didn't like it, because being a journalist in Ethiopia is very difficult. There was such a difference between my theoretical and my practical experience of journalism. You're always telling lies. You know what is going on in practice but you say the opposite all the time. You know the nature of the Derg and what is happening, you know how many people have died in the Ethiopian revolution, how many families have been separated, how difficult it is to survive economically, but as a journalist you have to say that the government is doing well, that the people are happy, and that there is progress. I myself was never happy. I was keeping going as a journalist despite this, but because I'm Tigrayan everything was dangerous in the office. I was afraid for my life. They can always find a reason for taking you to prison.

So, early one morning in Decenber 1986 I flew to Gonder leaving my husband and my baby behind. He wanted me to go to save myself. I had to hide because I had no pass papers, but I got my air ticket with my journalist's identity card. I knew an Amhara woman in Gonder whom I could trust. Even the Amhara are oppressed under the Derg. She arranged everything, including a peasant to take me for five hundred birr. There were three of us, and we walked for six nights and got to the EPDM liberated area. They asked us what we planned to do. I knew a little about TPLF, but not much real information. Some TPLF fighters who were there suggested that we go into Tigray, but after three weeks I went to Sudan.

In the beginning it was difficult in Sudan. I was very depressed. Everything was dark for me. You may not know Ethiopia – politically there is a problem, but culturally the people are free to do so many things. So it was difficult getting used to the culture in Sudan. When I came at first, the people made me frightened, "Don't wear this, wear that". Even Muslims in Ethiopia seem no different from Christians, even the women. But at first you don't have papers, you don't feel at home. But later, once you know people, they are kind. I know my neighbours, and can even speak a little Arabic. But your own homeland is best. Two months ago I went back to Tigray, to Adigrat and Makelle. You can go anywhere, do anything and no one will say anything whether it's the day or night.

I heard that REST wanted an information officer and I told them that I had been working as an Ethiopian journalist, so we suggested that it would not be too diffcult for me. I enjoy it; here you do not have to lie, and when you do things which you believe are right, you can be confident and satisfied.

I appreciate the revolution and the TPLF gives democracy. I have seen the Ethiopian revolution and that was not democratic, and not for the people. I think democracy is everything. If you talk to the people of Tigray they can think anything and do what they like.

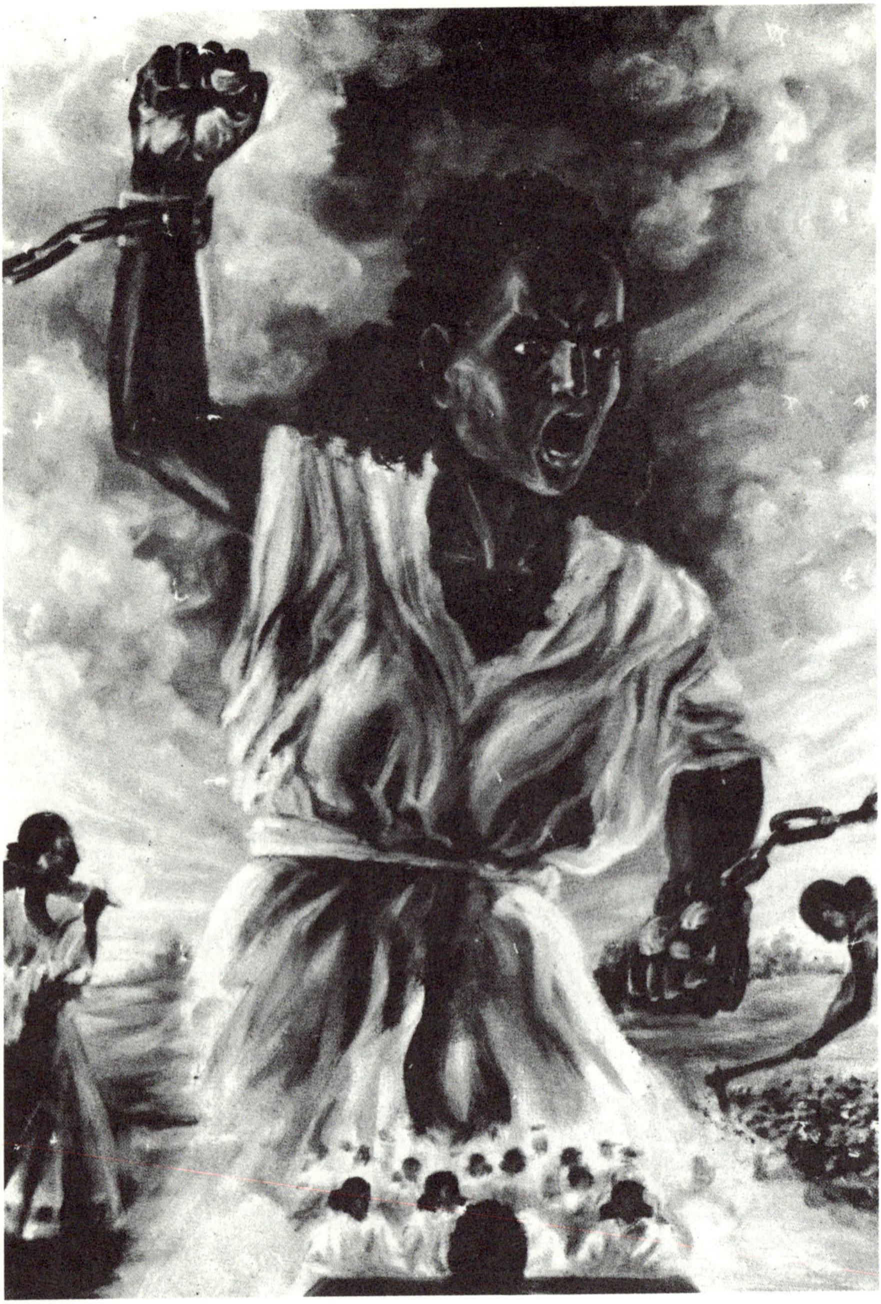

New developments

The political and military situation in Ethiopia is changing very rapidly. The most obvious development has been the liberation of the towns and the expulsion of the Derg from the whole of Tigray. Less visible, but even more important is the evolution of the struggle from one for regional autonomy to the larger struggle for a more just and democratic system in Ethiopia as a whole. "Outside Ethiopia," said Aregash to me, "people are approaching us to organise them and arm them against the Derg. Of course the enemy is out of Tigray now, but that is not the end of our aim, which is to destroy the enemy in the whole of Ethiopia and establish a democratic Ethiopia." One of the signs of this intensified resistance beyond Tigray was the formation in January 1989 of a new united front between TPLF and the Ethiopian People's Democratic Movement (EPDM), the liberation movement south of Tigray in Wollo and Gonder. The Ethiopian People's Revolutionary Democratic Front (EPRDF) has a broad democratic and anti-imperialist programme.

How is the TPLF going to balance the continuing problems of Tigray, particularly the economic problems of the newly liberated towns, with the demands of an extended struggle in Ethiopia? First of all, they see the problems of the towns as considerable but not insuperable. In the early days of the revolution, the process of mobilising and politicising the rural people was an arduous one until they could take responsibility for their own administration in the baitos. This is still going on in the Afar areas. However TPLF believes this process will be much shorter in the towns. In February, as the Derg was evacuating the last towns, the third Congress of the TPLF was deciding that the solution was an intensification of the democratic process. Experiences of life under the Derg, the fact that so many families have sons and daughters who are fighters, the increasing interaction with the politically conscious country people, will all combine to mobilise the townspeople to solve their own problems, so that baitos can be established at a much earlier stage than in the rural area.

Overall, the economic policies of the TPLF are based on the principle of self-reliance. This does not mean they refuse aid from outside Tigray – in fact they need it – but that they reject aid which affects their autonomy and therefore their self-reliance. In practice, this means they do not receive aid from overseas financial institutions and, as Gebru Asrat told me:

"*So far neither the US nor other imperialist countries have given us aid...as to the humanitarian aid, our people receive a little, but it is very small compared to what is given to the Derg and other governments in the area. This humanitarian aid is enough only for a limited number of those who are drought stricken or victims of war.*"

Income depends on four sources. By far the most important is the financial and material support of the people themselves; the second is the Ethiopian Government, inasmuch as all military equipment, weapons and ammunition are captured from the Derg, either in battle or in raids on military installations; thirdly, the TPLF run agricultural and commercial projects, such as the large TPLF farms in the west; the last category is aid from foreign donors.

One of the developments I observed in Tigray in 1989 was the increased influence of the Marxist Leninist League of Tigray (MLLT). On our first visit we had been aware of MLLT working alongside TPLF. The people often referred to *Malalit*, as they called the Party, and celebrated it in song. Two years later, MLLT was being identified with crucial policy changes. "The developments in Tigray," Meles told me, "are directly linked to the role that MLLT have been playing in the revolution over the past few years, in terms of mobilising the people, devising better tactics, and in deepening the democratic practice of the organisation of TPLF", and on another occasion, "We believe that the political participation of the people is a necessary precondition for the construction of socialism". What does this mean? In the West we are used to defining Marxist Leninism in terms of its practice in the Eastern Bloc or in China; it is seen, with some justification, as damaging to democracy, rather than an intensification of it as people's participation proves in Tigray. How can political theory be interpreted in such opposing ways as the 'top-down' autocracy of the Derg or the 'bottom-up' democratic developments under the Tigrayan revolution? Of course democracy in Tigray is participatory as well as representative, and is very different from democracy as practised in the West, where a vote every few years is the only opportunity the vast majority of people get to influence policies.

It seems fruitless to discuss here political theory which can be interpreted in such different ways and the comments of leaders mean little unless supported by evidence from the people. The proof of the political theory is in the practice. The TPLF Information Department has spent years studying previous revolutions in order to learn from their experience and avoid their mistakes. As the testimonies show, the basis of revolutionary practice in Tigray is the people's participation in all economic, social and political activities. The emphasis is never on enforcing change; it is a process, sometimes slow, sometimes faster, but always at the pace of the people. I was never aware of named leaders or figureheads. There are leaders, of course, elected to Central Committee and other posts of responsibility, but I never heard peasants refer to any by name and I was gently rebuked when I tried to find out who were the 'original' first fighters who started TPLF. Their progress towards socialist transformation depends, not on 'levelling-down' as we are taught in the West, but on a 'levelling-up' process, initially to the standard of the middle peasant. 'Participation' means everyone shares in constructing change as well as in the benefits it brings.

People's participation has also been expanded in other ways. The baito structure has been extended to the smallest social structure of the *kushette*, a group of about twenty or thirty families, which will have the power of resolving disputes and electing representatives to the *tabia* level. The *woreda* baito congress came together in the past to make laws and then dispersed; now it is to be a standing body.

The political principle of participation by the people in every aspect of the struggle has also led to a greater fusion of political and military tactics. The peasants have been involved in the armed struggle in a more direct way than before, as Lichy has described already. According to Meles this is, "more effective and less bloody". At the battles of Dejenna and Endaselassie, after the huge Derg armies had been fragmented and scattered by guerrilla forces, organised bands of mostly unarmed peasants were waiting to capture and disarm the fleeing soldiers and conduct them to prisoner of war camps. Prisoners of war are used to convince the peasants that the very enemy soldiers who have destroyed their homes are only instruments and are themselves victims. Meles again:

> They go to one village and say, 'We have burned your huts. We have huts like yours in our own village. We have been forced out of them. We came here. We have been given guns and ordered to shoot and burn your houses. If we didn't we would die. Of course we could have died without burning your houses, but after all it's human to try to save your life. So, in order to save our lives we had to burn your huts. That's very bad, it's criminal, and we regret it. But that's a fact.' A very simple statement like this would change the outlook of the peasants immediately. From a state of hostility you immediately see a state of sympathy towards the plight of the ordinary soldier, the fact that he has been forced to leave his wife and his children and his family, taken to a place he has never seen before and forced to fight.

In fact nobody wants to fight. People will use any channel they can to avoid such an extreme response as armed struggle, but if there are no democratic channels through which to resist oppression, even extinction, then people will fight with any means available to them. As Meley, a combat fighter said to us:

> We Tigrayans, like other people in the world, we need peace. But we are forced to fight because for so long our ancestors, our parents and we ourselves have been oppressed. We cannot live under these conditions; we have to change them – and the only way is to fight a war, to wage a long and bitter rural struggle. Under the Derg we can't do anything. There is no democracy. There is no legal way to struggle; we can only fight. We revolutionaries want peace. We want to hear our children singing in school, instead of hearing bombs. We want to see a developed and modern society.

The desire for peace was expressed by many Tigrayans we spoke to. After the expulsion of the Derg from Tigray, the third Congress of the TPLF resolved on a diplomatic initiative to bring about peace. An eight-point peace proposal was formulated in March 1989 and sent to the Derg. It has been included here in full. They show the importance to TPLF of democratic participation and basic democratic freedoms, but more than this, they demonstrate their repudiation of narrow nationalism and their willingness to work with other Ethiopian groups, including the Derg, for a constructive peace.

In early May there was an attempted coup supported mainly by the airforce in Addis Ababa and the Derg's Second Army in Eritrea. When this failed, the Second Army continued to resist. On May 17th, they broadcast a message on Radio Asmara calling for Colonel Mengistu to step down, for the problems of the people to be solved democratically and for the formation of a provisional government drawn from all organisations. The only organisation they mentioned by name was TPLF and they called on them for their support, expressing solidarity with their peace proposals. Although wary of military coups, TPLF responded positively but with certain conditions, that they "must prove in practice that you genuinely stand for the establishment of people's power". In fact the rebels were crushed, but their response to the peace proposals shows the significant growth in TPLF's say in the politics of the whole country. This received no publicity in the Western press.

The Derg has continued to announce to the world their intention to negotiate for peace, but they did not respond to the TPLF proposals until mid-August 1989 when they asserted a willingness to talk about peace, but with no specific suggestions as to how this might come about. At the same time there are reports from Wollo and Gonder of preparations, involving more than eighty thousand troops, for a massive new offensive.

Peace Proposals

In accordance with the resolutions and basic guidance of the third congress of the TPLF on the peaceful resolution of the Ethiopian situation, the Central Committee of the TPLF has decided to propose peace negotiations on the following terms:

1. An immediate cease-fire to be agreed among the warring forces and effectively implemented.

A. To bring about a peaceful solution a cease-fire must be accepted as an inseparable part of this process.

B. The cease-fire to be implemented once the whole peace package is agreed and to be enforced along with other points of this peace proposal. Detailed measures for implementation of the cease-fire to be decided by further discussions.

2. Freedom of speech, of the Press, the right to organise freely, and other basic democratic rights to be respected. All political organisations to be allowed to carry out political work freely among the people, freely and democratically.

A. All popular demands can only be satisfactorily resolved through the democratic participation of the people themselves. The basic democratic rights of the people to be implemented in practice, not simply written on paper and discarded as at present. Thus the concrete representation of democratic rights is an integral part of a peaceful solution.

B. For the people to decide their own future, it is essential that they be given the right and opportunity to understand, evaluate and choose from among different options presented by different political forces. One basic cause of the present war is the denial of such rights to the people. Therefore allowing all political forces to conduct political work freely and legally will be an essential element of a peaceful solution.

3. All political prisoners must be released. People who were forced to leave their country for political reasons and exiles who wish to return home must be allowed to return and conduct political activities freely and democratically.

4. In order to solve all problems peacefully and democratically, the repressive security institutions of the Derg must be dismantled.

5. The internal problems of the people of Ethiopia must be solved by Ethiopians themselves, and since foreign military intervention is an obstacle to the realisation of peace, all foreign military establishments must be closed down, and foreign military forces and experts immediately expelled.

6. A provisional government constituted from all political organisations to be established.

A. The provisional government must ensure the democratic rights of the people and allow all political organisations to operate freely. After a transitional period, a constitution to be approved by the people's free and democratic choice. This will be the main task of the provisional government, which will be the supreme administrative body throughout the transitional period.

B. Once the constitution has been approved by the people in a democratic forum and once a democratic government has been formed through elections, the transitional government will cease to exist.

7. To enable the people of Eritrea to freely and democratically decide their own fate for themselves and their decision must be respected by all parties.

8. The elected government will democratically solve all the demands of the people on the basis of the people's own wishes and decisions. This will be the final stage in the process of achieving a peaceful solution.

The Central Committee of the Tigray People's Liberation Front is ready and willing to discuss the above points for a peaceful solution with the concerned parties in open and declared forums at any time and place. But it is opposed to any secretive meetings and manoeuvres in the guise of peace and peaceful solutions.

The Central Committee of the Tigray People's Liberation Front
March 1989

GLOSSARY

Afar	minority nationality of nomadic Muslim people living in the eastern lowlands of Ethiopia
Agew	minority nationality living in southern Tigray
Amhara	dominant ethnic group in Ethiopia, about ten million people
baito	people's council, the administrative structure of the state
birr	Ethiopian dollar, worth about twenty pence
Derg	Amharic for 'committee', the Ethiopian government
Field	field of revolutionary activity, the liberated rural area
hakim	medical worker. healer
hamien	women using their poetic skills for begging
injera	basic food of Tigray, a fermented grain pancake
kebelle	Derg urban association
kushette	group of about a hundred families
kuta	one kind of Tigrayan shawl
Makelle Prison	notorious prison where first Haile Selassie and then the Derg imprisoned and tortured thousands of Tigrayans
mass	the Tigrayan people
Mass Bureau	TPLF department responsible for administrative and political relationships with the mass
melkesti	men and women poets skilled at giving the 'melkes' or funeral chant
MiG	Soviet fighter planes, MiG 21s and 23s, used for aerial bombardments by the Derg
Oromo	majority nationality in southern Ethiopia, about eighteen million people
Saho	minority nationality living north of Adigrat in Tigray
sewa	a beer fermented from sorghum and herbs
Shoa	Ethiopian province, the district around Addis Ababa
shig woyanit	'torch of the revolution', a peasant activist
tabia	village of about three hundred families, or three or four *kushettes*
teff	grain crop indigenous to the central highlands of Ethiopia
Terranafit	feudal-nationalist organisation defeated by TPLF in 1976
ululating	a high-pitched sound made by women together, in celebration or for joint action such as a battle
woreda	a district of seven to fourteen *tabia*
woyane	Tigrinya for 'revolution'

CELU	Confederation of Ethiopian Labour Unions
EDU	Ethiopian Democratic Union
ELF	Eritrean Liberation Front
EPDM	Ethiopian People's Democratic Movement
EPLF	Eritrean People's Liberation Front
EPRDF	Ethiopian People's Revolutionary Democratic Front
EPRP	Ethiopian People's Revolutionary Party
	Amharic acronym meaning All-Ethiopian Socialist Movement
MLLT	Marxist-Leninist League of Tigray
PMAC	Provisional Military Administrative Council
REST	Relief Society of Tigray
TNO	Tigrayan National Organisation
TPLF	Tigray People's Liberation Front
WFAT	Women Fighters Association of Tigray

SOME IMPORTANT DATES

1889 - 1913	Menelik II establishes the Ethiopian Empire
1916 - 30	Regency of Haile Selassie
1930 - 74	Rule of Haile Selassie
1943	Tigrayan uprising, the First *Woyane*
1962	Illegal annexation of Eritrea by Haile Selassie
197	Founding of TNO
1974	Overthrow of Haile Selassie; the Derg takes power
1975	February 18th, Tigrayan revolution starts
1975 - 6	Zemacha campaign, the Derg strategy, supposedly for rural education and land reform, in fact for dispersing student opposition
1977 - 78	Red Terror, Derg campaign of violence against all opposition groups
1986	February 8th: In the Agazi Operation, named after an early hero, the TPLF released eighteen hundred prisoners from Makelle prison
1988	February: TPLF gains control of all Tigrayan towns, except Makelle; Endaselassie and Adigrat reoccupied by the Derg
1989	February: TPLF defeats the Derg in the Battle of Endaselassie; Derg withdrawal from Makelle
March:	TPLF Peace Proposals sent to the Derg
May:	military uprising against the Derg in Addis Ababa, supported by the military in Asmara, Eritrea; military made contact with TPLF. Mutiny suppressed